Socrates and the Jews

Socrates and the Jews

Hellenism and Hebraism from Moses Mendelssohn to Sigmund Freud

MIRIAM LEONARD

University of Chicago Press
Chicago and London

The University of Chicago Press, Chicago 60637
The University of Chicago Press, Ltd., London
© 2012 by The University of Chicago
All rights reserved. Published 2012.
Paperback edition 2015
Printed in the United States of America

23 22 21 20 19 18 17 16 15 14   2 3 4 5 6

ISBN-13: 978-0-226-47247-8 (cloth)
ISBN-13: 978-0-226-21334-7 (paper)
ISBN-13: 978-0-226-47249-2 (e-book)
10.7208/chicago/9780226472492.001.0001

Library of Congress Cataloging-in-Publication Data

Leonard, Miriam
    Socrates and the Jews : Hellenism and Hebraism from Moses Mondelssohn to
Sigmund Freud / Miriam Leonard.
        pages. cm.
    Includes bibliographical references and index.
    ISBN 978-0-226-47247-8 (cloth : alkaline paper)
    ISBN 0-226-47247-7 (cloth : alkaline paper)
    1. Philosophy, Ancient—Influence. 2. Jewish philosophy. 3. Judaism and
philosophy. 4. Socrates—Criticism and interpretation. I. Title.
B181.L46 2012
180—dc23

                                                        2011050371

To Phiroze, with all my love

Contents

Figures

Note on Translations

In the interest of accessibility, all foreign-language texts appear in translation. I have used published translations where they exist; all other translations are my own.

Acknowledgments

It is a great pleasure to be able to thank the individuals and institutions who made the research and writing of this book possible. I started working on this project at the University of Bristol, where I was blessed with an extraordinarily rich intellectual community. The support, both emotional and intellectual, that I received from my colleagues there, and in particular, from Vanda Zajko, Ellen O'Gorman, Pantelis Michelakis, Duncan Kennedy, and Charles Martindale, was invaluable. The great majority of the work for the book was undertaken during a blissful sabbatical when I was a Fellow at the Stanford Humanities Center. I am immensely indebted to the staff and then director, John Bender, for providing such a congenial space for research. At Stanford I learned an enormous amount from my fellow fellows Jim Clifford, Faviola Rivera Castro, Benjamin Lazier, Christopher Rovee, and from the participants in the Seminar on Enlightenment and Revolution, especially Dan Edelstein, Yair Mintzker, and James Wood. I am especially grateful to Giovanna Ceserani for her friendship and intellectual companionship during that year as well as before and since. It was the generosity of my two chairs at my current institution, UCL, Christopher Carey and now Maria Wyke, which allowed me to take up my fellowship at Stanford. UCL has proved to be an immensely stimulating environment for completing this project and I am particularly grateful to my colleague Sacha Stern and to the students on our "Greeks and Jews" course for giving me so much to think about as I was drawing the threads together.

Versions of these chapters were delivered as papers in Santa Cruz, Stanford, St Andrews, Berlin, Bristol, Michigan, Northwestern, DePaul, Yale, Princeton, Leeds, London, Cambridge, and Oxford. I would like to thank my hosts and the audiences at all these places for the stimulating and instructive discussions which ensued. I am particularly grateful to Froma Zeitlin and Elizabeth Wingrove, who read the manuscript for the press and offered extremely insightful and generous comments. At Chicago it has been a great pleasure to work with my wonderful editor Susan Bielstein. Thanks also to my copyeditor, Therese Boyd. My mother, Irène Heidelberger-Leonard, commented on and greatly improved the manuscript from the beginning to the end. I owe special thanks to Yopie Prins and Daniel Orrells, who read portions of the manuscript with great acumen. Bonnie Honig gave me immensely helpful feedback on specific chapters and also, invaluably, challenged me to think harder and more deeply about the broader intellectual project. Charles Martindale's comments substantiantly improved the argument of an early draft. Jim Porter read substantial portions of the manuscript and offered characteristically brilliant insights. Simon Goldhill not only read the whole book in its many forms but also offered unstinting encouragement and a model of intellectual dynamism and generosity to which one can only aspire.

I would like to thank the University of Minnesota Press for allowing me to reprint a section of chapter 1 that appeared as "Greeks, Jews and the Enlightenment: Moses Mendelssohn's Socrates" in the special volume of *Cultural Critique* 74 (Winter 2010). A small section of chapter 2 appeared in "Derrida between Greek and Jew" in *Derrida and Antiquity*, ed. Miriam Leonard (Oxford University Press, 2010) and I am grateful to Oxford University Press for allowing me to reprint it here. I would like to thank Wiley-Blackwell for their permission to reprint a revised version of a part of my chapter "History and Theory: Moses and Monotheism and the Historiography of the Repressed" in *A Companion to Classical Reception*, ed. Lorna Hardwick and Christopher Stray (Blackwell, 2008) in a section of chapter 5.

I am grateful to my friends Katherine Angel and Vanda Zajko and particularly to Aude Doody, Katie Fleming, Annelise Freisenbruch, and Daniel Orrells for always being there. Thanks also to Dinoo, Arnavaz, Vikram, Shernaz, Zulfi, and Leia for all their encouragement.

Most especially my thanks go to Mark, Gabs, Noa, and Jakob, and to my parents Dick Leonard and Irène Heidelberger-Leonard for their love which knows no bounds.

Finally, and most of all, I am grateful to Phiroze Vasunia. He not only read and commented on every word but also lived through the drama of their creation. Without his love and daily support in Bristol, in Palo Alto, in London, and in Mumbai, none of it would have been possible.

Athens and Jerusalem

It was the Christian moralist Tertullian who perhaps gave European culture the most pithy formulation of its own cultural bifurcation: "What has Athens to do with Jerusalem?" Tertullian's rhetorical question, written in the third century CE, was part of a broader Christian project of drawing the boundary lines between classical and biblical cultures. If Christianity had emerged in the classical world and in self-conscious and violent opposition to it, how could the secular knowledge of Greco-Roman antiquity be reconciled with the new certainties of Christian revelation? In opposing Athens to Jerusalem, Tertullian would reaffirm the incommensurability of the pagan and Christian worlds.[1]

Tertullian's "quotation has echoed down the centuries" and "often its use is only tangentially connected with Tertullian himself."[2] Despite the broad cultural reach of Tertullian's antithesis, its immediate context ties it to a more specific opposition: "Quid ergo Athenis et Hierosolymis? Quid Academiae et Ecclesiae? Quid haereticis et christianis? [What indeed has Athens to do with Jerusalem? What has the Academy to do with the Church? What have heretics to do with Christians?]" [*De Praes.* 7.9]). Often read in conjunction with another of Tertullian's well-known proclamations: "credo quia absurdum est" ("I believe because it is absurd," in fact, a misquotation), this series of questions has led Tertullian to be branded "the enemy of argument and the apostle of unreason."[3] Athens is opposed to Jerusalem by Tertullian in a series

1. Recently, however, many critics have highlighted the rhetorical nature of Tertullian's formulation arguing that he did not, in fact, advocate an outright rejection of classical culture. See González 1974, Helleman 1994, Osborn 1997, and Dunn 2004.

2. Helleman 1994, 361.

3. Osborn 1997, 27. He actually writes in *On the Flesh of Christ* 5.4: "credibile est, quia ineptum est."

of antitheses that simultaneously place Plato's Academy in direct opposition to the Church and make the study of philosophy an act of heresy. Tertullian reduces the conflict between the Greco-Roman and Christian worlds to an argument about the status and the use of reason. Tertullian's clash of civilizations is played out in a contest between Socrates and the Christians.

Given its original focus on the question of rationality, it is no surprise that Tertullian's polarity between Athens and Jerusalem found a resonance in later Enlightenment debates about the (in)compatibility of faith and reason.[4] But there are a number of ironies involved in the transformation of Tertullian's question into its more recent incarnation. In an important essay on the modern Greek/Jew antithesis, Tessa Rajak has written that "the idea of the twin roots of European civilization, the one Hellenic and the other Hebraic, has served, from the second half of the eighteenth century on, both as a sophisticated theoretical and scholarly tool and as a widespread commonplace."[5] If by the mid-eighteenth century, as Rajak suggests, the opposition between Athens and Jerusalem had become a "commonplace" in both scholarly arguments and popular debates, it is all the more striking that Tertullian's question already had the familiarity of a rhetorical *topos* in the second century CE. The Athens/Jerusalem polarity was from the outset a cliché whose meaning extended well beyond its literal referents.

Moreover, despite his ostensible desire to demarcate the "Hellenic" from the "Hebraic," Tertullian's identity as a Christian writing under the Roman empire places him in an oblique relationship to both Athens and Jerusalem. Tertullian was a Roman subject writing long after the destruction of the Temple of Jerusalem and even longer after the apogee of Athenian philosophy. The opposition between Athens and Jerusalem formulated in the mouth of a Christian apologist has a quite different set of connotations from the debates about cultural assimilation that took place, for example, in the context of Hellenistic Judaism. Although there may be some continuities, Tertullian's questioning of the relationship between Athens and Jerusalem does not, for instance, share the same premise as Philo of Alexandria's attempts to understand the relationship between Plato and Moses. Philo's efforts to harmonize Greek philosophy and Jewish traditions stand in contrast to Tertullian's insistence on their incommensurability. The intense interrogation of the limits of "Hellenization" that took place in the aftermath of the Maccabean revolt in the second century BCE produced its own *Kulturkampf*.[6]

4. See Osborn 1997; Helleman 1994.
5. Rajak 2001a, 535.
6. See Hengel 1974, Momigliano 1994b, and Gruen 2009.

But although Philo and Josephus occasionally figure in modern accounts of the Greek/Jew antithesis, it is significant that the Enlightenment and post-Enlightenment figures who form the subject of this book rarely return to this historical period of cultural contact. For a variety of reasons that must include a desire to minimize the fusion of the two cultures, neither Josephus nor Philo, neither the second book of Maccabees nor the Letter of Aristeas, are the referents in the modern conflict between Athens and Jerusalem. Conversely, as Erich Gruen notes, "the terms 'Hebraism' and 'Hellenism' constitute a convenient and conventional dichotomy" today but "rarely surface in ancient texts as distinguishing concepts."[7] Instead of the historical encounter between Greeks and Jews it is the figurative dialogue between Athens and Jerusalem, a figurative dialogue given its most memorable formulation by a Christian, which finds prominence in the later accounts. Rome rather than Athens, Alexandria, or Jerusalem remains the starting point for the opposition between Greeks and Jews and the definition of Christianity is more often than not what is at stake in these dialogues.

Despite the importance of Rome for understanding Tertullian's formulation, it is a nice paradox that the dichotomy that would come to underpin the fractured sense of *European* identity was first voiced by a Carthaginian. It was on African rather than European soil that Tertullian coined his memorable phrase. The overt references to Athens and Jerusalem may obscure the implicit centrality of Rome to Tertullian's worldview, but it is important to ask which other cultures are pushed out of view by this "convenient dichotomy." The desire to demarcate the world into the opposing camps of "Greeks" and "Jews" had the effect of obscuring the reality of cultural diversity in both the ancient and modern imperial contexts. In modern European empires, just as in the Roman empire, the dichotomy between Athens and Jerusalem could not do justice to the multitude of religious and cultural identities. Was the impassioned debate between "Hellenism" and "Hebraism" in the nineteenth century a way, for instance, of not dealing with the "real" (not so) other of European culture, that is, Islam? In focusing their attention on the choice between Athens and Jerusalem, were figures in the European Enlightenment at the same time placing a limit on the plurality of pasts which Europe might choose to make reference to?

If one pole of the subject of this book is represented by Tertullian's third-century question, the other is provided by James Joyce's early twentieth-century aphorism: "Jewgreek is Greekjew." It hardly needs stating that a historical and conceptual gulf separates Tertullian's *De Praescriptionibus*

---

7. Gruen 2009, 129, 131.

adversus haereses omnes from Joyce's *Ulysses*.[8] Nor is it simply the case that
while Tertullian presents Athens and Jerusalem as irreconcilable opposites,
Joyce advocates a happy synthesis. If anything, the opposition between the
two worldviews had become even more reified in Joyce's day and it is precisely this context that makes his pronouncement so provocative: "Women's
reason. Jewgreek is Greekjew. Extremes meet."[9] Like Tertullian, Joyce sees
the relationship between Greeks and Jews revolving around the question of
"reason." But this time the inability to differentiate between Athens and Jerusalem becomes associated with the irrationality of women. Rather than assigning a privileged relationship to reason to one or other of the two cultures,
Joyce makes their confusion the marker of an inability to reason. But despite
the failure of rationality, their status as opposites is never really called into
question. They remain "extremes" even as they "meet."

Bryan Cheyette argues, "Joyce's *Ulysses* includes a cluster of 'Hebraic and
Hellenic' representations and employs them to explode any notions that an
Arnoldian grand synthesis of these oppositions is equivalent to the progress
of civilization."[10] As Cheyette indicates, Joyce's great epic was written in the
shadow of the most famous modern formulation of the Greek/Jew antithesis:
Matthew Arnold's "Hellenism and Hebraism," which formed the centerpiece
of Arnold's seminal work of cultural criticism *Culture and Anarchy*, published
in 1869. Arnold's influence makes itself manifest from the opening pages of
Ulysses. Theoharis, Cheyette, and Davison all demonstrate how it is Arnold's
conceptualization of Hellenism/Hebraism that provides a framework for
situating *Ulysses* as an intervention into the debate about modern European
culture. It is also Arnold's opposition that is the impetus for Joyce's radical
reevaluation of the power of Hellenism and the problematic representation
of Hebraism. "Unlike Arnold," writes Cheyette,

> Joyce in *Ulysses* does not attempt to synthesize "Hebraism with Hellenism"
> but deploys Hebraism as a means of disrupting the certainties implied in a
> unifying Hellenism. Bloom, as a "Jewgreek," is ambivalently constructed as
> both a universal "everyman"—the embodiment of modernity—and, at the
> same time, as a dark "other," repressed in the unconscious, who can not be
> assimilated into the grand narrative of modernity.[11]

8. For a fascinating account of one of the intervening figures in the history of this dialogue
between Hellenism and Hebraism see Grafton/Weinberg (2011). Grafton and Weinberg's portrait of Isaac Casaubon gives an invaluable insight into the history of Christian Hebraism and
classical learning which precedes the narrative of this book.

9. Joyce 1990, 504.

10. Cheyette 1993, 206.

11. Ibid., 210–11.

Although Arnold remains an essential reference point for understanding Joyce's characterization of modernity as an ambivalent struggle between "Hellenism" and "Hebraism," he is far from being his only model.[12] In his defense against the anti-Semitic attack of "the citizen" in the Cyclops episode, Leopold Bloom rattles out a list of influential Jews: "Mendelssohn was a jew and Karl Marx and Mercadante and Spinoza."[13] Jews, Bloom says, who "are like me." Mercadante was, in fact, no Jew at all but a Catholic. Mendelssohn, Marx, and Spinoza, for their part, were indeed all born Jews but they were not just controversial figures within the Jewish communities into which they were born. They also struggled to reconcile their religious heritage with a commitment to rationalism. As Davison argues: "Bloom's list has often been regarded as the prime example of his foggy thinking, here about 'his own people.' But this assumption again suggests 'Jewishness' as an either/or question of religion, which it is not. Joyce's joke is thus on the reader, not on Bloom. With the exception of Mercadante, each of the names suggests a 'Jewishness' similar to Bloom's."[14] Mendelssohn, Marx, and Spinoza were, in Arnold's terms, "Hellenized" Jews: Jews who saw the traditions of Western philosophy as an escape from the irrational legacy of their religion.

Unlike for Tertullian, Bloom's association with Jerusalem was no longer merely "an either/or question of religion." Although, as we have seen, a debate about faith and reason remains central even to Joyce's conception of the Greek/Jew polarity, the association of Athens with reason and Jerusalem with unreason no longer holds sway. Mendelssohn, Marx, and Spinoza are easily a match for the "Hellenic" Arnold in any pantheon of "Reason." The "Hellenization" of Jews since the Enlightenment and the Jewish Haskalah had radically altered the identity of Jewish intellectuals.[15] To be a Jew in post-Enlightenment Europe no longer implied a necessary championing of faith over reason. By placing himself in a genealogy with Mendelssohn and Marx, Bloom not only sidesteps Tertullian's choice between Athens and Jerusalem, but he also presents an alternative to Arnold's English liberal synthesis of "Hellenism and Hebraism." The tradition of German Hellenized Jews that Bloom elects as his ancestry provides an alternative genealogy—a genealogy which, from Moses Mendelssohn to Sigmund Freud, I shall be tracing in this book.

12. Davison (1996) claims that Joyce is influenced as much by Nietzsche's conceptualization of the opposition as he is by Arnold's.

13. Joyce 1990, 342.

14. Davison 1996, 219.

15. See Shavit's seminal work (1997) on the role of "Hellenism in the making of the modern secular Jew."

Bloom's encounter with the "citizen," then, seems to disrupt the terms of both Tertullian's and Arnold's polarities. For the question that introduces Bloom's discussion of his Jewish identity is not a question of religion but one of nation.

—Do you know what a nation means? says John Wyse . . .
—What is your nation if I may ask, says the citizen.
—Ireland, says Bloom. I was born here. Ireland.

Met with skepticism by his fellow drinkers he continues:

—And I belong to a race too, says Bloom, that is hated and persecuted. Also now. This very moment. This very instant . . .
—Are you talking about the new Jerusalem? says the citizen.
—I'm talking about injustice, says Bloom.[16]

As Cheyette writes:

[Joyce's *Ulysses*] scandalized its readers by placing the ultimate cosmopolitan, Leopold Bloom, at the heart of European culture. Joyce took to its logical extreme the Judaized rewriting of Greek mythology or Hellenism by making his Odysseus an unplaceable Jew. When confronted by the Citizen in Barney Kiernan's pub and forced to define his nationality (on pain of a beating), Bloom imagines himself in a long line of cosmopolitan non-Jewish Jews like himself.[17]

For Bloom the issue of nationality is bound up in a complicated way with his identity as a Jew. Zygmunt Bauman has argued that in the modern nation state the Jews "were the epitome of incongruity: a non-national nation, and so cast a shadow on the fundamental principle of modern European order: that nationhood is the essence of human destiny."[18] Confronted with the abuse of a nationalistic zealot, Bloom assumes a cosmopolitanism that forefronts his Judaism while at the same time refuses to align him straightforwardly with his "hated" and "persecuted" "race." The issue of "injustice," he argues, transcends both nation and people.

And yet, the exchange between Bloom and the citizen cannot be understood outside the context of the so-called Jewish question, which had linked the Jewish people to the question of the nation for well over a century before the publication of Joyce's *Ulysses*. Ever since the French Revolution, political debates about the admission of Jews into civil society had become a central

16. Joyce 1990, 331, 332.
17. Cheyette 2004, 41.
18. Bauman 1998, 153. One could think here of the connection to the question of Christian Zionism. It was Shaftesbury who coined the phrase, "a country without a people for a people without a country."

plank of the definition of modern European identity. Throughout the nineteenth century and across the whole of Europe, the issue of the treatment
of the Jews was inextricably bound up, on the one hand, with the project of
social and political reform, and, on the other, with the attempts to define
the integrity of the nation-state. Debates about Jewish emancipation that had
originated in Germany in the decades preceding the French Revolution led to
the granting of full citizens' rights to the Jews in France in 1791.[19] As a result
of the Napoleonic Wars these privileges were extended to many other European Jews but were successively repealed during subsequent years. Jewish
emancipation played a significant role in revolutions of 1848/49 and although
many Jews received legal equality by the middle of the nineteenth century,
the "problem" of the integration of the Jews remained a persistent preoccupation throughout the century and well into the next.[20]

The conflict between "Hellenism" and "Hebraism," which I explore in the
mainly philosophical works in this book, takes place against the background
of these political events. With the exception of Moses Mendelssohn and Karl
Marx, the figures I investigate in *Socrates and the Jews* by and large avoid a
sustained engagement with the issue of contemporary Jewish emancipation.
Indeed, one of the central preoccupations of the book is to explore how the
very urgent political debate about the treatment of the Jews gets transposed
into the abstract formulation of the Greek/Jew opposition. Despite willful
metaphorization, the contemporary situation not only provides a crucial
context for understanding the persistence of the Athens/Jerusalem polarity
but also is sometimes its motivating force. It is the imbrication and mutually
reinforcing nature of the philosophical and the political discourses surrounding Greeks and Jews which I aim to expose.

The history of Jewish emancipation, moreover, plays more than an incidental role in the biographies of a number of the writers explored in the
book. Moses Mendelssohn, the subject of the first chapter, dedicated much
of his life to advocating Jewish rights in Berlin. He was also read and admired
by the very French Revolutionaries who would grant citizenship to the Jews.
The radicals Heinrich Heine and Karl Marx were both so-called baptized
Jews, but their conversion to Christianity neither protected them from anti-
Semitism nor prevented them from entering into discussions about Jewish
integration. Sigmund Freud, the subject of the final chapter, may have been
a highly assimilated "Godless Jew" but his life and career were significantly
marked by his Jewish background not least in his forced exile from Vienna in

19. See Schechter 2003.
20. See Mosse 1981.

the aftermath of the Anschluss in 1938. *Socrates and the Jews* investigates the Greek/Jew opposition in a period that extends from the 1750s to the 1930s. The alternating histories of Jewish emancipation and persecution between 1791 and 1938, between the French Revolution and the Kristallnacht, act as a framing narrative of this book.

As is clear from these examples, a shifting sense of "Jewishness" develops in parallel with the fight for emancipation. The Enlightenment, as we have seen, played a crucial role in creating new possibilities of self-expression for Jews in Europe. But beyond the individual biographical choices of the figures I examine, the question of the "essence" of Jewish identity becomes an important subject of intellectual debate. The changing understanding of what it was to be a Jew explains how Mendelssohn's readers saw his Judaism as essential to his philosophy despite his adoption of the guise of Socrates, while a generation later Hegel could figuratively identify Kant's philosophy as Jewish. The individual trajectories of Bloom's precursors, the ambivalent "Hellenized" Jews whom I trace in the chapters, proceed in parallel to the non-Jewish mainly Christian accounts of the Hellenism/Hebraism opposition. Christians and Jews, of course, had different investments in this dichotomy but their various perspectives intersect in a unified project of philhellenism. Mendelssohn and Hegel, Renan and Freud may have been bitterly opposed in their attitudes to Judaism but they nevertheless share a deep attachment to Greek civilization and culture. Indeed, for Mendelssohn, Heine, Marx, and Freud, the question of "Hellenization" was inextricably bound up with the quest for a new sense of Jewish identity.[21]

The "Jewish question," on the one hand, and the evolving sense of Jewish identity, on the other, may go some way to explaining how the Athens/Jerusalem antithesis became caught up in the broader narrative of European history and the development of the nation-state. But although Joyce makes nationalism a crucial context for understanding Bloom's Jewish identity, he does not completely exclude the religious dimension either. For although, in his altercation with the "citizen," Bloom seeks to associate himself with a decidedly "free-thinking" set of Jews, his list has a rather unexpected coda: "Mendelssohn was a jew and Karl Marx and Mercadante and Spinoza. And the Saviour was a jew and his father was a jew. Your God." "Christ," he continues, "was a jew like me." "By Jesus," retorts the citizen, "I'll brain the bloody

---

21. Shavit (1997) explores this process in much greater detail. His study looks at the alternative narrative of Jewish secularization which intersects with my preoccupations but from a quite different perspective. His focus on the question of Zionism adds a crucial dimension that I have not been able to explore in this book.

jewman for using the holy name. By Jesus, I'll crucify him, so I will. Give us that biscuit box here."[22] For all the simmering violence that had characterized the debate about national identity, it is Bloom's assertion that "the Saviour" was a Jew, indeed, that the Christian God was a Jew, that threatens to tip the quarrel over into open confrontation.

Although European countries had since the French Revolution undergone a stark process of secularization, the nineteenth century was nevertheless marked by extraordinarily fervent religious debates. None was more controversial than the question of the Jewish identity of Christ. In many Christian accounts, the Jewish origins of Christianity were considered an aberration. With the growth of historical scholarship, the concrete connections between early Christianity and Judaism became the focus of scholarly inquiry. But since Greco-Roman society provided the matrix for the development of Christianity, this alternative cultural context could be contrasted with its "Jewish" theological content. Hegel and Renan would write very different accounts of the relationship between Judaism and Christianity. While Hegel's had as its goal the analysis of the essence of Judaism and its role in the development of the world history of "Spirit," Renan's was grounded in historical inquiry and guided by the new science of comparative philology. Nevertheless, both Hegel and Renan would foreground the role of Hellenism in the development of Christianity.

The assertion of Christianity's "Hellenic Spirit" became a powerful driving force for marginalizing Judaism. The affinities between Christianity and Hellenism had become so obvious to a Protestant theologian like Johann Kaspar Lavater that when Mendelssohn chose to associate himself with the figure of Socrates he assumed that this was merely a prelude to his conversion to Christianity. We have come a long way since Tertullian! Particularly in Germany, Protestant theologians would fashion Christianity as a new Hellenism, a new rational religion, and in the process simultaneously rescue Christianity for the Enlightenment and decisively exile Judaism from the domain of reason.

It is this narrative of the failure of secularism that constitutes one of the central arguments of this book, for, although Greco-Roman culture was repeatedly held up as a secular alternative to the Bible, it is the stubborn persistence of a Christianized account of Hellenism that needs to be understood and that I attempt to trace in this study. Many Enlightenment and post-Enlightenment writers I explore in this book would focus their critiques not on Christianity as such but on its so-called Judaic elements. The attempt to

22. Joyce 1990, 342.

construct a Hellenic genealogy for Christianity produced a detoxified religion more palatable to the sensibilities of the age. Philhellenism, then, was far from being a uniformly secular movement. Many of its most fervent adherents like Hegel, Schelling, and Hölderlin were simultaneously the representatives of the stance that come to be known as *Kulturprotestantismus*.[23] In choosing Athens over Jerusalem, these figures would not necessarily abandon Rome. Although the later chapters of *Socrates and the Jews* explore how the Greek/Jew antithesis played an important role in the transition from Christian anti-Judaism to secular anti-Semitism, it is the perseverance of Christianity as a central reference point and potent force in European culture which ultimately emerges from the analysis.[24]

While I am keen to emphasize the tenacity of Christianity in the intellectual and spiritual lives of many thinkers, as Frank Manuel argues, "old theological concerns were largely supplanted by historical, archaeological, and linguistic enquiries" during the course of the nineteenth century.[25] Although the essence of Christianity still remained a central preoccupation, the new methods of enquiry would give way to different nomenclatures. The introduction of the designations "Indo-European," "Aryans," and "Semites" would profoundly alter the nature of the opposition between Athens and Jerusalem. For a figure like Renan, issues of theological content and linguistic and racial typology were inextricably linked. In Renan's self-consciously historicist and rationalist account of the *Life of Jesus*, the "problem" of the Jewishness of Christ can only be answered with reference to the emerging fields of comparative linguistics and ethnology. A modern account of religion could not do without a terminology of race. The same is true of Nietzsche. Even this most decidedly post-Christian of authors would devote several of his later works to exploring the relationship of Christ to the ethics of Judaism. But for Nietzsche, this account of the genealogy of religion can only be narrated in a vocabulary of race. Outside the German and French contexts, Matthew Arnold unexpectedly maps his abstract concepts of Hellenism and Hebraism on to the ethnographic categories of "Indo-European" and "Semite."

These advances in philology would also play an important role in the disciplinary development of Classics. Suzanne Marchand has recently emphasized "the simultaneity of eighteenth-century Germandom's oriental and neoclassical renaissances," and yet already by 1807, Friedrich August

---

23. See Marchand 2009, 76–77. Goldhill (2011) is excellent on the Victorian context.

24. For an analysis of the development of the vocabulary of "anti-Semitism," see Pulzer 1988, 47–57.

25. Manuel 1992, 302.

Wolf, the scholar who is often considered to be the founding father of classical studies, had defined *Altertumswissenschaft* in stark opposition to the science of the "Orient."[26] The first volume of Martin Bernal's controversial *Black Athena* made the claim that the constitution of classics as an area of scholarly enquiry was systematically defined by the anti-Semitic prejudices of its nineteenth-century practitioners. While many of the details of Bernal's argument are questionable and have been held up to close scrutiny not least by Marchand in her own meticulous and careful study of German Orientalism, its broad outline remains helpful for understanding the imbrication of racial concepts and philological preoccupations in the nineteenth century. The ethnological divisions that would increasingly underlie the study of Classics in Germany intersected in complex ways with what Maurice Olender has named "the languages of paradise." As Olender makes clear, philological questions progressed in tandem with religious debates well into the age of reason. Wolf's student August Boeckh would argue against such a confusion: "As, in fact most men are Christians without being philologists and [as] Jews and Muslims have become excellent philologists, [it is clear that] one should not mix these things up."[27] The triumphant story of the secularization of classical studies as an emancipation from the strictures of biblical exegesis sits uncomfortably with the persistence of anti-Semitism as a pervasive force in the development of philological categories. Athens and Jerusalem remained important for shaping the contours of scholarly analysis even as their theological referents were increasingly downplayed.

Despite the significance of this wider cultural and institutional history, the primary aim of *Socrates and the Jews* is to understand the role of the *conceptual* opposition between Greeks and Jews. My aim has been to retrieve and reconstruct the persistent figural "work" done by the Greek/Jew couplet in giving form to a range of Enlightenment and post-Enlightenment philosophical, social, and political concerns. While I repeatedly trace how this antithesis finds itself played out in concrete historical and political debates, the focus of my analysis nevertheless remains rooted in the history of ideas. It is no accident that I started this introduction with a reference to Tertullian. The abstraction of Tertullian's question has been the source of its longevity, and the opposition between Athens and Jerusalem has been a powerful signifier in the history of ideas precisely because it has resisted being tied down to any identifiable signified. It is this same quality that has made the Greeks such a fertile resource for modernity. When we speak about the idealization

---

26. Marchand 2009, 54
27. Quoted in ibid., 79.

of Greece in German philhellenism it is this Greek predisposition to productive ambiguity that we name. As Friedrich Schlegel put it: "Jeder hat noch in
den Alten gefunden, was er brauchte oder wünschte; vorzüglich sich selbst
[Everyone has found in the ancients whatever he needed or wished for; especially himself]."[28] The mechanisms of abstraction in relation to the Jews have
been rather more pernicious. As Max Silverman points out

> "Jew" is one of the most malleable signifiers. Over the ages, it has been the
> name given to an extraordinary and bewildering number of conceptions. . . .
> The one common and persistent preoccupation is the construction of a "Jew-
> ish question," the resolution of which will ensure the well-being of society.
> "Jew" is the site on which unruly desire and ambivalence can, supposedly, be
> transformed into a coherent and univocal discourse.[29]

The challenge of this project has been to resist being enthralled to the metaphor while not ignoring the fact that the very power of the antithesis lies in
its philosophical abstraction. The politics of this negotiation are difficult. But
the Greek/Jew opposition is an exemplary case, if ever one was needed, of
how symbolic structures come to have consequences in the "real" world.

There is a further dimension to Tertullian's conceptualization of the problem that lies at the heart of *Socrates and the Jews*. The centrality of the concept
of reason to the Christian moralist's understanding of this cultural antithesis
has had a lasting effect on its reception in the modern period. By defining the
Greek/Jew opposition as a struggle between faith and philosophy, Tertullian
made this dichotomy central to the self-definition of the age of reason. In the
Enlightenment, Athens and Jerusalem became tropes both *within* philosophy and *of* philosophy. Where Tertullian pits Plato against the Christians,
his later Enlightenment and post-Enlightenment heirs will place Socrates in
confrontation with the Jews. The task of this book has been to explore how
this philosophical tradition lies behind many of the most important developments in intellectual and cultural history in the long nineteenth century.
The book investigates the narrative of the struggle between faith and reason
from Kant and Moses Mendelssohn, both of whom wrote celebrated essays
entitled "Was ist Aufklärung?," to Freud, whose theories of psychoanalysis
would put the final nail in the coffin of the rational subject. The conflict between Athens and Jerusalem from the mid-eighteenth century to the early
twentieth century, then, can also be mapped on to a much broader history of
the Enlightenment and its critique. The figures explored in this book (Kant,

28. Schlegel 1991, 31.
29. Silverman 1998, 197.

Hegel, Marx, Nietzsche, and Freud) are perhaps the most significant thinkers for understanding the triumph and the limits of reason.

This story, it will not have gone unnoticed, remains a determinably German one.[30] The opposition between Greeks and Jews, Athens and Jerusalem, Aryans and Semites, for sure, has other national inflections. Indeed, this book does not shy away from the paradox that the most memorable modern formulation of this antithesis, Matthew Arnold's essay "Hellenism and Hebraism," appears not in a tome of German philosophy but in one of the most important works of *English* cultural criticism. Nor do I ignore the central importance of a figure such as Ernest Renan whose peculiarly French story of disillusioned Catholicism and arms-length Hellenism maps imperfectly onto a German schema. Such supranational intellectual dialogues cannot be sidestepped. Indeed, I hope to show how Hellenism and Hebraism became important markers of national identity in the cultural rivalries and political conflicts between nation-states in nineteenth-century Europe. Nevertheless, at least three factors seem to me to explain why the Greek/Jew opposition came to take on a particular significance in Germany.

First, the story of modern philhellenism is dominated by Germany. Nowhere else in Europe did an affinity to the Greeks play such a profound role in the creation of cultural unity and the fostering of national feeling. In Germany the return to the Greeks was from the very outset a *vaterländisches Streben*, a patriotic pursuit. Simultaneously, the dominance of German scholars and institutions in the disciplinary history of Classics has inextricably tied the scientific study of ancient cultures to a German history. Within the German academy, moreover, the new field of Altertumswissenschaft defined itself in opposition to the methods of biblical exegesis which had dominated philological enquiry before the mid-eighteenth century. Second, the intellectual context of an "Enlightened" Protestantism had a specific investment in the relationship between philosophy and religion. This intellectual theology was motivated by a strong desire to unite faith and reason. Where in France the *philosophes* had to some extent positioned themselves as opponents of religion, Aufklärer like Kant and Mendelssohn would pursue an accommodation between belief and rationality. Indeed, so dominant was this culture that Nietzsche would argue that the most important task of his unbridled Hellenism was to wrest German philosophy away from the stranglehold of the Tübingen school—the seat of Kulturprotestantismus. Finally, the so-called

---

30. The political process of German unification runs in parallel to the cultural developments which are traced in this book. Philhellenism, as will become clear, played an important role in the development of a national identity in the long process of German unification.

Judenfrage is a quintessentially German question. German intellectuals were engaged in debates about Jewish emancipation long before their counterparts in most other European countries. If Germany gave rise to some of the most progressive voices in the debate about Jewish rights, it was also, of course, the site of the most violent betrayal of this tradition. In choosing the long nineteenth century as its focus, the book concentrates on a period of intense interaction between Germans and Jews.

Socrates and the Jews ends with an analysis of Freud's *Moses and Monotheism*, which was written in 1938 under the shadow of Nazism. The aim was not to give my argument a false teleology but rather to demarcate a distinct historical period in which the Greek/Jew antithesis came to take on a particular resonance. Although Freud's text was written on the eve of World War II and was unambiguously marked by this context, it nevertheless looks back to a series of preoccupations that were at the center of the nineteenth-century engagement with biblical and classical antiquity. The Shoah fundamentally changes the nature of this debate. It would have been possible to extend my analysis, for instance, to the role of the antithesis in the work of Heidegger or Auerbach or Adorno and Horkheimer or Leo Strauss.[31] But I have deliberately eschewed comprehensiveness in favor of a more focused intellectual history—a history that is intended to give a particular account of the aftermath of the European Enlightenment.

The German philosophical tradition I trace in this book from Kant through Hegel, Marx, and Nietzsche to Freud has played a fundamental role in narratives of European modernity. These figures have been no less central in defining a distinctive relationship to antiquity.[32] A dialogue with the classical past underpins many of the most important works in the modern history of ideas from Hegel's *Phenomenology of Spirit* to Freud's *Interpretation of Dreams*. And yet, scholars have simultaneously noted the striking presence of a different antiquity in these writings. The prominence of discussions of Judaism in Enlightenment and Idealist philosophy has been the subject of much recent work.[33] From Mendelssohn and Kant to Fichte and Hegel, the figure of the "Jew" is often articulated as a problem for the universalist precepts of philosophy. The philosophical engagement with Judaism, moreover, also plays an important role in Marx, Nietzsche, and Freud's critical dialogue with the philosophy of the Enlightenment. Through its sustained interaction

31. Some of this work has already been done in the case of Adorno and Auerbach by Jim Porter; see Porter 2008, 2010.

32. On the broad topic of modernity's relationship to antiquity see Morley 2009. For Marx, McCarthy 1990 and 1994; for Nietzsche, see Porter 2000; for Freud, see Armstrong 2005a.

33. See Rotenstreich 1964, 1984; Mack 2003; Rose 1993.

with both classical and biblical cultures, the German philosophy of modernity has been suspended between Athens and Jerusalem.

"Jerusalem against Athens has become the emblem for revelation against reason, for the hearing of the commandments against the search for first principles, for the love of the neighbour against explanation of the world, and for the prophet against the philosopher," writes Gillian Rose. "Yet, suddenly, in the wake of the perceived demise of Marxism, Athens, for a long time already arid and crumbling, has become an uncannily deserted city, haunted by departed spirits. Her former inhabitants, abandoning her justice as well as her reason, have set off in a pilgrimage to an imaginary Jerusalem, in search of difference or otherness, love or community, and hoping to escape the *imperium* of reason, truth or freedom."[34] The desertion of Athens may not have been as sudden as Rose suggests. From its very inception, the modern opposition between Greeks and Jews has been at the heart of a debate about the Enlightenment and its limits. The conflicts between justice and reason, universalism and difference, love and community have, ever since the end of the eighteenth century, found their expression in a conceptual opposition between Greeks and Jews. Moses Mendelssohn, for instance, did not have to wait for the demise of Marxism to defect from Athens and create his own imaginary Jerusalem. Mendelssohn's Jerusalem embraced justice and community, ethics and difference, without abandoning reason or freedom.

But what of Athens and Jerusalem today? Can we, like Mendelssohn, use this polarity to formulate an alternative universalism for our own post-Enlightenment age? Can we hope for a truly secular Europe not founded on the exclusionary principles of a Hellenized Christianity? Can we dare to imagine not just a new Jerusalem but a new Athens too? "Difficult to say 'Europe,'" wrote Derrida, "without connoting: Athens-Jerusalem-Rome-Byzantium."[35] *Socrates and the Jews* is an attempt to make sense of these European connotations. If this book demonstrates that it is difficult to speak of a European past without reference to Athens, Rome, and Jerusalem, will there be room for Byzantium and even for Tertullian's Carthage in a more inclusive European future?

34. Rose 1993, 1.
35. Derrida 1998, 4.

1

Socrates and the Reason of Judaism:
Moses Mendelssohn and Immanuel Kant

"There must be Jews who are not really Jews."
LESSING, *Die Juden*

In September 1784 the *Berlinische Monatschrift* published an answer to the question "What is Enlightenment?" The essay was written by the Berlin philosopher Moses Mendelssohn. Immanuel Kant's more celebrated answer to that same question, published in the same journal three months later, "marks" what Foucault has called "the discreet entrance into the history of thought of a question that modern philosophy has not been capable of answering, but it has never managed to get rid of, either."[1] "With the two texts published in the *Berlinische Monatschrift*" continues Foucault, "the German *Aufklärung* and the Jewish *Haskala* recognize that they belong to the same history; they are seeking to identify the common processes from which they stem. And it is perhaps a way of announcing the acceptance of a common destiny—we now know to what drama that was to lead."[2]

Foucault locates the beginning of a new philosophical era, indeed the beginning of modernity itself, in the collocation of these two essays, Kant's and Mendelssohn's, by the coincidence of the projects of the Aufklärung and the Haskalah. But, in Foucault's engagement with the question of Enlightenment, his own meditation on the destiny of a German and Jewish injunction to think soon gives way to an exclusive focus on Kant's work. If Mendelssohn is given little more than an anecdotal role in Foucault's master narrative of Europe's "impatience for liberty," he nevertheless looms in Foucault's essay as a reminder of a path not taken.[3]

Mendelssohn brings to the fore the intriguing role that Judaism assumed

---

1. On the institutional context of the coincidence of these two essays see Schmidt 1989.
2. Foucault 2003, 43–44.
3. Ibid., 57.

in the Enlightenment's wider interrogation of religion. As Nathan Rotenstreich puts it: "it is a curious fact that the major systems of German philosophy were preoccupied to such an extent with Judaism." For Rotenstreich,
the reasons for this "curious fact" are mainly historical.[4] He comments on
the coincidence of the historical emancipation of the Jews with the development of the most influential traditions of German thought. As Hannah Arendt observes: "The modern Jewish question dates from the Enlightenment;
it was the Enlightenment—that is, the non-Jewish world—that posed it."[5]
In France and Germany the philosophers' abstract questioning of liberty of
thought had its concrete concomitant in political debates about the admission of Jews into civil society.[6] Granting citizenship to the Jews became a test
case for the enlightened nation. In historical terms, Judaism was far from an
academic preoccupation for the new *philosophes*.

The near coincidence of Kant's and Mendelssohn's essays in the *Berlinische Monatschrift* in 1784 was not the first time that these two philosophers'
works had come into competition. In fact, Mendelssohn's precedence in this
debate merely repeats the pattern of an earlier encounter at the start of the
two philosophers' respective careers. Over twenty years earlier, Mendelssohn
had effectively launched his philosophical oeuvre with an essay, "On Evidence in the Metaphysical Sciences," which had defeated Kant's own essay
in the competition for a prestigious prize from the Royal Prussian Academy
of Sciences. In this work Mendelssohn had set out to prove that metaphysics
and the natural sciences share a methodology: the exercise of reason. This
classic statement of Enlightenment optimism followed the program of extending the Newtonian revolution from the natural to the human world.
Mendelssohn was thus, from the very start, the embodiment of an Aufklärer.
His work and life brought him into contact with every important figure of
his age—indeed a list of his intellectual and personal interlocutors reads like
a Who's Who of Enlightenment thought: Locke, Hume, Leibniz, Voltaire,
Rousseau, to say nothing of Lessing, Jacobi, Hamann, Herder, and Kant.[7] The
scope of his work was also impressive. In addition to his essays and books on

4. Rotenstreich 1984, vii. See also Brumlik 2000; Librett 2000. Librett (2000, 24–25) gives a
different account of this development that focuses more directly on theological concerns: "The
Enlightenment overcoming of Lutheran Protestantism . . . will pose (or be exposed to) the threat
of a *reemergence of Judaism as the privileged religio-cultural figure of literal, spiritual fulfillment*."

5. Arendt 2007, 3.

6. See in particular Hess 2002 for the German context and Schechter 2003 for the French
philosophes.

7. For the most important intellectual biographies of Mendelssohn see Altmann 1973, Bourel
2004, and Tree 2007.

metaphysics and epistemology he wrote extensively on political theory, theology, and aesthetics (it was Mendelssohn, for instance, who inspired Lessing to write his *Laokoon*).

And yet, it is perhaps Mendelssohn's alternative identity as the "Jew of Berlin" that has been his more lasting legacy. Mendelssohn's career, contacts, and works all speak to the universalism of the Enlightenment project. His writings on metaphysics, epistemology, and aesthetics are written in a shared language of eighteenth-century European thought.

And yet, it is his particularity rather than his embrace of universalism that has more often than not marked him out for note in our histories of thought. In both his age and our own it is what Willi Goetschel has termed (with reference to Spinoza) the "scandal of his Jewishness," which has made of Mendelssohn a figure of ambivalent fascination.[8] Many have seen in Mendelssohn's work at times an implicit and at other times an explicit attempt to find a mediating role between the poles of Enlightenment and Judaism, reason and religion. The theoretical framework for this venture has been found in his most influential work *Jerusalem, or on Religious Power and Judaism*. At the level of practice, Mendelssohn also engaged directly in the campaign of Jewish civil emancipation advocating equal rights and citizenship within the Prussian state.

His project of reformation had consequences on both sides of the ghetto walls. Mendelssohn's attempts to improve the social status of Jews was mirrored by a reformist attitude within the Jewish community that he also helped to cultivate.[9] His translation of the Psalms and Pentateuch into German was part of this attempt at greater cultural integration although he never followed a straightforward assimilationist stance.[10] Mendelssohn's German Bible was actually written in Hebrew script. The ambivalence of Mendelssohn's attitude to German-Jewish relations has no more eloquent an expression than his translation of the Torah. As Jonathan Sheehan puts it, Mendelssohn's translation

> was, in a complex and contradictory way, supposed to give largely Yiddish-speaking Jewish children a subtly rendered German text in order that they might have access to the Hebrew original. One cannot help sympathize with the rabbi who complained that such a work "induces the young to spend time

8. See Goetschel 2004, 4. Although Goetschel is talking here about Spinoza, he writes extensively about Mendelssohn's debt to Spinoza. For Goetschel, Mendelssohn follows Spinoza in his formulation of an "alternative universalism."

9. On Mendelssohn's relationship to the Berlin *Haskala* see Behm 2002.

10. See Altmann 1973, 368–83, 242–45, on the genesis of these translations.

reading Gentile books in order to become sufficiently familiar with refined German to be able to understand this translation."[11]

As Sheehan concludes: "The task was incredibly complex. Mendelssohn sought, at one and the same time, to train the Jews in German culture, to produce a German-Jewish literary monument, and to persuade Germans that the wisdom of the ancient Hebrews lived on in meaningful poetic and philosophical terms."[12] Just as Franz Rosenzweig and Martin Buber's translation of the Bible stands as a testament of German-Jewish ambivalence at the beginning of the twentieth century, so Moses Mendelssohn's German Torah in Hebrew letters expresses the ambiguous position of the enlightened Jew at the close of the eighteenth century.[13]

His role in this religious Enlightenment led Heinrich Heine to give Mendelssohn the title of the "Jewish Luther." But within Judaism, Mendelssohn has always been more important as a symbolic figure of cultural fusion than as a radical doctrinal innovator. Conversely within Enlightenment philosophy, Mendelssohn represents the acceptable face of Judaism in a largely anti-Judaic tradition. It is as an honorable exception to his race that he is admitted into the mainstream of Berlin intellectualism. Immortalized by Lessing in his *Nathan, der Weise*, Mendelssohn represents the Jew who rises above the limitations of his people to achieve the status of universal humanity: the Jew, in short, who is no Jew. And yet, it is easy to overstate the tokenism of Mendelssohn's role in the Aufklärung. He achieved a remarkable degree of integration and, far from being marginal, Mendelssohn was central to German thought in the second half of the eighteenth century. To his contemporaries he was not only an exceptional Jew but an exceptional thinker, one who was able to vie with Kant, after all, in the intellectual contests of his day. Mendelssohn was not only just a Jewish Luther or a wise Nathan, he was a "German Socrates."

In this chapter I want to take this term, "German Socrates," seriously as an incitement to investigate this fusion of Enlightenment thought and Judaism in a period of explosive German philhellenism. Through his identification with Socrates, Mendelssohn would attempt to secure for Judaism the same recognition that was accorded to Greco-Roman antiquity in this period. By claiming that ancient Jerusalem could act as a rival to the idealized

11. Sheehan 2005, 180.

12. Ibid.

13. On Mendelssohn and Rosenzweig see Funkenstein 1993, Hilfrich 2000, and now Rosenstock 2010.

societies of Athens and Rome, he insisted that its inclusions must have certain effects both for Judaism and for Enlightenment.[14] Mendelssohn's move
was bold—it challenged the monopoly of Christian Enlightenment thinkers
over the classical past. Mendelssohn would not only disrupt the binary of
Greece and Rome, he would also render these classical models in Jewish
rather than Christian terms.

Early in his career Mendelssohn set about writing a version of Plato's
Phaedo. Mendelssohn's own dialogue on the immortality of the soul was an
immediate bestseller; its first edition sold out within four months. It was sub-
sequently published in numerous editions and translated into Dutch, French,
Russian, Danish, Italian, and English all within Mendelssohn's life time. His
choice of dialogue is telling. The image of the steadfast Socrates calmly debating his own death with his anxious followers stages a classic scene of the
triumph of reason over fear and superstition. But the choice of a dialogue
on the immortality of the soul has a specific resonance within the religious
discourse of the eighteenth century. The belief in immortality was, in Alexander Altmann's words, "one of the few dogmas of natural religion."[15] Mendelssohn's task in his *Phaedon* was to provide a proof of the immortality of
the soul without reference to revelation. By putting his proofs in the mouth
of the pagan Socrates, Mendelssohn attempts to show how immortality can
be deduced from reason alone. Mendelssohn's dialogue thus steers a course
between the poles of Plato and Neoplatonism, between pagan reason and
Christian revelation. His *Phaedo* represents an attempt to reclaim Plato for
the Enlightenment. Mendelssohn wrests his Socrates away from the mysticism of the Neoplatonists and reinstalls him in the pantheon, so to speak, of
rationality.

And yet, Socrates remained a problematic figure for the *philosophes*.[16] For
his eighteenth-century readers Plato bridged the gap between philosophy and
theology. Through the Neoplatonist tradition, Socrates had come to embody
not so much the opposition as the compromise between reason and revelation. If Christianity could appropriate Socrates as a precursor to Christ, Judaism tended to adopt an alternative chronology. Since Philo of Alexandria
in the first century BCE, Plato had been identified as a follower of Moses.
As Numenius is supposed to have put it "What is Plato but Moses speaking Attic Greek?" Divine truth, according to Philo of Alexandria, could be

14. It would be interesting to read Mendelssohn's advocacy of Jerusalem against the background of an earlier tradition of political theory traced by Nelson (2010).

15. See Altmann 1973, 148–49.

16. Gay 1967, 82–83.

traced in an unbroken chain from Plato through Pythagoras back to Moses. Platonic doctrine, in this interpretation, was merely an elaboration of Old Testament wisdom. If Mendelssohn had so wished, it would have been easy for him to assimilate his Socrates to this theologizing tradition of Platonism. But there was more to this choice, for to choose to discuss the issue of immortality had a particular resonance in a German-Jewish context. Christians had long been critical of Judaism's neglect of the issue of the immortality of the soul. The Hebrew Bible, they observed, had nothing explicit to say on the issue. From the Christian perspective, the question of immortality was just one more indication of the essential lack of Judaism. Whether we see this as a lack or a virtue, immortality is a Greek—not a Jewish—idea. Paradoxically Philo had to recourse to Plato to fill in the gaps of Jewish theology. Platonism is not so much the antithesis as the supplement to Judaism. Plato hardly represented the dangerous lure of paganism. Jews needed Plato to become better Jews.

Socrates, then, is an ambivalent figure of reason. When Mendelssohn chose Socrates and when his contemporaries for their part chose to identify Mendelssohn with Socrates, there was more at stake than any simple conflict between Enlightenment and religion. The epithet "German Socrates" expressed or, better, covered over a complex series of questions and anxieties about Judaism and its relationship both to pagan Athens and Christian Berlin. The reception of Plato in the late eighteenth century calls into question the Enlightenment's embrace of a monolithic conception of reason. Moreover, the specific fusion of Platonism and Judaism in Mendelssohn's work announces a new chapter in the long history of Socrates' relationship to Moses.

The uneasy compromise between reason and revelation that preoccupies Mendelssohn in his *Phaedon* is also at the heart of his most famous work, *Jerusalem*. It is here that Mendelssohn explicitly defends Judaism against Christianity and sets out a vision of the ideal relationship between politics and theology. Mendelssohn's *Jerusalem*, according to Altmann, represents "the first attempt at a philosophy of Judaism in the modern period."[17] *Jerusalem*, in fact, tries to pull off the ultimate sophistic challenge: to show that Judaism was not only reconcilable to the Enlightenment but also provided its most compelling model of a life governed by reason. His argument is bolstered by a historical interpretation of the political organization of the ancient Jewish polity. Flying in the face of the accepted wisdom of his age, Mendelssohn posits monarchic Jerusalem rather than democratic Athens or republican Rome as his paradigm of the enlightened city.

17. Altmann 1983, 3.

But despite his unorthodox contribution to the debate about antiquity, Mendelssohn proclaimed skepticism about the rise of historicism as the dominant mode of argumentation among his peers.[18] Mendelssohn's analysis of Judaism came under sustained attack in the nineteenth century by his more historically minded readers. For Mendelssohn had maintained the autonomy of reason from the vagaries of historical development and was particularly hostile to the master theories of historical progress that were so important to Lessing, Kant, and later to Hegel. As Matt Erlin has put it, "Mendelssohn . . . not only rejects the idea of global human progress; he also refuses to acknowledge any substantive distinction between past and present and thus seems to deny the very possibility of a modern age understood in terms of qualitative historical difference."[19] Mendelssohn's complex use of history in *Jerusalem* has both an important philosophical role to play in the development of his own ideas about universalism and a wider resonance in the debates about the ruptures and continuities between antiquity and modernity in the eighteenth century.

Socrates and the Age of Enlightenment

If the twentieth century, in the wake of Freud's compelling reading of Sophocles, has been known as the "age of Oedipus," the eighteenth century could be called the age of Socrates. As Benno Böhm asserts, "Socrates is the 'hell fire,' which Eighteenth-century Man has to walk through" to come to a better understanding of himself.[20] Socrates' life and death have, of course, been a preoccupation for philosophers since the fifth century BCE. The eighteenth century, however, remains a distinctive moment in the transformation of Socrates into a figure of modernity. The age of Enlightenment witnesses, in Raymond Trousson's words, a Socratic "prise de conscience."[21] While at the beginning of the century Socrates could still be seen as a relatively marginal character in the history of philosophy (Aristotle and to a lesser extent Plato were the figures associated with the ancient tradition), by the time of the French Revolution Socrates had assumed a position of dominance. Already by the middle of the century three plays entitled *La Mort de Socrate* appeared in France in the space of six years.[22]

18. See Reill 1975; Meinecke 1972; Myers 2003; Hess 2002.

19. Erlin 2002, 85.

20. Böhm 1966, 3.

21. Trousson 1967, 17.

22. See Wilson 2007, 172.

On all sides, newspapers and periodicals glorying in the name of Socrates joined in the fray. Addison and Steele brought out a *Modern Socrates*; publications called *Socrates* appeared in Berlin, Dresden and Leipzig; Hamann wrote his *Mémoires Socratiques* [*sic*], Vernet wrote the *Dialogues Socratiques*; Fontenelle made Socrates converse with Montaigne; Toland, following Locke, founded a 'Socratic Society' open to free discussion as to every religious faith.[23]

For Alexander Nehamas, the "Socratic question" was not native to antiquity, it was an invention of the eighteenth century.[24]

The rise of Socrates as a figure of fascination mirrors the wider turn to antiquity that took place in this period. Socrates' rediscovery is in part the story of the discovery of classics as a discipline. The emergence of Socrates as a paradigm of reason can partly be accounted for by developments in the burgeoning field of philology. Philosophy's first martyr came to take on a particular form at this time in parallel with the availability of new source material and the development of the ever more technical analysis of ancient texts. At the dawn of the nineteenth century, Friedrich Schleiermacher saw this textual revolution as crucial to the rehabilitation of Plato: "For of all philosophers who have ever lived, none have had so good a right as Plato, in many respects, to set up the only too general complaint of being misunderstood, or not understood at all."[25] For Schleiermacher, rescuing Plato from misinterpretation entailed a return to the Platonic text. Schleiermacher's hermeneutic placed textual analysis at the cornerstone of interpretation. The figure of Socrates has a crucial role to play in the development of this literary critical methodology. For the exercise of liberating Socrates from tired second-hand accounts is at the heart of this project. Direct access to the texts of Plato and Xenophon should give us direct access to Socrates. Moreover, it is not just a case of going back to the original Greek texts rather than relying on poor Latin intermediaries; the project also involves peeling back the damage of harmful later accretions. Redeeming Plato, and especially redeeming Socrates, involves extricating them from the "misinterpretations" of history.

Neoplatonism was perhaps the most obvious of these historical deformations. If Schleiermacher champions a philological Plato, he does so in order to defend against a theological Plato. For, as Julia Lamm puts it, "claims about Plato's philosophy had to be grounded in the writings themselves— undefiled by dogmatic commitments, theological agendas or other philo-

23. Montuori 1981, 15. This is almost a direct translation from Trousson 1967.
24. Nehamas 1998, 93.
25. Schleiermacher 1836, 4.

sophical systems."[26] Despite Schleiermacher's own Christian sympathies, both he and his reading practices were heir to the Enlightenment's hostility to Neoplatonism. Schleiermacher may, as Nehamas suggests, be the first truly modern reader of Plato, but his philological rigor has its roots in earlier debates about the identity of Socrates. The task of dating and ordering Plato's dialogues, which had preoccupied Schleiermacher, had at its source a desire to identify the moment at which the thought of the historical Socrates was superseded by the doctrine of Plato. By pinpointing this transition it became possible to establish the distinctiveness of Socrates above and beyond his later appropriations from Plato right up until the eighteenth century.

By isolating the Socrates of the early aporetic dialogues from the transcendental turn of Plato's late style, contemporary philosophers were able to recast Socrates as a figure of Enlightenment. The virtue of the historical Socrates, writes Trousson, was "a wholly secular virtue, certainly not an atheist one, but one which was independent of the dogmas of the priests. . . . He became, thus, a sort of apostle of natural religion, the archetype of the free thinker in matters of faith, and the designated champion of Deism."[27] By reestablishing the historicity of a living Socrates one could return him to his pagan context far removed from the Christianizing imperatives of his later readers. But this historicist gesture itself needs to be historicized. Fifth-century Athens became assimilated to eighteenth-century Paris. Rousseau and Diderot found in Socrates a fellow sufferer in their battles with the state, while for Voltaire "the death of this master was the apotheosis of philosophy."[28]

According to Vieillard-Baron, Plato's dialogues were hardly read in the first half of the eighteenth century. Nevertheless, he argues, "major theological wars were fought in the name of Plato who was a figure who represented simultaneously a quasi-Christian pagan and the corruptor of authentic Christianity."[29] The rediscovery of Socrates in the middle of the century is intimately related to this theological war. Philology worked hand in hand with philosophy to extract a dialogic, aporetic Socrates from the doctrinaire Plato. Socrates as a rationalist skeptic was held up in opposition to the believing Plato that Christianity had already claimed for itself. But many of the depictions of Socrates, far from removing him from the Christian framework, only served to highlight it.

Beyond Neoplatonist philosophy, a separate, if related, tradition existed

26. Lamm 2005, 93. On the philosophical significance of Schleiermacher's hermeneutics see also Bowie 2005.

27. Trousson 1967, 18.

28. Voltaire 1994, 729.

29. Vieillard-Baron 1979a, 64.

FIGURE 1. Jacques-Louis David, *The Death of Socrates*, 1787. The Metropolitan Museum of Art.

that linked Socrates to the figure of Christ. More specifically, it linked the
heroic death of Socrates to the martyrdom of the Messiah. Long before Percy
Bysshe Shelley proclaimed Socrates "the Jesus Christ of Greece," Christian
writers had been drawn to accounts of Socrates' death as a precursor to
Christ's own agony. The exercise of favorably comparing Christ to Socrates
became a topos of early Christian writings.[30] But the assimilation of these
figures survived both late antiquity and the Middle Ages. Marsilio Ficino,
whose Latin translations of Plato were widely consulted by Enlightenment
philosophers, was the author of one of the most elaborate comparisons
between these two martyrs. As Emily Wilson recounts, the eighteenth century's iconographic representations of Socrates were reworkings of an older
thematic: "artists who might, a century earlier, have painted a *Deposition of
Christ* . . . now searched classical literature for a suitable death."[31] The zenith
of this tradition of "secular *pietas*" was reached when the Royal Academy of
France made the death of Socrates the topic of its grand prize in 1762. The
specter of a thousand dying Christs looms behind even Jacques-Louis David's
aggressively secular *Mort de Socrate* (see fig. 1) . The age of reason may have
worked hard to topple Jesus Christ from his position of authority and replace
him with the pagan Socrates. But this effort more often than not resulted in

30. See Hanfmann 1951, 214–18.
31. Wilson 2007, 172.

an insidious juxtaposition rather than a straightforward substitution. For all his enthusiasm for Socrates as the embodiment of a new religion, Voltaire, like everyone else couldn't help invoking Jesus as a counterpart to Socrates. It was Voltaire, after all, who named Christ the "Socrates of Palestine."

The question of religion, then, was never far from the surface of the Enlightenment's Socratic preoccupations. Although eighteenth-century intellectuals essentially turned to Socrates for a paradigm of an ethical life, they were also caught up in the pressing metaphysical and epistemological questions of their age. Discussions of Socrates in this period are an illustration of the complex entwinement of moral, ontological, and epistemic debates. Johann Georg Hamann's 1759 *Sokratische Denkwürdigkeiten* (*Socratic Memorabilia*) is a case in point. When Hamann, another of Kant's close associates, had a spectacular pietistic conversion experience during a failed business trip to London, Kant suggested to him that he set about translating some entries from the French *Encyclopédie* as remedy for his departure from rational methodology. Hamann responded to Kant in a letter which has "good claim to be the first clash between the *Aufklärung* and the *Sturm und Drang*."[32] In the letter he cast Kant in the role of Socrates and himself assumed the identity of Socrates' *daimon*—the figure of genius who speaks through Socrates.[33] Hamann's prophetic message announces the end of the tyranny of the Enlightenment and a return to faith and feeling. Hamann, thus, uses Socrates himself to voice the voice of inspiration that had been repressed in his Enlightenment reception. In his response to Kant, Hamann sarcastically topples Socrates as a figure of reason. The letter was only a prelude to his more extended identification with Socrates' spirit in his *Socratic Memorabilia*. Hamann's account of the life of Socrates is a full-frontal attack on the arrogance of the Enlightenment written in the name of its most favored representative. Composed in an obscure prose densely overlaid with biblical references, the *Memorabilia* represents Socrates' battle with the Sophists as a precursor to Hamann's own battle with Kant and his Enlightenment cronies:

> The opinion [*Meinung*] of Socrates can be summarized in these blunt words when he said to the Sophists, the learned men of the time, "I know nothing." Therefore these words are a thorn in their eyes and a scourge on their backs. All of Socrates' ideas, which were nothing more than expectorations and secretions of his ignorance, seemed as frightful to them as the hair of Medusa's head, the knob of the Aegis.[34]

32. Beiser 1987, 23.
33. See Nicholls 2006, 82ff.
34. Hamann 1967, 167.

Hamann can think of no more provocative a challenge to Kant than to proclaim his own ignorance. As frightful "as the hair of Medusa's head," the realization that "I know nothing" is the symbolic castration of the Enlightenment. The "secretions" of Socrates' ignorance were far more offensive to his
Sophistic contemporaries than a basketful of doctrines. Socrates' big idea is
his lack of ideas. Where Plato's Socrates labors the difference between belief
and certainty, truth and opinion, Hamann's Socrates defiantly contents himself with "Meinung" (opinion). Hamann has different oppositions to labor:

> The ignorance of Socrates was sensibility [*Empfindung*]. But between sensibil-
> ity and a theoretical proposition is a greater difference than between a living
> animal and his anatomical skeleton. The ancient and modern skeptics may
> wrap themselves ever so much in the lion skin of Socratic ignorance; never-
> theless they betray themselves by their voices and ears. If they know nothing,
> why does the world need a learned demonstration of it? Their hypocrisy is
> ridiculous and insolent. Whoever needs so much acumen and eloquence to
> convince himself of his ignorance, however, must cherish in his heart a pow-
> erful repugnance of the truth of it.[35]

Empfindung in Socrates' world is king. Sensibility is the governing principle of existence. But the equation of ignorance and sensibility has a peculiar
meaning in Hamann. The realization of one's own ignorance is tantamount
to the acknowledgment of a realm of faith that exists beyond the dominion
of reason. Enlightenment thought may have skepticism at its root, it may
see critique as the touchstone of its methodology, but real self-criticism remains beyond its scope. For genuine self-criticism (with "voices and ears")
would inevitably confront one with experiences that defy rational analysis.
Hamann's Socrates feels, and he understands that to feel is to acknowledge
that there is something that exceeds the grasp of a rational mind. There is no
eloquence, no "theoretical proposition" that could come close to capturing
faith; in his strikingly Protestant formulation, it is "an *immediate* experience,
one whose content is private, ineffable, and just given. . . . Faith is on a par
with our simple sense qualities such as the tangy taste of oranges, the sharp-
ness of a needle, the brightness of colour."[36]

> Our own existence and the existence of all things outside us must be believed,
> and cannot be determined in any other way. What is more certain than the
> end of man, and of what truth is there a more general or better attested knowl-
> edge? Nevertheless, no one is wise enough to believe it except the one who, as

35. Ibid.
36. Beiser 1987, 28.

Moses makes clear, is taught by God himself to number his days. What one believes does not, therefore have to be proved, and a proposition can be never so incontrovertibly proven without on that account being believed.[37]

The injunction to "believe" stands in stark opposition to the Enlightenment imperative to think. To Kant's *sapere aude*, Hamann answers *credere aude*. And Hamann chooses as his illustration the very issue of immortality, which will be at the core of Mendelssohn's engagement with Socrates. For all the advance of scientific reason, it has taken religion to convince man of the certainty of his own death. It is to God and not to reason that man looks to comprehend his own mortality. Hamann's argument is characteristically paradoxical. The faith on which he calls seems to lead us to believe in *immortality*, while reason is normally credited with the demonstration of mortality. But Hamann is not wrong to see that the converse is powerfully present here when the proponents of natural religion are busy trying to devise "proofs" of immortality, while Moses merely feels through God that "his days are numbered." Moses has direct access to God's wisdom without the intermediary of human reason. Religious knowledge is not a category of reason. And in Hamann's version, Socrates shares this knowledge with Moses:

What for a Homer replaces ignorance of the rules of art which an Aristotle devised after him, and what for a Shakespeare replaces the ignorance or transgression of those critical laws? Genius is the unanimous answer. Indeed Socrates could very well afford to be ignorant; he had a tutelary genius, on whose science he could rely, which he loved and feared as his god, whose peace was more important to him than all the reason of the Egyptians and the Greeks, whose voice he believed, and by means of whose wind . . . the empty understanding of a Socrates can become fruitful as well as the womb of a pure virgin.[38]

It is not difficult to see how Hamann's hymn to "genius" marks him out as precursor to Romanticism. Indeed, Hamann's whole portrait of Socrates in his *Memorabilia* seems unsettlingly modern. His untimely emphasis on ignorance and self-knowledge anticipates many of the obsessions of both the nineteenth and twentieth centuries' characterizations of Socrates.[39] But Hamann's notion of genius also articulates a cultural conflict. Socrates' "tutelary genius" is a more integral part of his identity "than all the reason of the Egyptians and the Greeks." Despite the reference to Homer, Hamann sees

37. Hamann 1967, 167.
38. Ibid., 171.
39. From Hegel to Lacan, as it were. See Leonard 2005, Kofman 1998, Harrison 1994, and Trapp 2007a, 2007b.

Socratic genius as distinctly "un-Greek." Not for the first time, Hamann allu-
sively suggests a communality between Socrates and Christ. Socrates' "empty
understanding" has the same promise as the "womb of a pure virgin." It is
almost as if Socrates' ignorance *is* the womb from which Christ will emerge.
Socrates' lack is more than compensated by his faith and this faith is the faith
of Christianity. Hamann, on the one hand, seems to be drawing an opposition between the reason of Greece and the "genius" of Moses and Christ.
Moses blocks his ears to the "theoretical propositions" of the Greek Sophists,
as the "pure virgin" stands immune to the reason of Greece and Egypt. The
Hebrew and the Greek embody two distinct and irreconcilable worldviews.
On the other hand, it seems obvious that Hamann's presentation of the life
of Socrates argues for a profound continuity between Hellenic and Christian culture. Although, as we have already seen, he was able to draw on an
extensive tradition of comparisons between Socrates and Christ, Hamann's
demonic Socrates has his own unique flavor. And despite the reference to
Moses, Hamann's vision of a Christian Socrates in democratic Athens largely
bypasses Jerusalem in his narrative of spiritual history. Christianity's affinity
to Hellenism is an exclusive affinity achieved at the expense of its relationship
to Judaism.

Hamann's Hellenic proto-Christ, then, voices a polemic against the Enlightenment and its adoption of Greece as the homeland of rationality. Locked
in a confrontation with Kant, Hamann's conceit was to assume the mantle of
Socrates to expose what he took to be the arrogance and hypocrisy of the age
of reason's philhellenic aspirations. "It is one of the exciting facts of cultural
history," writes O'Flaherty, "that in the year 1759, exactly at a time when the
Enlightenment was at the zenith of its influence, Hamann published his *Socratic Memorabilia*, a treatise presenting a version of Socrates in direct contrast
to the portrait of that philosopher presented by the Enlightenment."[40] Hamann's *Sokratische Denkwürdigkeiten* pulls Enlightenment time out of joint.
His Socrates is simultaneously premodern and postmodern. He embodies
both the devotion of the Middle Ages and the suspicion of the present.

By the time Hamann's Socratic rebuke appeared in press, Moses Mendelssohn's own Socrates project had already been conceived. In his biography, Alexander Altmann gives a compelling account of the gestation of
Mendelssohn's *Phaedon* and the difficulties of its execution.[41] Mendelssohn
is only one in a long line of thinkers who have been kept awake at night by

40. O'Flaherty 1967, 5.
41. Altmann 1973, 140–79.

the enigma of Socrates.[42] It was during this period of creative frustration that Mendelssohn surveyed the field of other contemporary Socrateses and wrote one of the three published reviews to which Hamann would respond. Mendelssohn's review (1843) is surprisingly positive. In fact, he goes so far as to praise Hamann's Greece as positively Winckelmannian:

> The way he writes reminds one of Winckelmann. It is the same grainy but dark style, the same subtle but noble irony, and the same familiarity with the spirit of antiquity. You will note in particular that our author has beautifully transposed the naïve disposition of Socrates. The description of his character seems to be very life like.[43]

When Mendelssohn wrote this review, Johann Joachim Winckelmann had only recently published his groundbreaking work *Gedanken über die Nachahmung der griechischen Werke in der Malerei und Bildhauerkunst* (*Reflections on the Imitation of Greek Masterpieces in Painting and Sculpture*) (1755). Winckelmann's literary style, his vivid descriptions of Greek art and culture, as well as his colorful life all contributed to his immense popularity in the Enlightenment and the Romantic period. It is frequently asserted that Winckelmann singlehandedly seduced Germany into its passionate affair with ancient Greece that would last more than a century. Winckelmann's praise of the "noble simplicity and serene grandeur" heralded what Suzanne Marchand calls "a social revolution against the baroque, aristocratic tastes and values of the old regime." As Ludwig Curtius argues, "The cure [for the corruption of society], which for Rousseau was the return to nature, for Winckelmann was the return to the Greeks. Here essential humanness was to be found, in which, without consideration of status or role, the noble and the beautiful in each person was recognized and cultivated."[44]

It is interesting to see Mendelssohn compare Hamann's depiction of the notoriously ugly Socrates to Winckelmann's almost erotic paeans to the beauty of the Greeks. Alex Potts sees the political radicalism of the late eighteenth century as one of the fundamental legacies of Winckelmann's aestheticism. He examines a "highly charged engagement with the classical ideal associated with the radical Jacobin phase of the French Revolution, which reconnects

---

42. Compare Nietzsche 1979, 127: "*Socrates* is so close to me that I am almost continually fighting with him"; or Lacan 1991, 101: "The effect of this exhaustion could not be better summarized than by the words that came to me one of these sleepless Sunday nights—*Ce Socrate me tue*. And a curious thing, I woke up in the morning feeling infinitely more cheerful."

43. Mendelssohn 1843, 4.2:99.

44. Marchand 1996, 9; Curtius 1954, 58 (translation from Marchand 1996, 9).

with Winckelmann's attempt to represent the beauty of the Greek ideal as an embodiment of political freedom." But for Potts, the Socrates of David's *Mort de Socrate* precedes the Winckelmannian moment of the French Revolution: "Ideas of heroic austerity, of virile nobility, could apply equally to the message of works such as the *Oath of the Horatii*, the *Death of Socrates*, and the *Brutus*. As spectators, we might wish to identify with and admire the Horatii, but we are not invited to desire them." Emily Wilson, on the other hand, identifies David's Socrates as groundbreaking in his sex appeal: "Far more than any of his artistic predecessors, David makes Socrates look attractive. He inspires his philosophers by his shining intelligence and his sexiness."[45] While Potts and Wilson argue over which side of the Winckelmannian threshold to place David's Socrates of 1787, nearly thirty years earlier Mendelssohn had already decidedly associated Hamann's Socrates with the Winckelmannian aesthetic. What is more, the question of Socrates' body will take on a central importance in Mendelssohn's own *Phaedo* and its reception.

But while, in this respect, Mendelssohn's invocation of Winckelmann points to the revolutionary foresight of Hamann's depiction of Socrates, in other respects his review underplays Hamann's radicalism. By associating him with Winckelmann's "familiarity with the spirit of antiquity," Mendelssohn tames Hamann's philhellenism. Hamann's Socrates does not embody the spirit of his age; rather, he is the radical loner who was born into the wrong age. Unlike Hegel's Socrates, Hamann's *did* grow "like a mushroom out of the earth." He did *not* "stand in continuity with his time." Elsewhere in the review, Mendelssohn criticizes Hamann for his paradoxical argumentation about proof and belief, but fails to see Hamann's arguments as a real threat to the principles of the Enlightenment. What Hamann characterizes as Socrates' devastating critique, Mendelssohn depicts as his "naive Laune." Perhaps it is Mendelssohn's own "naïve disposition" at stake here?[46]

In Altmann's account of the genesis of the *Phaedon*, it is precisely this selective reading of Hamann's work that guides Mendelssohn's own research. Altmann indicates Mendelssohn's approval of Hamann's remark that Socrates' sentences were "a great many small islands lacking bridges and ferries for linking them methodically." Altmann summarizes Mendelssohn's response: "'One cannot judge more accurately,' Mendelssohn observed, 'the great truths and untrustworthy arguments of Socrates.' Thus Mendelssohn's discontent with Socrates' (i.e., Plato's) proofs was already evident. Its natural

---

45. Potts 1994, 223, 224; Wilson 2007, 177.

46. Hegel 1974, 384. On the later reception (and misunderstanding) of Mendelssohn's work by Hamann see Feuchtwanger 2003.

corollary was a desire to substitute more convincing ones."[47] Mendelssohn's review at one level seems to spectacularly miss the point of Hamann's critique of the culture of proof and hypothesis. *Pace* Altmann, it is difficult to see Mendelssohn's resolve to find "more convincing proofs" as an adequate response to Hamann's assertion: "between sensibility and a theoretical proposition is a greater difference than between a living animal and his anatomical skeleton." If, for Mendelssohn, the desire for better proofs was a natural corollary, for Hamann, it was a definite wrong turn.

Mendelssohn's *Phaedo*

Perhaps Mendelssohn saw a more profound continuity between his own project and the *Sokratische Denkwürdigkeiten* lurking beneath the surface of these glaring incongruities. It is certainly striking that Mendelssohn appears to take over the form of Hamann's work by preceding his dialogue with an account of Socrates' life. Hamann had seemingly read neither Plato nor Xenophon when he embarked on his *Memorabilia*.[48] Although Schleiermacher may have been sympathetic to Hamann's Christian feeling, he would have been hostile to his philological credentials. His choice of writing a biography of Socrates seems in part to have been governed by the source material that was available to him. By contrast, in Mendelssohn's own version even its biographical narrative self-consciously parades its learning. The contrast between Hamann and Mendelssohn's works is perhaps most vivid in their respective accounts of Socrates' daimon:

> The opinion of scholars is divided about the guardian spirit [Daemon], which Socrates alleged to possess, and which, as he said, always deterred him from doing anything harmful. Some believe that Socrates allowed himself a little poetic license here, in order to gain the ear of the superstitious population; but this seems to dispute his usual sincerity. Others understand by this guardian spirit a keen sense of good and evil, which, through reflection, long experience, and constant exercise, became moral instinct, by virtue of which he could judge and test every act of free will by its probable results and effects, without being able to give an account of it through judgment. Several instances are found in Xenophon and Plato, however, where this spirit foretells things to Socrates, which cannot be explained by any natural power of the soul. These instances perhaps have been added by his students from good intention.[49]

47. Altmann 1973, 141–42.
48. See O'Flaherty 1967, 59–60.
49. Mendelssohn 2007, 54–55.

Mendelssohn's argument here is hedged in the rhetoric of philological learning. He situates his own text against the background of scholarly opinion whose differences he must adjudicate. The "guardian spirit" here is the subject of academic debate rather than theological conviction. Both he and Hamann highlight the controversy of this aspect of Socrates' biography but while Hamann uses it as a springboard for revolutionary intellectual history, Mendelssohn makes it a quandary for the community of scholars. Rather than leading his readers to the edge of reason, Socrates' daimon calls upon the faculty of reason to fathom it. What seems to be an appeal to mysticism can either be understood as "poetic license" or as moral reason by another name: "a keen sense of good and evil, which, through reflection, long experience, and constant exercise, became moral instinct, by virtue of which he could judge and test every act of free will by its probable results and effects, without being able to give an account of it through judgment." While Mendelssohn admits that Socrates' acts are driven by "instinct" and are unable to "give an account of [themselves] through judgment," he nonetheless insists that this "instinct" is based not only on "reflection" and "long experience" but even, after all, on "judgment." Despite himself, Socrates remains a Kantian *avant la lettre*. Even Socrates' most suspect idiosyncrasy is here brought in line with the rational imperatives of morality and the moral imperatives of reason.

And yet, Mendelssohn seems aware that Socrates' daimon at some level seems to resist the schema of Enlightenment thought:

Perhaps also, Socrates, who, as we saw, was disposed to raptures, was weak or enthusiastic enough, to transform this vividly moral feeling, which he didn't know how to explain, into an intimate spirit, and to attribute those forebodings to it afterwards, which arise from entirely different sources. Must then an admirable man necessarily be free from all weaknesses and prejudices?

In our days, it is no longer popular to mock apparitions. Perhaps, in Socrates' time an exertion of genius was necessary to do that, which he used for a more productive purpose. All the same, it was usual for him to tolerate any superstition, which did not lead directly to moral corruption. . . . The felicity of the human race was his only study. As soon as a prejudice or superstition gave rise to open violence, injury to human rights, corruption of morals, etc., nothing in the world could stop him from defying all threats and persecutions, to profess himself against it.[50]

Even Socrates nods. . . . But if Socrates is not "free from weakness and prejudice," what hope is there for the rest of us? Socrates' "enthusiasm" is used by

50. Ibid., 55.

Mendelssohn as a test case of how the Enlightenment should deal with its doubters. As Francesco Tomasoni argues:

> "Radical Enlightenment" has often been accused of having nurtured the impossible dream of an absolutely free and autonomous reason, forgetting that "imprinting," that "horizon" which defines us. Nevertheless, distinction is made between legitimate and illegitimate prejudice, and therefore the superior criterion of reason is re-proposed. . . . During the period of the Enlightenment, there emerged a far more articulate awareness than is commonly admitted of the play between reason and prejudice.[51]

Tomasoni shows how in different ways both Mendelssohn and Kant strove to demonstrate that the distinction between "convenient" and "harmful" prejudices involved the exercise of reason.[52] Moreover, the issue of "tolerance" that Mendelssohn ascribes to Socrates is clearly crucial to his vision of an enlightened society. Tolerance of prejudice has its limits, however, in the violations performed in its name. Where prejudice stands in opposition to "human rights," Mendelssohn declares, Socrates would be the first to denounce it. The paradox, of course, remains if we acknowledge that in the previous statement it is Socrates' daimon rather than his reasoning capacity that enables him to draw the line between the convenient and the harmful. Even in his most rationalizing of accounts, Mendelssohn fails to exorcise the specter of Hamann's irrational Socrates.

Mendelssohn's exegesis of the Socratic daimon exhibits the same ambivalent attitude toward historical distance and difference that will characterize his work more generally. While Hamann does away altogether with the armory of scholarly apparatus, Mendelssohn coats his arguments in erudition: Mendelssohn cites Plato and Xenophon where Hamann recklessly ignores them; Hamann openly draws a line between the Sophists and Kant, between Socrates and himself, while Mendelssohn maintains a distinction between Socrates' "day" and "our own"; Hamann provocatively plays havoc with chronology so Socrates can be a Christian before Christ and simultaneously be a citizen of eighteenth-century Prussia. Mendelssohn's conscious anachronisms are more subtle. A Socrates who will defy "all threats and persecutions" in the name of "human rights" is hardly the embodiment of a fifth-century Athenian citizen. But Mendelssohn's presentism is no naïve ahistoricism. Mendelssohn conceptualized his project precisely as a precarious balancing act between historical sensitivity and philosophical relevance. In his preface

---

51. Tomasoni 2003, 2–3.
52. Ibid., 3–4.

to the *Phaedon* he writes: "The dialogue of the Greek author which has the name *Phaedo* has a multitude of extraordinary beauties which deserve to be used—the best of the doctrine of immortality. I took advantage of its form, ordering and eloquence, and have only tried to adapt the metaphysical truths to the taste of our time." Plato's dialogue on the one hand represents "the best of the doctrine of immortality"; on the other hand, the question of immortality was such a pressing contemporary issue that it would have been irresponsible of Mendelssohn not to revivify Plato's arguments. Mendelssohn rejects the idea of a passive reception of the past. The relationship between antiquity and modernity has to be a dynamic one in which the moderns have a duty to critically reflect on their debt to the past:

> In the third dialogue I had taken my refuge completely in the moderns, and allow my Socrates almost to speak like a philosopher of the eighteenth century. I would rather commit an anachronism, than leave out arguments, which can contribute something to convince the reader. In such a way the following mean between a translation and my own composition arose.[53]

Anachronism in Mendelssohn's scheme is a small price to pay for metaphysical Enlightenment. But the issue is not just one of rhetoric. Behind the question of the historicity of Socrates is a larger controversy about universal versus historical truths which will preoccupy Mendelssohn in his *Jerusalem* and bring him into conflict with both Kant and Lessing. Mendelssohn is careful to highlight the limitation of Plato's style rather than the content of his arguments. He does not so much reject his "proofs" as adapt them to "the taste of our times." The object is one of persuasion, he does not call into question the validity of Plato's arguments, as such. Mendelssohn, like Hamann, maintains a continuity between Socrates' convictions and his own. His task is to uncover the transhistorical truth that lies hidden beneath the ruptures of history. Neither Socrates in fifth-century Athens nor Mendelssohn in eighteenth-century Berlin can lay an exclusive claim to this insight. Both their philosophies are mere expressions of "the tastes of their times" striving to access the timeless ethical doctrine that unites them.

Mendelssohn and Socrates are thus united in their attempts to prove the immortality of the soul without reference to revelation. But in striving to do this through Socrates, Mendelssohn is pulled in unexpected directions. In particular, Mendelssohn's assimilation to Socratic rationality has surprising consequences for the relationship of Judaism to the Enlightenment. The investment in the question of the afterlife, as has already been mentioned,

53. Mendelssohn 2007, 42.

plays a dual role for Mendelssohn. The concept of immortality was key to the religious self-definition of the Aufklärung. Mendelssohn's program of updating Socrates' arguments for the imperishable soul was directly in line with the wider rationalist agendas of Gottfried Leibniz and Christian Wolff. In his *Phaedon* Mendelssohn claims to do for the question of immortality what he and others had done for the existence of God. It was the project of finding metaphysical proofs for God's existence that had preoccupied Mendelssohn in the so-called prize essay, which had seen him triumph over Kant.[54] Kant had his own victory when much later Mendelssohn called his dismissal of such proofs in his *Critique of Pure Reason* "weltzermalmend [world crushing]."[55] Kant's objections to Mendelssohn's proof of the immortality of the soul would turn out to be equally cataclysmic.

At the end of the second dialogue of the *Phaedon* Mendelssohn puts forth one of his most distinctive arguments for the imperishability of the soul. In a clear departure from the tenets of Platonic philosophy, Mendelssohn's Socrates argues for the simplicity of the soul's composition:

> We would neither remember, nor reflect, nor compare, nor be able to think, indeed, we would not even be the person that we had been a moment before, if our conceptions would be divided among many and were not encountered together somewhere in their closest connection. Therefore, we must at least hypothesize one substance which unites all concepts of the component parts. But will this substance be able to be composed from parts?
>
> Impossible, otherwise we need again a combining and contrasting, in order that from the parts becomes a whole, and we come back to the point from where we started.
>
> It will therefore be simple?
>
> Necessarily.
>
> Also unextended? For the extended thing is divisible, and the divisible is not simple.
>
> Right!
>
> There is, therefore, in our body at least one single substance, which is not extended, not compound, but is simple, has a power of intellect, and unites all our concepts and our desires, and inclinations in itself. What hinders us from calling this substance our soul?[56]

Mendelssohn claims in his preface that it was the Neoplatonist Plotinus who inspired this passage, but it clear that Leibniz's *Monadology* also lies behind

---

54. See Tomasoni 2004.
55. See Wood 1992; Adams 1998.
56. Mendelssohn 2007, 119–20.

Socrates' words here. Critics have been quick to note that Mendelssohn's is a bastardized Leibniz but it remains obvious that Leibniz's metaphysics provide the intellectual basis of Mendelssohn's rewriting of Plato. The argument about the simplicity of the soul follows from Mendelssohn's earlier assertions about the infinite divisibility of the body:

> Therefore nothing is lost with the dissolution of the animal body the disintegrated parts continue to exist, to act, to suffer, to be combined and separated, until they change through infinite transitions into parts of another composition. Some become dust, some become moisture, the former rises into air, the latter passes into a plant, wanders from the plant into a living animal, and leaves the animal, to serve as nourishment for a worm.[57]

What is death of the body other than its dissolution into its constituent parts? As the soul has no such fragments, dissolution is impossible and its immortality is secure. Socrates' high materialism in this passage is nonetheless predicated on an extreme dualism. It was this "proof of the permanence of the soul" developed by Mendelssohn that Kant refutes so decisively in his *Critique of Pure Reason*:

> In his [Mendelssohn's] *Phaedo* he endeavoured to prove that the soul cannot be subject to such a process of vanishing, which would be a true annihilation, by showing that a simple being cannot cease to exist. His argument is that since the soul cannot be diminished, and so gradually lose something of its existence, being by degrees changed into nothing (for since it has no parts, it has no multiplicity in itself), there would be no time between a moment in which it is and another in which it is not—which is impossible. He failed, however, to observe that even if we admit the simple nature of the soul, namely that it contains no manifold of constituents external to one another, and therefore no extensive quantity, we yet cannot deny to it a degree of reality in respect to all its faculties ... [which] may diminish through all the infinitely smaller degrees.[58]

"Thus the permanence of the soul . . . ," Kant concludes, "remains undemonstrated, and indeed indemonstrable." Kant applies the same dismissal to this Leibnizian proof of immortality as he had done to the project of providing a metaphysical proof for the existence of God. For Kant such metaphysical certainty lay beyond the boundaries of human thought. The limits of reason make any such demonstration impossible. Yet, far from a declaration of atheism, Kant's skeptical attitude to the rationalist project was rooted in his desire to return to religious feeling. In a phrase that recalls Hamann, Kant asserted

57. Ibid., 93.
58. Kant 1929, B413–14.

that "he had to deny knowledge, in order to make room for *faith*." And like Hamann, Kant will explicitly link this profession of the limits of reason to the figure of Socrates: "There is an inestimable benefit, that all objections to morality and religion will be forever silenced, and this in Socratic fashion, namely by the clearest proof of the ignorance of the objectors."[59] Where for Mendelssohn Socrates becomes a mouthpiece for the power of theoretical reason in the service of God, for Kant Socrates proclaims the limits of science in the service of religion and morality. As Robert Merrihew Adams puts it:

> The faith Kant has in mind is a purely rational faith, but it is grounded in practical (action-guiding, moral) reason rather than in theoretical reason. In Kant's view the inability of our theoretical faculties to prove the truth or falsity of religious claims leaves room for our practical reason to determine our religious stance. He welcomes this because he thinks it crucial for religion to be controlled by moral considerations.[60]

It is in this spirit that Kant puts forward his own contrasting argument for immortality in his *Critique of Practical Reason*:

> The realization of the summum bonum ["highest good"] in the world is the necessary object of a will determinable by the moral law. But in this will the perfect accordance of the mind with the moral law is the supreme condition of the summum bonum. . . . Now, the perfect accordance of the will with the moral law is holiness, a perfection of which no rational being of the sensible world is capable at any moment of his existence. Since, nevertheless, it is required as practically necessary, it can only be found in a progress in infinitum towards that perfect accordance, and on the principles of pure practical reason it is necessary to assume such a practical progress as the real object of our will.[61]

Kant argues that the ultimate aim of a human life is the attainment of certain moral ends that we must believe are capable of fulfillment. But the perfection of our virtue, Kant believes, is not realistically possible in the context of a human lifetime:

> This endless progress is only possible on the supposition of an endless duration of the existence and personality of the same rational being (which is called the immortality of the soul). The summum bonum, then, practically is only possible on the supposition of the immortality of the soul; consequently this immortality, being inseparably connected with the moral law, is a postulate of pure practical reason (by which I mean a theoretical proposition, not demonstrable as such, but which is an inseparable result of an unconditional a priori practical law.)

59. Ibid., Bxxx.
60. Adams 1998, vii–viii.
61. Kant 1998, 147

This principle of the moral destination of our nature, namely, that it is only in an endless progress that we can attain perfect accordance with the moral law, is of the greatest use, not merely for the present purpose of supplementing the impotence of speculative reason, but also with respect to religion.[62]

For Kant, a belief in immortality is a necessary condition of moral self-improvement. A world in which annihilation were a certainty would in, Kant's estimation, be a much less ethical one. Although it mirrors the moral precepts of Christianity, Kant's position is not simply reducible to it. The belief in the afterlife as the moral compensation for a mortal life of virtue is not what is envisioned here. Kant's ethics remain firmly rooted in the here and now of mortality. The afterlife in Kant's scheme does not represent a rupture with the ethical aspirations of this life, rather it merely represents an extension in time. Kant, thus, takes the question of immortality away from a metaphysical toward an ethical plane. While Mendelssohn's commitment to rationalism leads him to find ever more refined "proofs" for the undying soul, Kant's own commitment to reason leads him to dismiss such proofs as ultimately misguided. Immortality becomes in his scheme a necessity for the ethical precepts of the Enlightenment.

While Mendelssohn never quite abandoned the rationalist project of metaphysical demonstration, his task of reconciling Judaism to the demands of reason takes an increasingly ethical turn. Despite Kant's attempt to make Mendelssohn's Leibnizian proof of immorality the centerpiece of the *Phaedon*, there is good evidence that the wider reception of Mendelssohn's dialogue prioritized its moral preoccupations. Mendelssohn's decision to speak through the medium of the pagan Socrates exemplified a desire to create a new ethical discourse which, while not transcending the concept of religion itself, attempts to move beyond the differences between religions. Mendelssohn's Socrates makes of reason and ethics a common language. The Jewish philosopher voices a Leibnizian proof through the mouth of an Athenian pagan and thus enacts a universalism that defies proof. Mendelssohn's *Phaedon* represents a double challenge to the high Protestantism of rational theology. Although Mendelssohn never addresses the question of Judaism explicitly in this work, in writing the dialogue, he nevertheless indirectly implies that Judaism has a role to play in the Enlightenment's reevaluation of religion. A Jew can be as self-critical as the most rationalist of Protestants.[63] Not for nothing has Mendelssohn been called the Jewish Luther.

---

62. Ibid., 148.

63. On the full complexity of Mendelssohn's encounter with Lutheran Protestantism see the excellent account of Librett 2000.

Beyond such metaphysical preoccupations, Mendelssohn sees Judaism playing a crucial role in the discourse of religious ethics. We have already explored the irony of a Jew tackling the issue of immortality. Mendelssohn, like Philo before him, immerses himself in Plato in order to elaborate a Jewish philosophy of the afterlife. Platonism thus allows Judaism a passage into the common language of religious devotion. Where Christianity sets the standard for what counts as religion, Judaism could not help but find itself lacking. But there may be a further irony to Mendelssohn's deep investment in the life and afterlife of the soul. In contrast to his great Jewish predecessor Baruch Spinoza, philosopher of immanence, Mendelssohn wholeheartedly appropriates the dualism that underwrites Plato's dialogue. In the guise of Socrates, Mendelssohn shows how a Jew can become all soul and no body. As Jeffrey Librett argues: "One can readily discern in Mendelssohn's early texts a sustained attempt to speak, although he is a Jew, as a 'spirit,' as a substantial inwardness."[64] In contrast to the anti-Semitic stereotype of the extreme embodiment of the Jew, Mendelssohn's dialogue on the flight of the soul from the body frees Judaism from the charge of materialism.

The question of materialism and its relationship to the Greek/Jew opposition has a particular resonance in the context of the visual representation of Socrates in the post-Winckelmannian age. The aestheticized image of Greece that dominated German accounts in the wake of Winckelmann's beguiling descriptions of ancient art had such an effect on artistic expression that by the end of the eighteenth century even the famously ugly Socrates had become sexy. Where Socrates' lack of beauty was at one with Plato's philosophy of disembodiment, this same ugliness was decidedly at odds with the Enlightenment's classical aesthetics, which allied goodness with physical beauty. David, in other words, had no choice but to make Socrates beautiful. Even when it came to the representation of Socrates, Plato's commitment to dualism could not compete with the resolutely antidualist aesthetic of Enlightenment Hellenism.

When it came to the visual representation of the "German Socrates," what was to become of these considerations? The image of Mendelssohn as Socrates' doppelgänger was so compelling that it even left its mark on of the artistic representations of the thinker. In one much copied picture (see fig. 2) by the Jewish painter and engraver Michael Siegfried Löwe, Mendelssohn and Socrates are represented in profile facing each other in a contest for wisdom. Above them is a haloed owl in flight, before them stands a skull with a butterfly resting on its head. The skull and the butterfly repeats the theme of

64. Librett 2000, 43.

SOCRATES · MENDELSSOHN

FIGURE 2. Frontispiece image of Mendelssohn and Socrates, from J. Heinemann, *Moses Mendelssohn. Sammlung theils noch ungedruckter, theils andern Schriften zerstreuter Aufsätze und Briefe von ihm, an und über ihn*, Leipzig 1831. (Classmark: Hh.40.62.) Reproduced by kind permission of the Syndics of Cambridge University Library.

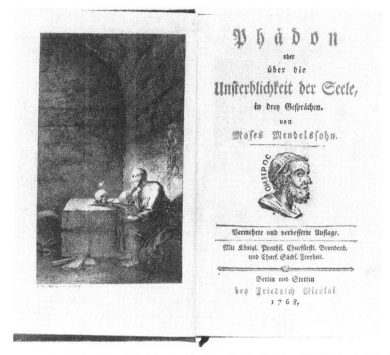

FIGURE 3. Frontispiece Moses Mendelssohn, *Phaedon oder über die Unsterblichkeit der Seele in drei Gesprächen*, Berlin 1767. (Classmark: 7180.e.39.) Reproduced by kind permission of the Syndics of Cambridge University Library.

the frontispiece of Mendelssohn's *Phaedon* (see fig. 3) where, in a sketch by Johann Wilhelm Meil, Socrates is depicted alone in his cell contemplating a skull with a butterfly flying above. Meil's picture appears to be heavily inspired by Rembrandt's etching of "St Jerome in a dark chamber"[65] (see fig. 4) and the presence of the butterfly confirms the relationship to this earlier explicitly Christian theme. The butterfly was a symbol of resurrection, representing the flight of the soul from the body to the promise of an afterlife. In Löwe's depiction of Mendelssohn, then, Hellenic, Christian, and Jewish symbolism vie for attention. Mendelssohn and Socrates mirror each other's philosophical physiognomy (the high brow, the arch of the eyebrows) while both retain their individual traits: Socrates his famous snubbed nose, Mendelssohn his unmistakably stereotypical Jewish one. The closer they are brought into proximity, the more important their differences. Christian doctrine appears as the synthesis of the antithetical attitudes of the Hellenic and Jewish sage.

65. My thanks to John Bender for this observation.

FIGURE 4. Rembrandt *Saint Jerome in a Dark Chamber*, 1642. Museum of Fine Arts, Boston.

But such a science of the face was brought to a new level by the publication of Johann Caspar Lavater's *Essays on Physiognomy: Designed to Promote
the Knowledge and Love of Mankind* in 1775. The Swiss theologian's great oeuvre in four volumes caused a sensation in its time.[66] Lavater claimed to detect
in the facial features of his subjects their underlying character. His methodology is memorably encapsulated in his analysis of Goethe's nose: "The nose
was full of expression and productivity—taste and love—that is, of poetry."
In Goethe's poetic nose resides a vocation. Although Lavater's treatise had
pretensions to be a general handbook of domestic science—a review from
1801 in the *Scots Magazine* makes the claim that "a servant would, at one time,
scarcely be hired till the descriptions and engravings of Lavater had been consulted in careful comparison with the lines and features of the young man's
or woman's countenance"—the majority of his examples come from the exploration of the features of great men.[67] Socrates is prominent among them.
Lavater acknowledges that "there can be no doubt of the ugliness of Socrates"
and concedes that this striking discrepancy between outer "deformity" and

66. See Shookman 1993.
67. Quoted in Graham 1979, 61.

inward wisdom poses a problem for the precepts of physiognomy.[68] But for Lavater it is precisely this dissonance that requires the expert eye of a physiognomist:

> "Characters pregnant with strong and contending powers, generally contain in the great mass, the prominent features of the face, somewhat of severe, violent or perplexed [sic]; consequently are very different from what the Grecian artists, and men of taste, name beauty. While the signification, the expression, of such prominent features are not studied and understood, such countenances will offend the eye that searches only for beauty." The countenance of Socrates is manifestly of this kind.[69]

Although Winckelmann is quoted on the facing page, it is precisely his ideal of "Greek beauty" that Lavater appears to be challenging. Lavater simultaneously upholds and discredits the mind-body problem which physiognomy had been enlisted to solve.

If Lavater sees Socrates' unconventional beauty as a test case of the science of physiognomics, he sees in the analysis of Mendelssohn's silhouette (see fig. 5) its ultimate vindication:

> Supposedly you know the silhouette? I can hardly conceal from you that it is exceedingly dear to me! Most expressive! . . . Can you say, can you hesitate a moment as if wanting to say: "Perhaps a fool! A vulgar, tactless soul!" One who could say a thing like this or could bear another saying so should close my book, throw it away—and permit me to stop thinking lest I pass judgment on him! I revel in this silhouette! My glance welters in the magnificent curve of the forehead down to the pointed bone of the eye. . . . In this depth of the eye a Socratic soul is lodged! The firmness of the nose; —the magnificent transition from the nose to the upper lip—the height of both lips, neither protruding beyond the other, oh! How all this chimes with another to make the divine truth of physiognomy perceptible and visible to me. Yes, I see him, the son of Abraham, who some day, in unison with Plato and Moses, will recognize and worship the crucified Lord of Glory![70]

Despite Lavater's enthusiasm, his imaginary observer seems to profess the same incredulity when faced with Mendelssohn as he had earlier imagined in the encounter with Socrates. For the unschooled eye, both Socrates and Mendelssohn could be presumed to be vulgar fools. But although Lavater goes into great detail about Socrates' superficial ugliness, no explanation is

---

68. Lavater 1848, 114.
69. Ibid., 115.
70. Lavater 1775, 243–44; translated in Altmann 1973, 319.

FIGURE 5. Silhouette of Moses Mendelssohn, from Johann Caspar Lavater, *Physiognomische Frag-mente, zur Beförderung der Menschenkenntnis und Menschenliebe*, Translated by H. Hunter, 3 vol. London, 1789–98. (Classmark: Hunter.a.78.10–12.) Reproduced by kind permission of the Syndics of Cambridge University Library.

given for the reaction to Mendelssohn. Could the layperson in Lavater's account be drawing his opprobrium from a more general profile of the "sons of Abraham"? Elsewhere in the treaty Lavater quotes an "observation" by the *Sturm und Drang* writer Jakob Michael Lenz: "It appears remarkable that the Jews should have carried with them the marks of their country and race to all parts of the world; I mean their short, black, curly hair, and brown complexion.— Their quickness of speech, haste and abruptness in all their actions, appear to proceed from the same causes. I imagine the Jews have more gall than other men."

Lavater continues in his own name, "I add, as a characteristic of the national Jewish countenance, the pointed chin, pouting lips, and well-defined middle line of the mouth." In this description Lavater falls silent on the topic of the Jewish nose—the famous "hawk nose" which Sander Gilman has called "the sign of the pathological Jewish character for Western Jews." Elsewhere, however, Lavater has this to say of the down-turned nose: "Noses which are much turned downwards are never truly good, truly cheerful, or noble, or great. Their thoughts and inclinations tend to earth. They are closed, cold, heartless, incommunicative; often maliciously sarcastic, ill humoured, or extremely hypochondriac, or melancholic. When arched in the upper part, they are fearful and voluptuous." Just as Goethe's poetic nose captured a propensity to genius, the Jewish hawk nose intimates a predisposition for depravity. As Judith Wechsler observes, "The Jews depicted in Lavater's physiognomic volumes are shown, with one exception, in profile—the better to delineate the nose."[71]

Despite a distinct downward tilt, Mendelssohn's nose escapes such harsh analysis. But although Lavater "revels" in Mendelssohn's physical features, it is ultimately his "Socratic soul" that draws his attention. Lavater sees through Mendelssohn's Jewish body to his Greek soul. And it is through the exposure of this inner Hellene that Lavater discerns his route to salvation. "The divine truth of physiognomy" turns out to be a prelude to conversion. The antithesis of Mendelssohn's Jewish body and Greek soul is resolved in the synthesis of Christianity.

Lavater's physiognomical analysis is the hopeful extension of his earlier attempt to make Mendelssohn see that his adoption of Platonism had its logical conclusion in the "recognition" and "worship" of the "crucified Lord of Glory." For, his remarks here rehearse the notorious "Lavater affair" that unfolded in 1769.[72] Encouraged by Mendelssohn's arguments about the immortality of the soul in his *Phaedon*, Lavater saw in his work the same possibility of a proto-Christianity that he identified in Plato's own dialogue. Lavater decided to append a "dedicatory epistle" addressed to Mendelssohn to his translation of a book by Charles Bonnet that had itself criticized Mendelssohn's discussion of the soul in his *Phaedon* for falling short of the revealed truths of Christianity. In this open letter he urges Mendelssohn "to refute publicly in case you find the *essential* arguments adduced in support of the facts of Christianity to be incorrect: in case, however, you find them correct, to do what prudence, love of truth, and honesty bid you to do; —what *Socrates* would have done, had he read this treatise and found it irrefutable."[73] In other words, just as Socrates would have converted to Christianity had he only had the historical benefit

---

71. Lavater 1848, 352–53, 472; Gilman 1991, 181; Wechsler 1993, 112.

72. The affair and its aftermath is discussed at length in Altmann 1973, 201ff.

73. Mendelssohn 1929–38, 7:3, translated in Altmann 1973, 209.

of being born after the Messiah, so Mendelssohn, Lavater argued, should ret-
rospectively profess the limits of his religious acculturation and embrace the
doctrines of Christ. Socrates thus assumes the position of the good Jew, the
Jew who transcends his own perversity and pertinacity and accepts conversion to Christianity.

Mendelssohn publicly responded with his own letter in which he indig-
nantly defended Judaism against Christianity in terms he would later develop
in *Jerusalem*. But Mendelssohn was not alone in his indignation with Lavater. Charles Bonnet himself, Johann David Michaelis, Herder, Hamann, and
Goethe all wrote with disapproval about the incident. And beyond the immediate responses, the aftershocks of the affair continued to shape the theological debates of the Enlightenment. Outside the purely theological sphere,
the question of conversion would never be far from the surface of debates
about Jewish emancipation and integration over the decades to come. Lavater
had violated the Enlightenment principle of tolerance. He had made conversion a condition of the Jews' acceptance into intellectual and civic society.
Lavater's persuasive technique in the "dedicatory epistle" to the Charles Bonnet volume had obviously fallen on deaf ears and it is in his physiognomy
that Lavater attempts to show that Mendelssohn was not just intellectually
but somatically predisposed to Christian deliverance. Mendelssohn's desire
to transcend the body and achieve immortality through the soul in his *Phaedon* became implicated both in the anti-Jewish stereotype that contrasted the
materiality of Judaism to the spirituality of Christianity and in the aesthetic
idealization of ancient Greece that saw the beauty of the Hellene's body as a
window onto his noble soul.

Emily Wilson has argued that "Mendelssohn's *Phaidon* had been an attempt to reclaim the death of Socrates—as well as Socrates' views of death—
for all the people of Europe, Jewish and Christian alike."[74] Certainly Mendelssohn's investment in the discourse of rational theology and his emphasis on the question of immortality represent an effort to show how Judaism
could contribute to the Enlightenment's wider interrogation of traditional
religion. By assuming the mantle of the pagan Socrates, Mendelssohn argues
that reason should be able to hold all religions to account for their moral
and theological precepts. But as Lavater's reading shows, any tension between
Judaism and Enlightenment that Mendelssohn's encounter with Socrates
could be seen to exemplify was resolved into a debate about Christianity. The
Greek/Jew antithesis rather than giving an alternative answer to the question
"What is Enlightenment?" merely becomes a new expression of Christian-

74. Wilson 2007, 190.

ity. Lavater's response to the *Phaedon* represents the failure of assimilation. Mendelssohn cannot as a Jew claim a distinctive voice in the religious debates of the age.

For a figure like Lavater, Mendelssohn's reflections on the reason of Judaism are merely a pretext for demanding that he abandon Judaism all together and embrace the doctrines of Christ. As Librett phrases it: "Mendelssohn, merely by presenting himself as a rational man, even if he is outwardly a Jew . . . , has already in principle declared his readiness to convert to Protestantism."[75] For Kant, on the other hand, the very concept of reason that Mendelssohn hopes to elaborate in the *Phaedon* is itself wrong-headed. Kant condemns Mendelssohn's metaphysical program in the name of an ethics of practical reason. Where Mendelssohn co-opts Socrates to the cause of rational religion, Kant reclaims him as a figure of ethical self-knowledge. Socrates, in Kant's version, exposes the limits of science to reveal an alternative program of moral Enlightenment.

Religion within the Limits of Reason Alone

Mendelssohn's attempt to insert Judaism into the Enlightenment's discussion of metaphysics and morality in his *Phaedon* had ultimately resulted in a call for his conversion to Christianity. In retrospect the widespread popularity of the dialogue could be seen to result from just such a reading. Mendelssohn's discussion of immortality had the great benefit of being compatible with the dominant religion. As Vieillard-Baron puts it: "In fact, everyone could agree on the topic of the immortality of the soul."[76] Mendelssohn's Hellenic disguise had been interpreted as an acquiescence to the teachings of Christianity. Far from a symbol of reason Socrates was, at best, a mediating force between different modes of spirituality.

The so-called Lavater affair forced Mendelssohn to address this question head on. Where his *Phaedon* can be seen as an implicit defense of Judaism against its Christian detractors, Mendelssohn's *Jerusalem; or on Religious Power and Judaism* is explicit in its vindication of Judaism. In his masterwork Mendelssohn moves the argument away from metaphysics and morality toward history and politics. From the very first page Mendelssohn announces the stakes of his investigation: "State and religion—civil and ecclesiastical constitution—secular and churchly authority—how to oppose these pillars of social life to one another so that they are in balance and do not, instead,

75. Librett 2000, 32.
76. Vieillard-Baron 1979b, 442; see also Vieillard-Baron 1974.

become burdens on social life, or weigh down its foundations more than they help to uphold it—this is one of the most difficult tasks of politics."[77] In this work Mendelssohn will take on the "task of politics" and, what is more, he will do so with open reference to the Jewish question ancient and modern. Jerusalem in both its concrete historical and symbolic guises will guide his investigation of "liberty of conscience" and its relationship to church and state.[78]

The task of finding a role for religion in the new polity had preoccupied Enlightenment thinkers. If a commitment to a secular state had become a given of political philosophy, the question of the boundaries of public and private conscience had not yet, in Mendelssohn's terms, "been accurately fixed."[79] The problem of reconciling religious and civic identities was, of course, one that concerned reform-minded Christian Europe. But the task of circumscribing the role of Christian belief in a new blueprint of citizenship presented less obstacles to the *philosophes* than the challenge presented by Judaism. The condition of being a Jew seeped so far into the fabric of his personhood that there was simply no accommodation possible with the demands of civic loyalty. Where Christian Europe had "yet to fix the boundaries," the charge against Judaism was that it was congenitally ill-disposed to make any such discrimination. When the prospect of conversion was dangled before the recalcitrant Mendelssohn more was at stake than a realignment of personal belief. The potential of becoming a modern citizen was dependent on his abandonment of Judaism.

In his *Jerusalem* Mendelssohn aligns himself to the project of Jewish emancipation that rejected the idea that civic loyalty was incompatible with Judaism. But where others, including Mendelssohn's friend and collaborator Christian Wilhelm Dohm, had made their case for extending citizen rights to the Jews on the basis of an argument for tolerance, *Jerusalem* takes a much more polemical stance.[80] Advocates of the Jews had typically seen Jewish emancipation as the ultimate test case for the enlightened nation and its commitment to secular universalism. If even Jews could be incorporated into the civic fabric of the modern state, their project of tolerance could be deemed a success. Mendelssohn, on the other hand, argues that Judaism is not just reconcilable to such a progressive vision of the state but could actually provide its most attractive model. Mendelssohn states that the tenets of Enlighten-

77. Mendelssohn 1983, 33.

78. On Mendelssohn's theory of the state see Goetschel 2007.

79. Ibid., 33.

80. Dohm had published his important work *Über die Bürgerliche Verbesserung der Juden* in 1781, on which see Hess 2002.

ment thought are integral to the Jewish religion. Unlike Christianity which, through its belief in revelation, makes intellectual demands on its followers which fly in the face of reason, Judaism has no such aspirations:

> I recognize no eternal truths other than those that are not merely comprehensible to human reason but can also be demonstrated and verified by human powers. Yet, Mr. Mörschel is misled by an incorrect conception of Judaism when he supposes that I cannot maintain this without departing from the religion of my fathers. On the contrary, I consider this an essential point of the Jewish religion and believe that this doctrine constitutes a characteristic difference between it and the Christian one. To say briefly: I believe that Judaism knows of no revealed religion in the sense in which Christians understand this term. The Israelites possess a divine legislation—laws, commandments, ordinances, rules of life, instruction in the will of God as to how they should conduct themselves in order to attain temporal and eternal felicity.[81]

The insistence that Judaism is a system of revealed legislation rather than revealed religion recasts Judaism as a code of action which accords with the truths of reason. Mendelssohn derives from Spinoza his vision of the Sinaitic revelation:

> Judaism boasts no *exclusive* revelation of eternal truths that are indispensable to salvation, of no revealed religion in the sense in which the term is usually understood. Revealed *religion* is one thing, revealed *legislation*, another. The voice which let itself be heard at Sinai on that great day did not proclaim, "I am the Eternal, your God, the necessary, independent being, omnipotent and omniscient, that recompenses men in a future life according to their deeds." This is the universal *religion of mankind*, not Judaism; and the universal *religion of mankind*, without which men are neither virtuous or capable of felicity, was not revealed there.[82]

In his *Tractatus Theologico-Politicus*, Spinoza had made the case that the divine commandments had set in place a Jewish commonwealth, a political organization. Mendelssohn agrees with Spinoza that adherence to these commandments was a matter of obedience rather than faith.[83] But despite their common understanding of revelation, Mendelssohn parts company with Spinoza when he asserts that the Law of Moses could be reduced to a purely political code. Mendelssohn wants to argue that Judaism, unlike Christianity, is free from dogmatic imposition. But this does not mean that Judaism has no relationship to the truths of natural religion. Judaism may have no "ex-

81. Mendelssohn 1983, 89–90.
82. Ibid., 97.
83. For Mendelssohn and Spinoza, see Goetschel 2004 and Zac 1989.

clusive" access to these truths, but it nonetheless has access to them through its scriptures: "Although the divine book that we received through Moses is strictly speaking meant to be a book of laws containing ordinances, rules of life and prescriptions, it also includes, as is well known, an inexhaustible treasure of rational truths."[84] For Mendelssohn the eternal truths of reason coincide with those of the Bible.

Mendelssohn relies in this presentation of Judaism on a particular understanding of history which distinguished him from many of his contemporaries. He found himself opposing a consensus of eighteenth-century historicism which saw history as an onward march of progress:

> I, for my part, cannot conceive of the education of the human race as my late friend Lessing imagined it under the influence of I-don't-know-which historian of mankind. One pictures the collective entity of the human race as an individual person and believes that Providence set it to school here on earth, in order to raise it from childhood to manhood. In reality, the human race is—if the metaphor is appropriate—in almost every century, child, adult, and old man at the same time, though in different places and regions of the world.[85]

For Mendelssohn, unlike Lessing, the truths of reason are independent from the development of history. He holds on to a belief in autonomous reason that is independent from the vagaries of history. Hannah Arendt, in her essay on "The Enlightenment and the Jewish Question," makes the case that Mendelssohn's skeptical attitude to history has its roots in the Jews' experience of history:

> This elimination of reality is closely bound up with the factual position of the Jew in the world. The world mattered so little to him that it became the epitome of what was unalterable. This new freedom of reason, of formation, of thinking for oneself, does not change the world at all. The "educated" Jew continued to regard the historical world with the same indifference felt by the oppressed Jew in the ghetto.[86]

For Arendt, "the failure of the Jews to appreciate history" was "based in their fate as a people without history and nourished by an only partially understood and assimilated Enlightenment."[87] Arendt's stereotype of the unhistorical Jews had been fully elaborated in a long history of German thought. The

---

84. Ibid., 99.
85. Ibid., 95–96.
86. Arendt 2007, 8.
87. Ibid., 8.

notion of a people whom history had left behind was central to the Enlightenment's characterization of the Jews as uniquely incompatible with modernity. The Jews' problematic history places them in an oblique relationship to the conflict between ancients and moderns. The dialogue between antiquity and modernity that animated the Enlightenment's engagement with Greco-Roman culture relied on a notion of historicism that the Jewish experience appears to sidestep. Modernity, for all its desire to distinguish itself from the past, was predicated on a conception of historical continuity that brought it into a competitive relationship with the classical world. The Enlightenment's portrayal of the Jews as a nation without a history made any such dynamic exchange impossible. More problematic still was the fact that the Jews as a people could not be bounded in history. Unlike the civilizations of Greece and Rome, which could be safely confined to a distant past, the Jewish experience was an ongoing one. A paradoxical opposition between the historical Greeks who were confined to the past and the unhistorical Jews who persisted into the present thus emerged.

Mendelssohn, I believe, had a much more polemical aim in mind in his underplaying of historical progress.[88] It was only by undermining the teleological view of history that he would be able to rescue Judaism from the narratives of Christian triumphalism that he was so keen to refute. The narrative of human progress that Lessing and others subscribed to had as its inevitable corollary the belief that Christian salvation superseded the primitive religion of Jerusalem and consigned it to irrelevance. Even supporters of the Jews such as Dohm wanted to divest the Jews of their history to make them more acceptable to the modern state. But Dohm constructs his argument against history on an argument based on historical example. In a counterintuitive move he makes the destruction of the Temple of Jerusalem by the Romans the crucial moment in the history of Jewish emancipation. The Roman conquest of Jerusalem becomes, in Dohm's scheme, a paradigmatic moment of modernity. With its ethics of civic tolerance and its clear demarcation of church and state, the Roman empire appeared as the perfect antecedent to the modern enlightened nation. In Jonathan Hess's words:

> Dohm's archetype for the modern, secular state was the conquering power that destroyed Jerusalem and initiated the final Jewish Diaspora, and the symbolic significance of this identification with the imperial power cannot be underestimated: in its emancipation of the Jews, civic improvement sought to reenact the fall of Jerusalem.[89]

88. See also Erlin 2002, and Honig 2009, 40 – 43 .
89. Hess 2002, 33.

The abandonment of Jerusalem thus becomes the necessary condition of the Jews' accession to modernity.

For Mendelssohn, unlike Dohm, Rome could never be a model. His description of the destruction of the Temple by the Romans has a quite different flavor:

> In plundering the Temple, the conquerors of Jerusalem found the cherubim on the Ark of the Covenant, and took them to be the idols of the Jews. They saw everything with the eyes of barbarians, and from their point of view. In accordance with their own customs, they took the image of divine providence and prevailing grace for an image of the Deity, the Deity itself, and delighted in their discovery.[90]

Earlier in this passage Mendelssohn likens the Romans to contemporary Enlightenment anthropologists: "Our own travellers may very often make similar mistakes when they report to us on the religion of distant people."[91] In contrast to Dohm's depiction of humane tolerance, Mendelssohn highlights the arrogant expansionism of the Romans. He compares the Roman imperial project to the contemporary ethnographic mission of the Enlightenment and suggests both may be blind to the real otherness they encounter, seeing always a mirror of themselves and assuming the image there is true or universal. Implicit in Mendelssohn's critique of Rome is a suspicion of the universalist fantasies of empires ancient and modern and of the (political) imperialism of universalism (ethical or rational). Just as the Romans saw things only "through the eyes of barbarians" and "from their point of view," their modern Enlightenment successors were ready to shoehorn Jerusalem into their own paradigms of religion and nationhood. Mendelssohn compares Jerusalem to Rome in order to rescue a different understanding of rationality, an alternative universalism.

Mendelssohn's resistance to Lessing's teleological history served the purpose both of salvaging Judaism from narratives of Christian triumphalism and of redeeming Jerusalem as a potential rival to the great civilizations of Greece and Rome. His resistance to the so-called rise of historicism was also strategic in placing the question of contemporary Jews firmly on the agenda.[92] Despite his interest in the civic structures of ancient Jerusalem, Mendelssohn has no desire to resuscitate the theocratic state of the historical Jews. Instead he hoped to draw on the ethical exemplarity of Jerusalem. Unlike the citi-

---

90. Mendelssohn 1983, 114.
91. Ibid., 114.
92. See Reill 1975, Myers 2003, Hess 2007.

zens of Athens and Rome, those inhabitants of ancient Jerusalem had a living presence in modern Europe. The contemporary Jews' albeit-distorted historical memory of an ancient Judaism provided them with an exemplar of freedom of conscience that they could strive to emulate. As Jonathan Hess argues:

> Presented in this manner, Judaism is no longer the political system Orientalists relegate to the historical past but a religion whose purification by Jews can serve as a model for the modern distinction between church and state. No longer the primitive, superseded origin of the West, the Orient apparently contains an archetype for liberty of conscience that needs to become the foundation stone for the politics of modernity.[93]

Mendelssohn thus established Jerusalem as a contrast both to Christianity and to the secular paradigms of statehood that his contemporaries sought in the classical world.[94] Despite the explicit opposition to Christianity he voices in *Jerusalem* in response to the Lavater affair, many of Mendelssohn's more sympathetic readers were prone to represent his reading of Judaism as an acquiescence to Christianity. As Hess goes on to claim: "Those willing to accommodate Jews or Judaism in their version of universalism tended to neutralize Mendelssohn's challenge, recasting his attempt to 'purify' Judaism as precisely the sort of step towards Christian universalism it was Mendelssohn's goal to undermine."[95] Immanuel Kant was chief among them. Like Mendelssohn, Kant was in search of a rational theology that accommodated liberty of conscience. He shared with Mendelssohn an investment in a religion that prioritized practical ethics over metaphysical principle. But Kant vociferously opposed Mendelssohn's identification of Judaism as just such a religion. Thus Kant wrote in a letter to Mendelssohn dated 1783:

> Mr [David] Friedländer will tell you how much I admire the penetration, subtlety, and wisdom of your *Jerusalem*. I regard this book as a proclamation of a great reform that is gradually becoming imminent, a reform that is in store not only for your people, but for other nations as well. You have managed to unite with your religion a degree of freedom of thought that would hardly have been thought possible and of which no other religion can boast. You have at the same time thoroughly and clearly shown it necessary that every religion have unrestricted freedom of thought, so that finally even the church will have to consider how to rid itself of everything that burdens and oppresses man's conscience, and mankind will finally be united with regard to the essential

93. Hess 2002, 109
94. See also Witte 2007.
95. Hess 2002, 135.

point of religion. For all religious propositions that burden our conscience
are based on history, that is, on making blessedness contingent on belief in the
truth of those historical oppositions.[96]

The letter anticipates many of the themes that Kant would develop in his
own great work on religion, *Religion within the Limits of Reason Alone*, which
appeared a decade later. For Kant, Mendelssohn's *Jerusalem* represented an
inspired attempt to show that religion could be thought within the boundaries of reason. In his view, *Jerusalem* successfully pulls off the challenge of reconciling Judaism to the Enlightenment. The question is, at what cost? Kant's
praise for Mendelssohn is laced with an implicit threat. Where Mendelssohn
had been keen to show that there was a religion that could be conceived on
the basis of reason alone, and this religion was Judaism, Kant instead foregrounds Mendelssohn's reformist agenda.[97] For Mendelssohn, *Jerusalem* describes the rational potential of Judaism as it was and is, but for Kant it rather
prescribes what Judaism (or religion in general) could be. Kant repeatedly
moves from the particular to the universal, from the specificity of Judaism to
the generality of religion. Jews, like "other nations," find themselves on the
eve of "a great reform that is gradually becoming immanent." These Jews, in
other words, will have to come into line with other nations in order to make
such progress possible. More exactly, they will have to "unburden" themselves from the weight of their specific history. When the Jews recognize that
their religious particularity is a product of history and history alone, they
will be able to move along the same road of reform that all other nations are
engaged in. Judaism, in Kant's version, is history.

History plays a fundamentally different role in the analysis of reason and
religion for Mendelssohn and Kant. According to Mendelssohn Jewish history predisposes Jews toward rational morality; according to Kant it is the
impediment Jews will need to overcome in order to accede to a new rational religion. For Mendelssohn Judaism *is* the reform that religions must undergo. For Kant all religions are in need of reform, but Judaism especially so,
because of its historical "burden." In fact, Kant famously believed that "Judaism is not really a religion at all." "The Jewish faith" he argues,

> was, in its original form, a collection of mere statutory laws upon which was
> established a political organization. . . . That this political organization has
> a theocracy as its basis . . . and that therefore the name of God, who after
> all is here merely an earthly regent making absolutely no claims upon, and

---

96. Kant 1967, 107–8.
97. Rotenstreich 1984, 23–36. See also Witte 2007, 23.

no appeals to, conscience, is respected—this does not make it a religious organization.[98]

To Kant the external character of Jewish moral commandments bars Judaism from the realm of ethics. Judaism is not a religion but a system of legislation. And since in Judaism moral actions are performed in accord with the external demands of the law rather than through internal "appeals to conscience" there is in Judaism no recourse to the all-important autonomy of practical reason.

The conditional enthusiasm that Kant expresses for Mendelssohn's *Jerusalem* in the letter is developed into a more explicit critique in the *Religion*. Although Mendelssohn is again praised for his "ingenuity," Kant essentially insists that he abandon his commitment to Judaism in order to undertake a joint search for the true rational religion. Kant's interpretation of Mendelssohn's refusal to convert to Christianity could not be more idiosyncratic: "He means to say: first remove Judaism from your *religion* (though in the historical teaching of faith it must always remain as an antiquity) and then we shall be able to take your proposal under advisement. (In fact nothing would then be left over, except pure moral religion unencumbered by statutes)."[99] In Kant's vision Judaism can only remain as "an antiquity," a historic and obsolete stage in the development of religion. Access to "pure moral religion" can only be gained by abandoning Judaism. Kant's own narrative enacts this process of "removing Judaism":

> For this purpose, therefore, we can deal only with the history of the church which from the beginning bore within it the germ and the principles of the objective unity of the true and *universal* religious faith to which it is gradually being brought nearer.—And it is apparent, first of all, that the *Jewish* faith stands in absolutely no essential connection . . . with the ecclesiastical faith whose history we want to consider, even though it immediately preceded it and provided the physical occasion for the founding of this church (the Christian). The *Jewish faith*, as originally established, was only a collection of merely statutory laws supporting a political state; for whatever moral additions were *appended* to it, whether originally or only later, do not in any way belong to Judaism as such. Strictly speaking Judaism is not a religion at all but simply the union of a number of individuals who, since they belonged to a particular stock, established themselves into a community under purely political laws, hence not into a church.[100]

98. Kant 1998, 130.
99. Ibid., 162–63n.
100. Ibid., 130.

"The true universal *religion*" of Christianity, then, stands for Kant in direct opposition to the inward-looking particularism of Judaism. But Kant does not just oppose the outlooks of Judaism and Christianity; he has a more genealogical claim. He aims to prove that Judaism has "no essential connection" to the development of Christianity. Far from seeing Judaism as integral to the development of Christianity, Kant sees their relationship as little more than a historical and geographical accident. Judaism precedes and "provides the physical occasion" for the founding of the Christian Church but can lay no claim of kinship. Kant constructs this argument on a deliberately reductive reading of Mendelssohn's depiction of ancient Jerusalem. Sharing Mendelssohn's backward gaze to Spinoza, Kant reconstitutes Jewish history as a political history. But unlike Mendelssohn, Kant will see the civic identity of ancient Israel as completely removed from any moral dimension. Ethics "do not belong to Judaism as such":

> [I]n this government [the Jewish theocracy] the subjects remained attuned in their minds to no other incentive except the goods of this world and only wished, therefore to be ruled through rewards and punishments in this life—nor were they in this respect capable of other laws except such as were in part imposed by burdensome ceremonies and observances, in part indeed ethical but only inasmuch as they gave rise to external compulsion, hence were only civil, and the inferiority of the moral disposition was in no way at issue. . . . Now there suddenly appears among these very people, at a time when they were feeling the full measure of all evils of a hierarchical constitution, and were feeling it as well, perhaps, because of the Greek sages' moral doctrines on freedom which, unsettling as they were for the slavish mind, had gradually gained influence over them and had induced most of them to reflection—they were thus ripe for revolution—a person whose wisdom, even purer than that of the previous philosophers, was as though descended from heaven.[101]

The material and "this-worldly" aspirations of the Jews are presented by Kant as just one more aspect of their inability to develop into an ethical community. The external compulsion that functioned as their primary motivator stood as the antithesis to Kant's principle of autonomous reason. But as before, Kant allies this philosophical observation about the limits of Judaism to a historical claim about the history of Christianity. Kant represents the onset of the "Christian revolution" as a "sudden" and decisive break with the Judaic past. And yet, Kant's narrative does not seem to be able to function without some sort of historical catalyst. He detects a certain incipient dissatisfaction among the Jews with their existing moral circumstances. Despite

101. Ibid., 95.

their resolutely amoral natures, these same Jews were able to perceive the "full measure of the evils of a hierarchical constitution." Given their inherent shortcomings, such a realization could not be self-generated. Kant locates this transformation of the "slavish mind" at the moment of its contact with the Greek "sages' moral doctrines on freedom." Hellenism becomes the mid-wife of ethical self-knowledge for the Jews:

> Thus from Judaism—but from a Judaism no longer patriarchal and uncon-taminated, no longer standing solely on a political constitution (which also had already been shattered); from a Judaism already mingled rather, with a religious faith because of the moral doctrines which had gradually gained public acceptance within it; at a juncture when much foreign (Greek) wis-dom had already become available to this otherwise still ignorant people, and this wisdom presumably had had the further effect of enlightening through its concepts of virtue, and in spite of the oppressive burden of its dogmatic faith, of making it ready for revolutions which the diminutions of the priests' power, due to their subjugation to the rule of a people indifferent to every foreign popular faith, occasioned—it was from a Judaism such as this that Christianity suddenly though not unprepared arose.[102]

Judaism had to be tempered by the humanizing wisdom of the Greeks in or-der to make it the acceptable matrix of Christianity. Greece saves Christianity from the taint of Judaism in more than one way: first by helping transform Judaism itself into something different and then by offering to Christianity the idea of an autochthony. Like Hamann, Kant sketches a continuity be-tween Hellenism and Christianity, a continuity that is based on the antitheti-cal characteristics of Judaism and Christianity.

Despite his professed enthusiasm for *Jerusalem*, in his *Religion* Kant chal-lenges both Mendelssohn's philosophical representation of Judaism as a re-ligion based on "mere reason" and his historical narrative, which insists on the decadence of Christianity from its Jewish source. But while Kant has a great deal to say about the religious dimension of Mendelssohn's work, he fails to address its urgent political plea. Yet, as Hess writes, "even in its strictly demarcated concern with Judaism rather than Jews, the *Religion* was obvi-ously more than a treatise on religion. Given the atmosphere in which it was published, the contention that Judaism was incompatible with morality and incapable of producing moral human beings was a distinctly political argu-ment about modern Jewry as well."[103] Kant seems to be implying in the *Re-ligion* that a Judaism that had not yet internalized an ethical code based on

---

102. Ibid., 132.
103. Hess 2002, 156.

the precepts of autonomous reason would be incompatible with the demands of citizenship in an enlightened state. In his reconstituted historical narrative the Jews had to become Greeks before they could become citizens. The "Greek sage's moral doctrines of freedom" were a prerequisite to unshackling themselves from the slavery of their "hierarchal constitution." Kant's concept of citizenship is based on a profound continuity between ethics and politics. It is a paradox that Mendelssohn's attempt to restore political rights to the Jews by insisting on their predisposition to politics becomes the very stumbling block to them achieving such an aim in Kant.

Kant's over-literal reading of Mendelssohn restores Jerusalem as a political entity and thereby denies it access to the ethical knowledge required of the modern citizen. As Nathan Rotenstreich has noted, this will not be the first time that Mendelssohn will become the victim of his own persuasive rhetoric:

> Mendelssohn's image of Judaism was accepted as hard currency by Kant, Hegel, Feuerbach, Bruno Bauer, Marx and others; each of them incorporating its contents into their own conceptual framework. Obviously Mendelssohn is not to blame for the opposition to, and criticism of, Judaism. . . . However, the nineteenth century regarded him as the man who confirmed the Christian conception of Judaism.[104]

Kant's position on civic emancipation remains implicit in the *Religion*, in *The Conflict of the Faculties*, however, the association between religious history and contemporary debates is spelt out more clearly:

> So we can consider the proposal of Ben David, a highly intelligent Jew, to adopt publicly the religion of *Jesus* . . . a most fortunate one. Moreover it is the only plan which, if carried out, would leave the Jews a distinctive faith and yet quickly call attention to them as an educated, civilized people who are ready for all the rights of citizenship and whose faith could be sanctioned by the government. . . . The euthanasia of Judaism is pure moral religion, freed from all ancient statutory teachings, some of which were bound to be retained in Christianity. . . . But this division of sects too, must disappear in time, leading, at least in spirit, to what we call the conclusion of the great drama of religious change on earth (the restoration of all things), when there will be only one shepherd and one flock.[105]

This passage could be summed up by an observation in Lessing's *Die Juden*: "there must be Jews who are not really Jews." It is only by "publicly" adopt-

---

104. Rotenstreich 1964, 45. See also Munk 2006, which makes the same point about Mendelssohn's influence over Kant.

105. Kant 1979, 95.

ing Christianity that the Jews will be able to prove to society what we should know already—that they are "ready for the rights of citizenship." Kant's rhetoric here is decidedly slippery. He first calls for the conversion of the Jews and then characterizes them as an "educated, civilized people." Kant sees the conversion of the Jews as one step toward the spiritual emancipation that he hopes his fellow citizens will undergo. "The euthanasia of Judaism" is crucial to achieving a "pure moral religion." Ultimately Kant expresses a desire to move "beyond such sects," to move beyond Christianity itself in his search for a rational theology. But his language of universalism here is itself an expression of the universalism of Christianity that Kant praises elsewhere. It is precisely this hegemonic aspiration that Mendelssohn had sought to disrupt. *Jerusalem* expresses the hope of an alternative universalism where tolerance reigns and many shepherds are left to rule over many flocks.

Mendelssohn and the French Revolution

Mendelssohn's identification as the German Socrates is deeply implicated in a complex of associations that governed the theological and political discourse of the Enlightenment. At one level he represents in the guise of Socrates the figure of reason who was allowed to escape the ghetto and enter the learned society of Berlin. At another level, his association with Socrates became the medium through which his supporters and detractors alike sought to persuade him to abandon his outdated religion and embrace the doctrines of Christ. Socrates is the Greek who Mendelssohn would have to become in order ultimately to recognize his true identity as a Christian. But such deliberations about Mendelssohn's and Socrates' identities could not be isolated from the political debates these respective figures would come to inspire. Mendelssohn and Socrates would in their own ways each come to play a role in the political revolution that was engulfing France. Ironically the German Socrates would have to become a French citizen to bring about the political reforms he had so desired in his own homeland.

Where Mendelssohn's Socrates spends his dying hours seeking metaphysical Enlightenment, David's Socrates is above all else a political figure. Painted in 1787 in the immediate run up to the revolution, *La Mort de Socrate* represents a heroic self-sacrifice in the name of the fatherland. Socrates' death is portrayed as an act of political resistance. Defying the tyrannical state in the name of truth and virtue, he embodies a new social order, a different relationship between the individual and the state and a revolutionary model of citizenship. Socrates thus not only represents the aspirations of Enlightenment reason, he also prefigures a new understanding of civil society that has its roots in the classical polity. Marx famously proclaimed that the French Revolution was acted out in Roman costumes and with Roman phrases, but it was the ancient Greek model of citizenship that was promoted in the revolutionaries' desire for radical democracy.[106] Despite the irony of the historical Socrates' opposition to democracy, in David's picture and elsewhere his death became associated with this thirst for Greek freedom. The question of how much like Socrates a Jew like Mendelssohn could be had become political.

The Jews' exclusion from civil society and indeed from citizenship was one of the most hotly debated political questions of the prerevolutionary period. Mendelssohn spent much of his life campaigning for Jewish emancipation, arguing, as we have seen, that ancient Jerusalem as much as classical Athens could provide a model for the modern city. While his writings had some influence on the political landscape of Prussia during his lifetime, it is with his posthumous reception in the French Revolution that he had the most direct success in pushing his agenda. Mendelssohn's ideas had such a profound effect on the revolutionary comte de Mirabeau that he was driven in 1787 in the immediate aftermath of Mendelssohn's death to write a fifty-eight-page biography of the Berlin Jew before he put forward his own case for political reform permitting the Jews to exercise rights that he deemed universal.[107] While David was painting the death of Socrates, Mirabeau was writing a eulogy to the figure he called "le Platon moderne."[108] Accounts of the French Revolution have stressed the absence of a sustained intellectual argument about the position of the Jews in France before the 1780s and highlight the importance of German debates in formulating the demands of the new revolutionaries. So Delpech writes, "in this still unfavorable context, the first serious impulses came from Berlin" and goes on to say specifically of Moses Mendelssohn: "The idea of a reform of the Jews owes a great deal to his example and to the writings of his admirers."[109] The German Socrates is credited with having put the issue of the emancipation of the Jews on the table for the French Revolution.

Mirabeau's biography of Mendelssohn draws on many of the familiar tropes of his representation by contemporaries. In particular, Mendelssohn's singular journey from the generalized misery of the Jewish condition toward the heights of social and intellectual recognition is stressed. "A man, thrown

106. On classical antiquity and French Revolution see Mossé 1989, Vidal-Naquet 1990, and Hartog 2005.

107. See Schechter 2003, 95–101.

108. Mirabeau 1968, 1.

109. Delpech 1976, 7–8.

by nature into the heart of a demeaning horde . . . raised himself to the rank of one of the greatest writers that this century has seen born in Germany" opens Mirabeau's account. But Mirabeau's wider argument will need to underline the exemplarity rather than the exceptionalism of Mendelssohn's trajectory. Mirabeau maintains that if all Jews were given access to the civic benefits that Mendelssohn was able against all adversity to avail himself to, they too would become a benefit to the society that had so mistreated them. In a familiar move, Mirabeau bases his argument for future emancipation on an analysis of the historical condition of the Jews. In a passage that recalls Christian Dohm, he elects Rome as the prototype of an enlightened society:

> The Jews were useful subjects in the Roman Empire. Conquered and therefore consequently slaves, they acquired considerable privileges such as admissions to all civil and military offices and, among other things, they obtained permission to live in accordance of their own laws. They preserved for nearly four centuries the enjoyment of unlimited citizen rights; it is enough to say that they fulfilled its duties.[110]

The Jews' rise from the status of slaves to the full honor of citizenship is testimony to the wisdom of the political Roman constitution. By granting the Jews the privilege of citizenship, the Romans reaped the reward of the Jews' service to the state. Such an argument from expediency, Mirabeau hoped, could sway the minds of even his most bigoted contemporaries. If the Roman Republic was to become a blueprint for postrevolutionary France, this act of emulation would have to be faithful to Rome's commitment to religious tolerance.

Five years after Mendelssohn's death, in September 1791 France would grant full citizen rights to the Jews, the first European nation to do so. For the first time in modern European history Jews were extended a seemingly unconditional welcome into the nation. France would appear to be a place where even Jews who still wanted to be Jews could be accepted. And yet, as Ronald Schechter has argued, a question still lingers as to

> whether the 'emancipation' that the Revolution enacted was good or bad for the Jews. Historians have repeatedly asked, implicitly or explicitly, whether the National Assembly's famous decree of September 1791, was the origin of a long tradition, tragically interrupted by the Dreyfus Affair and the Vichy regime, of hospitality toward the Jews, whom the French thenceforth regarded

---

110. Mirabeau 1968, 67–68.

as compatriots; or rather the prelude to assimilation, the death sentence of a traditional Jewish identity and therefore merely a bloodless means of eliminating the Jews.[111]

Would revolutionary Paris really be able to honor the alternative universalism of Mendelssohn's Jerusalem or would it only be an reenactment of the hegemonic universalism of the Roman empire?

Mendelssohn's promise had yet to be fulfilled and the ever-receding goal of "true" emancipation became one of the ongoing projects of modernity. But what this chapter has tried to show is that the Jewish question, the question that Foucault suggests dragged Europe into modernity, needed the examples of classical Greece and ancient Rome to find an adequate formulation. At stake has been Moses Mendelssohn's double identity as not just a German but a Jewish Socrates. He is the one who both stealthily reveals the Greek limits of philosophy by exposing reason to its Hebraic other and draws citizenship away from its inescapably Greek legacy by claiming Judaism as the preferred resource of the modern city. For Mendelssohn and Kant the question of autonomous reason and ethical duty were mapped onto a historical narrative where Hebraism and Hellenism would come into conflict. "Many things in our experience," Foucault claims, "convince us that the historical event of the Enlightenment did not make us mature adults." If anything, I would argue, it returned us to our childhoods in Athens, Rome and Jerusalem.[112]

111. Schechter 2003, 150.

112. Foucault 2003, 56. It is interesting that the first section of Peter Gay's 1967 classic tome on the Enlightenment is provocatively entitled "Hebrews and Hellenes." In Gay's chapter, "Hebrews" refers to Christians and "Hellenes" to enlightened secularists. I hope to have shown some of the complexities of the terms and the ambivalent role that Judaism and Hellenism played in this conflict between Christianity and secularism.

2

Noah and Noesis:
Greeks, Jews and the Hegelian Dialectic

"Moses Mendelssohn's *Jerusalem*," writes Werner Hamacher, "must be recognized as a key point of reference for Hegel's first philosophical sketches."[1] The previous chapter explored the ethical and political consequences of Mendelssohn's and Kant's debate over the place of reason in Judaism. In this chapter I investigate how Hegel's early theological writings develop a distinctive approach to the question of reason through a dialogue with Kant and Mendelssohn. The works known as the Berne and Frankfurt essays were written as Hegel was emerging from his theological studies at Tübingen where, together with his classmates Schelling and Hölderlin, he was assimilating the impact of Kant's *Critique of Pure Reason*.[2] It is in these essays written in the 1790s that we find Hegel's most sustained analysis of the essence of Judaism.[3] Hegel's earliest writings stage an encounter between

1. Hamacher 1998, 22. The central role of Mendelssohn in Hegel's early writings was first commented on by Hermann Nohl who worked on the manuscripts and published them as *Hegels Theologische Jugendschriften* in 1907. See also Rosenstock 2010, 209–14, and Pöggeler 1974, who writes: "From his student period onwards Mendelssohn's *Jerusalem* became one of the key books which he used to explain his own ideas" (530).

2. For the classic account of the development of Hegel's thought in this period see Harris 1972.

3. "Judaism," as his biographer Rosenkranz famously put it, "vexed him (Hegel) as a dark riddle throughout his life." Hegel returns to an analysis of Judaism in the *Philosophy of Right*, the *Lectures on the Philosophy of History*, the *Lectures on Aesthetics*, and especially in the late *Lectures on the Philosophy of Religion*. Explicit references to Judaism are almost completely absent from the *Phenomenology of Spirit*. Although Hegel's evaluation of Judaism changes across these different works, most scholars agree that the critique of Judaism elaborated in his early works plays a significant role in the development of his later thinking. Cf. Yovel

Socrates, Jesus, and the rabbis, but it is in his 1798–99 essay "The Spirit of Christianity and Its Fate" that the full significance of his engagement with the Enlightenment's preoccupation with Judaism emerges. Writing against the backdrop of the French Revolution, Hegel places an opposition between Greeks and Jews at the heart of his investigation of the moral and political identities of Judaism and Christianity. Hegel's central philosophical precepts are articulated in these essays through the relationship he constructs between the Jewish, Christian, and Hellenic worlds. Freedom and beauty, reason and subjectivity, tyranny and love, masters and slaves, immortality and citizenship all find their form in a conflict between the Greek and the Jew. In Hegel's early writings, then, Athens and Jerusalem have become philosophemes.

"The Spirit of Christianity" also plays a crucial role in the development of the dialectical method that will become so central to Hegel's analysis of history. The Greek/Jew antithesis occupies a central position at the origin of Hegelian dialectics and thus plays an important role in his later elaboration of the philosophy of history. So Jean-Luc Nancy writes: "the place of the Jew in Hegel's thought is the place of the *relevé* par excellence: it is the place of the overtaken, of the denied and recuperated as a superior form, beyond its negation. *Aufgehoben*: suppressed and sublime, suppressed in order to be sublime, sublime as a result of its suppression."[4] Hegel's incipient dialectics ultimately find their expression in "The Spirit of Christianity" in a comparison between Greek and Jewish tragedy. In the final section of this chapter, I explore Hegel's early preoccupation with tragedy and contrast it to Nietzsche's own discussion of Greeks and Jews in the *Birth of Tragedy*. Through an analysis of their respective philosophies of the tragic, I show how the genealogy of Greeks, Jews, and Christians becomes pivotal to Hegel's conceptualization of the philosophy of history.

1998, 21: "The young Hegel believed that Judaism represented only the negative aspects of religion, everything that must be rejected in it. In maturity he revised his view and attributed to Judaism a crucial positive role in the history of religion and the human spirit, but a role that has long since been consummated and left behind in the train of history. . . . This suggests that, consciously or not, the mature Hegel continued to assign a negative role to Judaism, to the point of making it a theoretical scapegoat for the ills of *all* religion." For the opposite point of view see Fackenheim (1973), who sees a "sharp" distinction between Hegel's early writings and his discussion of Judaism in his "mature philosophy of religion" (163). For a more detailed exploration of the evolution of Hegel's thinking on Judaism see Hodgson 2005, 228–37.

4. Nancy 2005, 11.

Socrates and Christ, Kant and Hegel

Kantianism is, in this respect, structurally a Judaism.

DERRIDA

"Socrates," Hegel writes in the so-called Berne Fragments, "who lived in a republican state where every citizen spoke freely with every other and where a splendid urbanity of intercourse flourished even among the lowest orders, gave people a piece of his mind in the most natural manner imaginable. Without didactic tone, without the appearance of wanting to enlighten, he would start an ordinary conversation, then steer it in the most subtle fashion toward a lesson that taught itself spontaneously."[5] Even in Hegel's earliest writings, his Socrates stands on the threshold of a new conception of reason. The Socrates of the Enlightenment had become the embodiment of the Kantian subject. The Athenian philosopher subjected his interlocutors to the court of reason where each was called upon to give an account of himself that went beyond the lazy dictates of public opinion and superstition. Socrates in the age of reason was the principled self-governing individual who stood bravely against both church and state. Hegel's Socrates is a different sort of individual. His teachings are still seen as "Enlightenment" but this is Enlightenment by stealth. Socrates' lesson needs no court of reason; rather it is "a lesson that taught itself spontaneously." Already in this early formulation (1793–94), Hegel's Socrates has taken on the attributes of his later incarnation in the *History of Philosophy* (1805–6): "Consciousness had reached this point in Greece, when in Athens the great form of Socrates, in whom subjectivity of thought was brought to consciousness in a more definite and more thorough manner, now appeared."[6] Socrates' "subjectivity of thought" stands in opposition to the universality of Enlightenment of reason.

Socrates may have introduced the "infinitely important element of leading the truth of the objective back to the thought of the subject," but his trajectory should not be confused with simple individualism. Indeed, one of the most striking elements of Hegel's characterization of Socrates is that he is deeply embedded in the social fabric. His method is represented as a reflection of the prevailing social order. Socrates' dialectics are, for Hegel, an expression of republicanism. Enlightenment thinkers had been prone to distance Socrates from the oppressive society that surrounded him, to see him in a sense as an enlightened martyr of an unenlightened age. Hegel, on the other

5. Hegel 1984, 59.
6. Hegel 1974, 384.

hand, represents Socrates as an extension of the existing civic structures. As
he puts it in the *History of Philosophy*: Socrates "did not grow like a mushroom out of the earth . . . he stands in continuity with his time."[7]

Hegel's journey with Socrates in his career is a journey toward the formulation of his own philosophy. Socrates is a constant companion from his frag-
mentary juvenilia to his posthumously published lecture notes. But despite
the continuities in Hegel's depiction of the Athenian sage, these early preoccupations with the philosopher need to be contextualized in his youthful explorations of politics and religion. The specificity of Socrates' dual identity in
Hegel as the originator of "the subjectivity of thought" and the embodiment
of harmony between individual and state has wider resonance in Hegel's writings from the earliest periods of his writing when he was based in Berne and
then in Frankfurt. Hegel's Socrates is fully implicated in his meditations on the
shortcomings of Christianity and the "beautiful totality" of the Greek state.
The immediate context of this depiction of Socrates as the happy republican
conversationalist pits the Greek ideal against the cacophonous dystopia of the
synagogue. The passage quoted from the Berne Fragments above continues:

> The Jews on the other hand, in the tradition of their forefathers, were long ac-
> customed to being harangued in a far cruder fashion by their national poets.
> The synagogues had accustomed their ears to direct instruction and moral
> sermonizing, and the squabbles between scriptural authorities and the Phari-
> sees had inured them to a much coarser mode of refuting one's opponents.
> Hence to their ears a harangue that began "You serpents and breed of vipers,"
> delivered even by someone who wasn't a Pharisee or Sadducee, sounded less
> harsh than it would have done to Greek ears.[8]

The "splendid urbanity" of democracy is opposed to the "traditions of the
forefathers" as free speech is contrasted to "crude harangue." Just as Socratic
dialectics are openly assimilated to a republican politics, Jewish sermonizing
is implicitly equated with despotism. The violence of Jewish persuasion could
not be further from the benign surreptitiousness of Socratic instruction.[9] But
Hegel's meditations on Socrates and the rabbis soon gives way to the more
familiar dyad of Socrates and Christ. Here Hegel uses not Christ himself but
his followers to extend the theme of the radical disparity between Judeo-
Christian and ancient Greek modes of sociality:

7. Ibid., 386, 384.
8. Hegel 1984, 59–60.
9. Hegel's ignorance of the dialogic practices of rabbinic Judaism is remarked upon by Fackenheim 1973, 181.

Christ had twelve apostles, and this number stayed the same despite the fact that the number of his disciples was far larger. And the apostles alone enjoyed his intimate acquaintance, divesting themselves of all other ties in favor of his companionship and instruction, striving to become as totally like him as possible, and seeking to gain, by virtue of his teaching and living example, eventual possession of his spirit. How narrow-mindedly Jewish, how utterly worldly were their initial expectations, their hopes, their ideas. How slow they were to lift their gaze and their hearts from a Jewish messiah who would found an empire complete with generals and assorted high officials. How hard they found it to rise above the selfishness that always thinks of "me" first, and to enlarge their perspective to encompass the ambition of becoming mere fellow citizens of the Kingdom of God.[10]

In Hegel's denunciation of Christ's relationship to the apostles he draws on many of the established tropes of the Enlightenment representation of Judaism: "How narrow-mindedly Jewish, how utterly worldly." The condemnation of the exclusionary nature of Judaism is here allied to a critique of its materialism. In line with Spinoza, Mendelssohn, and Kant, Hegel represents Judaism as a polity "an empire complete with generals and assorted high officials." But unlike Kant, at this stage in his career Hegel stresses the profound continuity between Judaism and Christianity. Christ is a "Jewish messiah" with a quintessentially Jewish "selfishness," and his disciples share the Jewish predisposition to "always think of me first." Hegel's Judaism may be a politics, but it is a politics that cannot see beyond the individual to his "fellow citizens under God." Jewish (and Christian politics) are no rival to their Greek counterpart. It seems an irony that it is Socrates whom Hegel elects as the prototype of the happy civility of the classical *polis*:

Socrates, on the other hand, had disciples of all sorts — or rather he had none at all. He was merely a teacher and a master, just as every individual who distinguishes himself by means of exemplary integrity and superior reason is a teacher for all. While he was bent on instruction, on enlightening and enlivening the people regarding matters that ought to awaken their most intense interest, one did not hear him speak *ex cathedra* or preach from a mountain top — indeed, how could it ever have occurred to him to preach in Greece?[11]

Socrates' pedagogy is the pedagogy of the Republic. Hegel contrasts the sermonizing of Christ and the rabbis to the gentle Enlightenment of the Athenian sage. Greece with her innate predisposition to freedom would not tolerate the condescension of a preacher. "Among the Greeks," Hegel puts it

10. Hegel 1984, 61–62.
11. Ibid., 62.

simply, "he would have been an object of laughter."[12] Socrates may have set
himself up as an opponent of the democratic state, but the method of his instruction could not have been more in tune with its fundamental principles.
Hegel's Socrates is a profound egalitarian. As Georg Lukács phrases it: "Jesus
took his disciples out of society, out of life, cutting them off and turning them
into men whose chief characteristic was precisely their disciplehood. In the
case of Socrates, his disciples remain social, they stay as they are, their individuality is not remoulded artificially. They return therefore into public life
enriched."[13] But even more striking than Hegel's rehabilitation of Socrates as
a model citizen is the distinction he draws between the material aspiration of
Christ and his disciples and the spiritual outlook of Socrates:

> Just before he died—he died as a Greek, sacrificing a rooster to Aesculapius
> . . . —Socrates spoke with his disciples about the immortality of the soul.
> He spoke as would a Greek, appealing to the reason and imagination of his
> hearers, and with such animation—showing them what he hoped for so com-
> pletely, intimately, and convincingly—that [it seemed to them that] they had
> been gathering the premises of the postulates of their lives.[14]

It is no surprise that the Socrates we find Hegel lionizing is as much Mendelssohn's Socrates as Plato's. Hegel had read Mendelssohn's *Phaedon* in his
youth and was deeply affected by it. The spiritualized Socrates of Hegel's Berne
period is directly inspired by the Socrates of the *Phaedon*, the very figure who
had led so many of Mendelssohn's readers to believe that he was proposing a
conversion to Christianity. But like Mendelssohn, Hegel does not view Socrates' concern with the afterlife as an expression of crypto-Christianity. For
Hegel, Socrates' Greek rationality has a higher claim to spirituality than the
earthbound gaze of Christ's apostles. And yet, despite his otherworldly preoccupations, it is Socrates' deep rooting in Greek society that Hegel chooses to
emphasize again. Hegel famously interprets Socrates' final act of sacrifice to
Asclepius as an example of his commitment to the religion of fellow compatriots. As Harrison puts it: "Hegel depicts a Socrates as a good son of his time,
which is to say a good and courageous free citizen of Athens, who also fulfilled
all the customary religious obligations." Hegel's ultimate aim in aligning Socrates with the religious outlook of his time arises from his more general task
of defining the appropriate religion for a free people. Socratic reason finds its
counterpart in the folk religion of Greco-Roman antiquity: "The doctrines

---

12. Ibid., 63.
13. Lukács 1975, 49.
14. Hegel 1984, 63–64.

of folk religion even if resting on the authority of some divine revelation, must of necessity be constituted so that they actually are authorized by the universal reason of man kind."[15] In Mendelssohn's hands Socrates emerges as a figure of reason who transcends Christian revelation; his Socrates is, nevertheless, also put at the service of a new expression of a Hellenized Judaism. Hegel's Hellenic Socrates, on the other hand, stands in opposition to both Judaism and Christianity.

> But Socrates nonetheless so quickened this hope . . . that it was almost as if he were a spirit from the grave who climbed out and informed us concerning divine justice, giving us more of an earful than the very tablets of Moses and all the oracles of the prophets carried in our hearts. And even if, contrary to the laws of human nature, such could really have taken place, Socrates would not have needed to fortify his comrades by means of a resurrection; only in impoverished spirits, with whom the premises of this hope (namely the idea of virtue and of the highest good) are not alive, is the hope of immortality so feeble.[16]

Socrates in Hegel's early writings assumes the mantle of an alternative spiritual leader. His teachings about the immortality of the soul have the capacity to outdo both the Ten Commandments and the resurrection. It is Socrates and not Moses or Christ who has the greatest claim to our attention. Socrates' power asserts itself precisely because "it is not something that can be drummed into us by preaching," precisely because he "left no Masonic signs, no mandate to proclaim his name." Socrates succeeds where Moses and Christ have failed because "dispensing with mediators, he led the individual only to himself without asking him to provide lodging for a guest."[17]

Hegel's discussion of immortality appropriates the Socrates of Mendelssohn's *Phaedon* only to highlight the irrelevance of Moses. In Hegel's scheme Athens towers above Jerusalem. "The Greek and Roman religions were religions only for free peoples."[18] The Jewish and Christian traditions stand against the freedom of the classical citizen. The moral strictures it imposed from the outside prevented the intellectual and political autonomy of the subject. Christ had demanded of the soul that it "provide lodging for a guest." The Jewish and Christian insistence on disciplehood insures that we

---

15. Harris 1972, xvii; Harrison 1994, 40; Hegel 1984, 49.

16. Ibid., 64.

17. Hegel 1984, 65. As Jim Porter suggests to me, there may be a pun here on the German for guest, "Gast," and the German for Spirit, "Geist."

18. Hegel, in Lukacs 1975, 45.

are no longer masters in our own home. Despite his analysis of the shortcomings of Christianity "which reads almost as an anticipation of the Nietzschean critique, Hegel is still a Christian philosopher."[19] Ultimately Hegel fails to follow through the logic of his own critique. His championing of Socrates as a spiritual alternative to Christ and Moses falls short of its promise:

> What would we lack if we took Socrates as our exemplar of virtue? Wasn't Socrates a man with powers not exceeding our own? Could we not undertake to imitate him, confident that in the course of our lives we can attain his level of perfection? By contrast, what did Christ's help to the sick cost him, aside from a few words? . . . Be that as it may, when our understanding coldly pursues such a line of reasoning, our imagination simply pays no heed. It is precisely the admixture, the addition of the divine, that makes the virtuous individual Jesus fit to be an ideal of virtue. Without the divinity of the person we would only have the man; whereas here we have a truly superhuman ideal.[20]

Reason makes of Socrates a superior moral exemplar to Christ. Following our heads we could only conclude that it is Socrates who is a better source of inspiration. Where Socrates' moral teachings are the result of the hard labor of reasoned argument, Christ's words to the sick "cost him nothing." Socrates, like the rest of us, possesses nothing beyond his intellect to help him on his path to perfection, Christ on the other hand owes all his power to his relationship to the divine. Nonetheless, in world historical terms, it is Socrates' "lack" that characterizes him. Socrates' human, all-too-human, reason stands in the way of achieving the status of an ideal. Moreover, Hegel contrasts the Socratic "cold pursuit of reason" to the "heedless imagination" of Jesus. Hegel's rejection of cold reason in favor of the imagination of the divine in this passage further deepens his challenge to a particular characterization of Enlightenment thought.

In Hegel's Berne Fragments, then, we see the genesis of his complex relationship to Socrates, to Moses and to Christ. Hegel's early theological writings repeatedly return him to the conflicted intersection of the Greco-Roman world and the development of Judeo-Christianity. Throughout this period, Hegel seems to be involved in a precarious balancing act between the intellectual precepts of the Enlightenment and the formulation of its critique. In his contrast with Christ, Socrates still seems to possess all the attributes of the Kantian autonomous subject. Socrates' independent search for reason contrasts with the depiction of Christianity as a series of moral strictures

---

19. Harrison 1994, 32.
20. Hegel 1984, 88.

imposed from the outside. On the other hand, it is the very "subjectivity" of Socratic thought that directs it away from the Enlightenment's relentless appeal to universality. By leading the thought of the subject back to the self, Socrates liberates reason from what Hegel characterizes at this stage in his career as the oppressive externalism of the categorical imperative.[21] Socrates, to use Hegel's vocabulary, opposed "positivity"—that is, he stood against all authority handed down and accepted as fact. Socrates' "subjectivity" was the antithesis of Jesus' "positivity."

In his essay "The Positivity of Christianity" (1795–96), Hegel sought to answer a question that had preoccupied liberal Protestants: why Christianity had encouraged its followers to be guided by external authority rather than the exercise of reason. In the spirit of Kantian Protestantism, Hegel would have liked to strip religion bare of all its institutional trappings, its myth, ritual, and ceremony, and return it to its state of nature. In analyzing the genesis of religion's enslavement to "statutory laws," Hegel like Kant, is driven inexorably to Judaism. Since Judaism for Hegel, is the religion of pure positivity:

> The Jews were a people who derived their legislation from the supreme wisdom on high and whose spirit was now [in the time of Jesus] overwhelmed by a burden of statutory commands which pedantically prescribed a rule for every casual action of daily life and gave the whole people the look of a monastic order. As a result of this system, the holiest of things, namely the service of God and virtue, was ordered and compressed in dead formulas, and nothing save pride in this slavish obedience to laws not laid down by themselves was left to the Jewish spirit.[22]

The moribund religion of the Jews is characterized by its legalism. The spirit of Judaism was being crushed beneath the weight of the law. The Jews' complicity with an unquestioned adherence to the dictates of external authority condemned them to slavery. But for Hegel, Judaism had already reached the moment of its own exhaustion. An incipient current within Judaism could already glimpse a beyond:

> In this miserable situation there must have been Jews of a better heart and head who could not renounce or deny their feelings of selfhood or stoop to become lifeless machines, there must have been aroused in them the need for nobler gratification than that of priding themselves on this mechanical slavery, the need for a freer activity than an existence with no self-consciousness, than

21. Hegel's later, more sustained critique of Kant's Categorical Imperative in the *Philosophy of Right* is centered around his accusation of "empty formalism." On which see Sedgwick 2011.

22. Hegel 1948, 68.

a life spent in monkish preoccupation with petty, mechanical, spiritless, and trivial usages. Acquaintance with foreign nations introduced some of them to the finer blossomings of the human spirit.[23]

Some Jews, then, Hegel surmises must have been able to rouse themselves from this mechanistic existence. But such an awakening to self-consciousness was, of course, not self-generated. In this respect the Jews compare unfavorably with the other representatives of the "Oriental Spirit" with whom they are associated. Lack of self-consciousness is one of the hallmarks of Hegel's depiction of the ancient Egyptians in his *Philosophy of History*.[24] And yet, Hegel's Egyptians have an intimation of their own limitations:

> An Egyptian priest is reported to have said that the Greeks remain eternally children. We may say on the contrary, that the Egyptians are vigorous *boys*, eager for self-comprehension, who require nothing but clear understanding of themselves in an ideal form in order to become *Young men*. In the Oriental Spirit there remains as a basis the massive substantiality of Spirit immersed in Nature. To the Egyptian Spirit it has become impossible—though it is still involved in infinite embarrassment—to remain content with *that*. The rugged African nature disintegrated that primitive Unity, and lighted upon the problem whose solution is Free Spirit.[25]

The Egyptians, like the "Jews of better heart," found it "impossible . . . to remain content with *that*" but in Hegel's narrative the Egyptians themselves are able, as it were, to reach beyond their own Spirit and glimpse the possibility of freedom. Egyptian existence is, thus, presented by Hegel as being at war with itself. The impulse toward self-consciousness is restlessly battling to free itself from its "rugged African nature." In the case of Judaism, however, such a self-liberation remains impossible. On the one hand the Jews' relationship to "Nature" has been definitively corrupted by the manmade edifice of legal stricture. The "immersion" in Nature that Hegel sees as a key characteristic of the "Oriental Spirit" had from the start already been circumvented by Judaism's insistence on the exclusive relationship between a chosen people and their God. On the other hand, the potential for self-improvement that Hegel sees as integral to Egypt is resolutely denied to Judaism. The "Jews of better heart" who seek an escape from the enslavement from their tyrannical religion had to look to an external culture. Without the impact of "foreign

---

23. Ibid., 69.

24. On the connection between Hegel's discussion of the Jews and his analysis of Egypt see Newman 1993.

25. Hegel 1902, 296–97.

nations" even the best of the Jews would have remained condemned to their enslavement. As we saw in the previous chapter, like Kant before him Hegel locates the moment of Judaism's transformation at the point that it comes into contact with Greco-Roman culture. The advent of Jesus cannot be seen as an organic development within the history of Judaism; rather, it results from the powerful impulse to freedom that classical culture held out as a promise to its neighboring people.

> Jesus, who was concerned till manhood with his own personal development, was free from the contagious sickness of his age and his people; free from the inhibited inertia which expends its one activity on the common needs and the conveniences of life. . . . He undertook to raise religion and virtue to morality and restore to morality the freedom which is its essence.[26]

Jesus has to turn his back on the sickness of his people to reach such a moment of self-realization. It is *qua* Greek that he comes to understand the "essence" of religion. Ironically it is Jesus' individualism that saves him from the collective contagion of his people. Like Socrates, Jesus sees the care of the self, the "subjectivity of thought," as the root to his own Enlightenment but, unlike Socrates, Jesus must conduct this self-scrutiny in absolute isolation from his own community. In his bid to rid himself of the corrupting "positivity" of Judaism, Jesus' moral teachings must take their inspiration from paganism. For if Judaism represents the religion of pure positivity, classical paganism provides its most potent antidote:

> Greek and Roman religion was a religion for free peoples only. . . . As free men the Greeks and Romans obeyed laws laid down by themselves, obeyed men whom they themselves appointed to office, waged wars on which they had themselves decided, gave their property, exhausted their passions, and sacrificed their lives by thousands for an end which was their own. They neither learned nor taught [a moral system] but evinced by their actions the moral maxims which they call their very own. In public as in private and domestic life, every individual was a free man, one who lived by his own laws.[27]

As Lukács puts it, "Hegel's central ideological problem is . . . what he calls subjectivity in contrast to positivity. . . . The freedom and independence of the people is the source of the non-positive, non-fetishized, non-objective character of classical religion."[28] Jesus achieves his moment of self-consciousness by removing himself from the Jewish community and turning his thoughts

26. Hegel 1948, 69.
27. Ibid., 154.
28. Lukacs 1975, 47, 48.

toward himself. But what Jesus finds when he begins to contemplate himself turns out already to have been there in the pagan culture that surrounded him. Socrates' program of internalization far from turning its back on the wider community is actually fully in tune with the instinctive "subjectivity" of Greek and Roman thought. When Jesus turns himself inward he discovers the Greek that he already was. It is by identifying himself as a Greek and repudiating his identity as a Jew that Jesus could become a "teacher for a purely moral religion, not a positive one."[29]

Hegel's initial strategy, then, is to make of Judaism the repository of positivity in order to absolve Christ of this charge. If Christianity retains the burden of positivity it is because Jesus' followers were not as successful in overcoming their Judaism as he was: "how narrow-mindedly Jewish." But as the essay develops, Hegel renounces this position and actually locates the moment of Christianity's turn to positivity in Jesus' own lifetime. Despite his early promise, Hegel argues that Christ increasingly corrupted his rational moral religion by giving it an authoritative form. It was Jesus' decision to reject the Socratic model and to teach *ex-cathedra* that divested Christianity of its moral core and eradicated its predisposition to freedom. Christ's intention may have been to liberate monotheism from its Jewish externality, but through his teaching he unwittingly reintroduces into Christianity the ills of its Judaic predecessor. As Yirmiyahu Yovel phrases it:

> At this point the young Hegel demonstrates the quasi-dialectical pattern that was to characterize his future writings—namely the opposition between content and form, between an essence and its actual shaping. Here we observe the ironic opposition between Jesus' intention and what it had produced. Such incongruity of intention and meaning was typical of what the mature Hegel saw in the pattern of history.[30]

"In Greek religion, or in any other whose underlying principle is a pure morality, the moral commands of reason, which are subjective, were not treated or set up as objective rules with which the understanding deals. But the Christian religion has taken the subjective element in reason and set it up as a rule as if it were something objective."[31]

Christianity, then, in Hegel's *Positivity*, has the content of Hellenism but the form of Judaism. In this respect, Christianity shares the same shortcomings as Kantianism: "Reason sets up moral, necessary, and universally valid

29. Hegel 1948, 71.
30. Yovel 1998, 29.
31. Hegel 1948, 143.

laws; Kant calls these objective. . . . Now the problem is to make these laws subjective."[32] For Hegel to move beyond Kant one must first move beyond positivity. "Kantianism," Derrida writes provocatively, "is, in this respect, structurally a Judaism."[33] As Derrida speculates elsewhere paraphrasing the Jewish Kantian Hermann Cohen: "Who is Kant? He is the holiest saint of the German spirit, the deepest innermost inner sanctum of the German spirit, but he is also the one who represents the innermost affinity with Judaism."[34] Despite the antipathy to Judaism that marks Kant's own writings, in Hegel's scheme Kant becomes a "Jew" by virtue of the "positivity" of his ethics. In stripping Christianity of its formal and abstract morality, Hegel simultaneously expels the specter of Judaism from world history and the specter of Kant from his moral philosophy. Christ's return to Socrates depends on Hegel exiling the figure whom Hölderlin would call the "Moses unserer Nation" from his thought. For Christianity to realize its Hellenism, Hegel must first emancipate himself from the "Jewish" Kant.[35]

Noah and Deucalion

The impression made on men's hearts by the flood in the time of Noah must have been a deep distraction and it must have caused the most prodigious disbelief in nature. . . . If man was to hold out against the outbursts of a nature now hostile, nature had to be mastered; and since the whole can be divided into idea and reality, so also the supreme unity of mastery lies either in something thought or in something real. It was in a thought-product that Noah built the distracted world together again.

HEGEL

Noah is the concept. By a bad wordplay, Jewish-Greek, à la Joyce, and mixing in a little gallicism (Noé), one would say noesis.

DERRIDA

Encoded in Hegel's critique of Judaism is paradoxically a critique of reason. In his most vociferously anti-Judaic work, "The Spirit of Christianity and Its Fate" (1798–99), Hegel develops an analysis of Judaism that simultaneously

32. Ibid., 143–44.

33. Derrida 1986, 34. On which see Critchley 1997, 202, 212–14.

34. Derrida 1991, 58. Derrida responds to the irony of Kant's Judaism by arguing somewhat unconvincingly that "the fact that the *Anthropology from a Practical Point of View* includes at least one properly anti-Semitic note (literally anti-Palestinian) is not incompatible with Kant's quasi-Judaism" (1991, 69).

35. See also Legros, who writes, "Let us try and focus on and question the principle of this strange hierarchy whereby Kant is almost equated with Jewish religion and the religion of Jesus with Greek paganism" (1997, 16–17).

calls into question Enlightenment reason and its relationship to the ethical life. He discovers in the figure of Abraham an antithesis both to Socrates and to Christ: "With Abraham, the true progenitor of the Jews, the history of this people begins, i.e. his spirit is the unity, the soul, regulating the entire fate of his posterity."[36] The soul of Abraham is key to understanding the Jewish people as an ethical community and a political entity. But although Abraham will be the main protagonist in Hegel's investigation of the "Spirit of Judaism," the Jewish patriarch soon gives way in Hegel's opening formulation to a different originary pair: Noah and Nimrod. For Hegel sees Abraham's authority as a symptom of the "loss of the state of nature."

Abraham emerges from "the important period in which men strove by various routes to revert from barbarism" after the "unity" between man and nature "had been broken." The destiny of the "Jewish spirit," which takes its form in the figure of Abraham, cannot be understood without reference to the time of Noah and the flood: "Formerly friendly or tranquil, nature had now abandoned the equipoise of her elements, now requited the faith the human race had in her with the most destructive, invincible, irresistible hostility; in her fury she spared nothing; she made none of the distinctions which love might have made but poured savage devastation over everything."[37] In Hegel's account, during the flood man is cruelly severed from his state of symbiosis with his natural environment. From the start, Hegel develops the ethical vocabulary that will be integral to his analysis of the fates of the Jewish and Christian spirits. Where his previous essay had opposed the poles of "positivity" and "subjectivity," Hegel's new lexical antithesis has become "hostility" and "love." For Hegel, the spirit of Judaism is forged in this cataclysm of "hostility."

Noah and Nimrod respectively represent two Jewish attempts to "master" "a nature now hostile." For Noah, the mastery will above all be intellectual. He represents the tyranny of the "idea":

> It was in a thought-product that Noah built the distracted world together again; his thought-produced ideal he turned into a [real] Being and then set everything else over against it, so that in this opposition realities were reduced to thoughts, i.e. to something mastered . This Being promised him to confine within their limits the elements which were his servants, so that no flood was ever to destroy mankind.[38]

36. Hegel 1948, 182.
37. Ibid.
38. Ibid., 183.

Noah creates a God to protect mankind from nature. But as a "thought produced ideal" God is from the very start set up in a hostile, tyrannical relation to his dominion. Noah's relationship to God is established as an exclusive one that in its very essence "opposes" itself to all "realities." Moreover, man's pact with God is immediately accompanied by a "subjection to the law." God's mastery of nature had its corollary in his demand that man be obedient to his command. The injunction "not to kill one another" is God's condition for protecting man from the ravages of nature. When man is given the gift of dominating nature he is himself in turn dominated by God. Noah's flood heralds the development of Judaism as a positive religion. Judaism thus has the dual characteristic of an intellectual mastery that pits man against the world of reality and a legal mastery that opposes him to the inner ethical life of subjectivity.

Noah's flood, for Hegel, thus becomes a parable of the Enlightenment notion of reason and the Kantian conception of ethics. The belief in an autonomous rational subject who "divides the whole" into "idea" and "reality" represents for Hegel the limitations of Enlightenment reason. Moreover, man's submission to an abstract ideal is reproduced in his deferral of ethical responsibility to a regime of law and abstract command. The moral decision not to kill is first rationalized and then reified. In Hegel's narrative of the development of Judaism both God and the ethical life are effects of hypostatization.

In contrast to Noah, Nimrod chooses a more direct path to domination. Where Noah creates a God to protect man from nature, Nimrod strives to protect man from God: "Nimrod placed the unity in man and installed him as the being who was to make the other realities into thoughts. . . . In the event of God's having a mind to overwhelm the world with a flood again, he threatened to neglect no means and no power to make an adequate resistance to Him."[39] Nimrod, according to Eusebius as Hegel informs us, orders the survivors of the flood to build for themselves a tower that will loom over the destructive forces of nature and protect man from her vengeance. Like Noah, Nimrod opposes violent nature to his controlling thought world; like Noah, Nimrod mandates a respect for life. But unlike Noah, Nimrod does not delegate responsibility for man's survival to a divine power:

> He united men after they had become mistrustful, estranged from another, and now ready to scatter. But the unity he gave them was not a reversion to a cheerful social life in which they trusted nature and one another; he kept them

39. Ibid., 184.

together indeed, but by force. He defended himself against water by walls; he was a hunter and king. In his battle against need, therefore the elements, animals, and men had to endure the law of the stronger, though the law of a living being.[40]

As it says in the Bible, Nimrod destroys, Noah saves. But for all their differences, Noah's and Nimrod's solutions to the flood are united under the sign of tyranny. Noah's domination of nature is transferred onto man's own domination by the divine law. Furthermore, Noah's conception of a tyrannical God has its mirror image in Nimrod's society kept together by force. Judaism is a religion held together, with or without God, by "the law of the stronger." The Jews' metaphysical servitude to an abstract authoritarian divinity is reproduced in their political servitude to a "king."

Ultimately, what Noah and Nimrod have in common is the perpetuation of hostility:

> Against the hostile power [of nature] Noah saved himself by subjecting both it and himself to something more powerful; Nimrod by taming it himself. Both made a peace of *necessity* with the foe and thus perpetuated the hostility. Neither was reconciled with it, unlike a more beautiful pair, Deucalion and Pyrrha, who, after the flood in their time, invited men once again to friendship with the world, to nature, made them forget their need and their hostility in joy and pleasure, made a peace of *love*, were the progenitors of more beautiful peoples, and made their age the mother of a newborn natural life which maintained its bloom of youth.[41]

Where Hegel at first seems to represent Noah's and Nimrod's two opposing worldviews, this opposition is at closer inspection merely illusory. The Noah and Nimrod couple are themselves opposed to their true antithesis: the "more beautiful pair Deucalion and Pyrrha." Noah and Nimrod thus represent a false dialectic; rather than clashing in a process of productive mutual education, their respective solutions merely represent two different versions of irredeemable failure. As Joseph Cohen has argued:

> Judaism is described as the negative origin of the world. For the good beginning is that of the "beautiful ethical totality" represented by the Greek city, where the divine is always already united and reconciled in and through what is humane, that is what is universal in all its particularity. The bad beginning, the beginning of Judaic separation, has condemned man to submission and has defined him as being of unadulterated ugliness. For the Hegel of Frank-

40. Ibid.
41. Ibid., 184–85.

furt, the Jew is ahistorical, he has nothing to do with the history of *Geist* and the historical unveiling of Spirit.[42]

Noah and Nimrod, according to Cohen, represent pure negativity. Unlike the "schöneres Paar" from Greek mythology, the protagonists of the biblical narrative can only react to force with force. A tense status quo is maintained but progress remains impossible. From the Greeks' experience of adversity emerges "friendship," "joy," "pleasure," and most important for Hegel, "love." "Love" will become *the* ethical virtue against which the spirit of Judaism is systematically opposed. But Hegel's Greek/Jew antithesis also engenders a distinctive philosophy of history. He locates the Greek mythological pair in a narrative of historical progress. Deucalion and Pyrrha, beautiful themselves, "were the progenitors of more beautiful peoples." But more than a mere genealogical narrative of self-preservation, the beautiful pair carry the burden of world history: they "made their age mother of a new born natural life which maintained its bloom of youth." The Greeks embody the paradoxical position of progressing while still staying the same. They are able to become "mothers" while at the same time forever retaining the "bloom of youth." The gift of eternal youth is coupled with a privileged role in the narrative of cultural maturation. In his representation of the Hellenic spirit, Hegel thus allies the clichés of Winckelmannian aestheticism to his own idiosyncratic narrative of ethical and historical progress. Hegel, as it were, had no choice, the Greeks of his era were all inescapably "schön." But he is able to transform this aesthetic valorization not just into an ethical discourse, which was in any case already more than implicit in Winckelmann and his many admirers, but also, and much more originally, into an account of the historical progress of the world spirit. With Hegel the Greek's beauty comes hand in hand with the responsibility for the development of ethical self-consciousness.

Paradoxically, Hegel's account of the development of reason in its relationship to nature reverses the cultural troping of a more recent account of the emergence of Enlightenment reason. J. M. Bernstein observes: "Taking due account of the opening passages of the 'Spirit' essay reveals how proximate its argumentation is to the genealogy of reason that Max Horkheimer and T. W. Adorno offer in *Dialectic of the Enlightenment*."[43] "Enlightenment, understood in its widest sense as the advance of thought, has always aimed at liberating human beings from fear and installing themselves as masters,"

42. Cohen 2005, 23.
43. Bernstein 2003, 16.

write Adorno and Horkheimer. "Yet the wholly enlightened earth is radiant with triumphant calamity. Enlightenment's program was the disenchantment of the world."[44] But in their account it is paradoxically the Greeks and not the Jews who come to embody the violence of instrumental reason. Adorno substitutes Hegel's mythological pair with the Homeric Odysseus in his own narrative of the Greeks' relationship to the natural world: "The pattern of Odysseus' guile is the mastery of nature. . . . The formula of Odysseus's cunning is that the detached instrumental mind, by submissively embracing nature, renders to nature what is hers and thereby cheats her." What better demonstration of the Hegelian "List der Vernunft," the "guile of reason"? For Adorno, Odysseus shares none of the guileless trusting of Deucalion and Pyrrha. To their "friendship" and "love" is opposed Odysseus' "cunning" and "cheating." Instead of submitting himself to nature in a gesture of "peace," Odysseus rather feigns submission only to better master her. Perhaps this is why Adorno provocatively states later in the essay that "Odysseus already bears features of the Jew."[45]

Abraham and the Greek Republics

The dialectic between Greek mythology and biblical narrative that launches his exploration of the spirit of Christianity is repeated in Hegel's analysis of Abraham. As Derrida writes:

> The Greek flood has more affinity than the Jew with the spirit of Christianity: reconciliation, love and the founding of the family. The opposition of Jew and Greek is pursued, precisely regarding the family. The contrast between Abraham on the one hand, Cadmus and Danaus on the other, reproduces in its signification the contrast between Noah and Nimrod on the hand and Deucalion and Pyrrha on the other.[46]

But despite Derrida's emphasis on the familial dimension of Hegel's Greek/Jew antithesis, it is the political question that is given more immediate prominence in his exploration of the founding of nations. It is in terms of the fatherland that Hegel pursues the disparate fates of Abraham and his Greek counterparts. To be more precise it is the dialectic of family and nation, father and fatherland that Hegel explores in continuing investigation of the Hellenic and Hebraic spirits.

44. Horkheimer and Adorno 2002, 1.
45. Ibid., 45, 54. On which see Porter's fascinating 2010 essay.
46. Derrida 1986, 40.

Abraham, born in Chaldea, had in youth already left a fatherland in his father's
company. Now, in the plains of Mesopotamia, he tore himself free altogether
from his family as well, in order to be a wholly self-subsistent, independent
man, to be an overlord himself. He did this without having been injured or
disowned, without the grief which after a wrong or an outrage signifies love's
enduring need, when love, injured indeed but not lost, goes in quest of a new
fatherland in order to flourish and enjoy itself there.[47]

Hegel's Abraham repeats Noah's acts of mastery and self-mastery. Like the
injured Noah in the wake of the flood, Abraham seeks to emancipate himself
from relationships of trust and dependency. His aim is to become "an overlord" himself. But unlike Noah, Abraham acts without any provocation. No
flood, no injury, no "irresistible hostility" spurred his own act of hostility. By
the time of Abraham, the Jewish spirit has so internalized its recourse to hostility that it has become entirely spontaneous and self-generating. "Love's enduring need" is as alien to Abraham's world as it is integral to Deucalion and
Pyrrha's. And the absence of love is precisely what makes Abraham's transition from his father to his fatherland possible: "The first act which made
Abraham the progenitor of a nation is a disseverance which snaps the bonds
of communal life and love. The entirety of the relationships in which he had
hitherto lived with men and nature, these beautiful relationships of youth
(Joshua xxiv.2), he spurned."[48] The abandonment of family and the founding
of the nation are not contingent factors in Abraham's rise. Severance from the
family and the denial of love are the constitutive forces "which made Abraham the progenitor of a nation." Abraham has to kill his father, to kill the
very concept of fatherhood and its ties to a vocabulary of familial love, to become himself a progenitor. Abraham is the father who emerges from the suppression of fatherhood, just as his nation is the community that is founded in
the moment of the severing of "communal" ties. The Jewish father is at best a
legal fiction, the Jewish community at worst an impossible one.

Abraham's political exile has its end rather than its beginning in hostility. Rather than being forced to leave his community and adopt a new one
in response, Abraham himself deserts his homeland in order to free himself
from the burdens of companionship. His Greek counterparts represent the
opposite trajectory:

Cadmus, Danaus, etc., had forsaken their fatherland too, but they forsook it
in battle; they went in quest of a soil where they would be free and they sought

47. Hegel 1948, 185.
48. Ibid.

it that they might love. Abraham wanted *not* to love, wanted to be free by not loving. Those others, in order to live in pure, beautiful, unions, as was no longer given to them in their own land, carried these gods forth with them. Abraham wanted to be free of these very relationships, while the others by their gentle arts and manners won over the less civilized aborigines and intermingled with them to form a happy gregarious people.[49]

Cadmus and Danaus thus share with Abraham a thirst for freedom. But the Greek freedom is a freedom to love, the Jewish, a freedom to hate. The Greeks export the best of their culture, their freedom, their beauty and their love and "with their gentle manners" win over the "less civilized." The happy Greeks are not just happy because of their blessed superiority to the peoples around; they are happy because they seek to win over these people to their way of life. Abraham is guided by the same hostility that drove him away from his family in his encounters with foreign peoples during the rest of his life. His alienation from other people is an alienation from the world itself: "He was a stranger on earth, a stranger to the soil and to men alike."[50]

Hegel's description of Abraham anticipates his characterization by the twentieth-century philosopher Emmanuel Lévinas. Abraham as the paradigm of the exile has been contrasted by Lévinas with the figure of Ulysses: "To the myth of Ulysses returning to Ithaca we can oppose the story of Abraham leaving his fatherland forever for an unknown land and forbidding his servant to lead even his son to the point of departure."[51] For Lévinas, while Odysseus' adventures represent a circuitous return home, Abraham's exile is one of absolute alienation. This Greek/Jew opposition represents for Lévinas a parable for the very itinerary of philosophy. As Lambropoulos writes of Ulysses:

> His career which is but a return home, represents the central concern of Greek and most Western thought, from Parmenides to Heidegger: the search for the self, truth, and being as the *algos* of *nostos*. Philosophy has long aspired to the totality of homeliness, the ideal of at homeness (*Heimatlichkeit*) in one's entire existence, and has found its model in the Greek objective (self) representation.[52]

A conception of philosophy that represents a central plank of Hegel's philhellenism: "Philosophy is being at home with self, just like the homeliness of the

49. Ibid.
50. Ibid., 186.
51. Lévinas 1986, 348.
52. Lambropoulos 1993, 215.

Greek; it is man's being at home in his mind, at home with himself."[53] Philosophy, for Hegel, is necessarily Greek because it is essentially an activity of the home. The state of exile is antithetical to the philosophical life. So Lévinas confirms: "Philosophy's itinerary remains that of Ulysses, whose adventure in the world was only a return to his native island- a complacency in the Same, an unrecognition of the other."[54]

Abraham, as Cohen phrases it, has an allergy to the "chez-soi." His nomadic existence embodies the inability of the Jews to feel at home. The experience of alienation was a constitutive part of the Jewish spirit. Hegel thus transposes into philosophical idiom the theological and political discourse of the "wandering Jew." The Jews' inability to form national ties became implicated in the contemporary political debate about whether it would be possible to integrate them into the nation. For Hegel's Abraham, his inability to engage in the here-and-now is the byproduct of his all-exclusive relationship to God. Abraham's devotion to a tyrannical God stands in the way of any relationship to another person:

> The whole world Abraham regarded simply as his opposite; if he did not take it to be a nullity, he looked on it as sustained by the God who was alien to it. Nothing in nature was supposed to have any part in God; everything was simply under God's mastery. Abraham, as the opposite of the whole world, could have no higher mode of being than that of the other term in the opposition, and thus he was likewise supported by God. Moreover, it was through God alone that Abraham came into a mediate relation with the world, the only kind of link with the world possible for him.[55]

Regarding the "whole world" as one's opposite stands directly against the "beautiful totality" of the Hellenic spirit. The integrated life of the Greeks puts into relief the essential rupture that characterizes the life of the Jews. Where the Greeks worshiped their gods as a celebration of their happy symbiosis with the natural world around them, Abraham's religious life severs him from the world. And yet, it is only through his religion that he is able to have any relation to the world at all. Abraham's relationship to God stands in the way of an involvement in the world but, at the same time, it provides the only conduit back to it. Man can only experience the world through the mediation of his God. No spontaneous connection can develop between a people

53. Hegel 1974, 152.
54. Lévinas 1986, 349.
55. Hegel 1948, 187.

and their surroundings without the intermediary of the divine. Abraham, like Noah then, represents the "thought-produced" ideal. His involvement in the here-and-now is not only mediated through the intellect, but this very process of intellectualization involves an act of violent domination: "his Ideal subjugated the world to him." This injunction to mastery even corrodes the natural ties of the ethical community of the family:

> Love alone was beyond his power; even the one love he had, his love for his son, even his hope of posterity—the one mode of extending his being, the one mode of immortality he knew and hoped for—could depress him, trouble his all exclusive heart and disquiet it to such an extent that even this love he once wished to destroy; and his heart was quieted only through the certainty of the feeling that this love was not so strong as to render him unable to slay his beloved son with his own hand.[56]

Abraham can only understand love as a power that he needs to master. The love of a son is so threatening to him precisely because it escapes the grasp of his command. Hegel's depiction of the earthbound aspirations of the Jews finds its expression in Abraham's limited conception of immortality. Abraham knows of no other "mode of extending his being" than through his son. Hegel's characterization of the Jewish patriarch chimes with the wider prejudice against Judaism as a religion confined to worldly experience. Like Mendelssohn's contemporaries, Hegel cannot envisage a Jewish conception of an afterlife. But even such a limited conception of afterlife is beyond Abraham's comprehension. Abraham's extension of his being through Isaac is only rescued because he knows ultimately that he is able to do without it. His rooting in the material world goes unchallenged. Isaac is saved from his sacrifice because Abraham is comforted by the knowledge that after all he is not able to love. As Cohen puts it: "the 'sacrifice' of the son is said to have been interrupted not by an excess of love but by a deficit." Isaac's sacrifice, therefore, is in fact no sacrifice, because as he is unable to love, the Jew cannot truly experience the loss of a son.[57]

"The Jews have no share in anything eternal," asserts Hegel.[58] It is at this juncture in the argument that Hegel makes his most explicit reference to Mendelssohn. Mendelssohn, as we have seen, had been an important influence on the young Hegel and his reading of *Jerusalem* played a pivotal role

56. Ibid.
57. Cohen 2005, 55. Hegel is no doubt building on the commonplace analogy between Isaac and Jesus here.
58. Hegel 1948, 195.

in the formulation of his thoughts on religion during this period. "Hegel's characterization of the Jews and Judaism in 'The Spirit of Christianity and its Fate' and his other early theological writings," writes Rosenstock "is a direct assault upon Mendelssohn's presentation of Judaism in *Jerusalem* as an exemplary enlightened form of sociality." "The young Hegel follows Kant . . . ," argues Yovel, "turning a great Jew he admired into a witness against his people."[59] The Enlightenment critique of Judaism had led Mendelssohn in his *Phaedon* to reaffirm the universality of a belief in the immortality of the soul, and yet, for Hegel, Mendelssohn's legacy merely substantiates his vision of the earth bound aspirations of Judaism:

> Other reflections on the human spirit, other modes of consciousness, do not present themselves in these religious laws, and Mendelssohn reckons it a high merit in his faith that it proffers no eternal truths. "There is one God" is an assertion that stands on the summit of the state's laws, and if something proffered in this form could be called truth, then, of course, one may say: What deeper truth is there for slaves than that they have a master? But Mendelssohn is right not to call this a truth, since what we find as truth among the Jews did not appear to them as truths and matters of faith. Truth is something free which we neither master or are mastered by.[60]

Mendelssohn's depiction of Judaism as a system of revealed legislation stands in opposition to Hegel's presentation of Christianity as the religion of truth. Mendelssohn had argued that its freedom from metaphysical dogma left the followers of Judaism free for rational pursuits. Hegel sees this as confirmation that truth eluded the Jews. Hegel ignores Mendelssohn's insistence to the contrary: "Although the divine book that we received through Moses is strictly speaking meant to be a book of laws containing ordinances, rules of life and prescriptions, it also includes, as is well known, an inexhaustible treasure of rational truths."[61] For Mendelssohn, the eternal truths of reason coincide with those of the Bible, whereas for Hegel the Jews are structurally barred from truth by their lack of freedom. For Hegel, truth is the very essence of freedom and the Jews' submission to a series of "prescriptions" and "ordinances" makes them incapable of apprehending it.

> The existence of God appears to the Jews not as a truth but as a command. On God the Jews are dependent throughout, and that on which a man depends cannot have a form of truth. Truth is beauty intellectually represented. . . . But

---

59. Rosenstock 2010, 207; Yovel 1998, 44; see also Pöggeler 1974, 530
60. Hegel 1948, 195–96.
61. Mendelssohn 1983, 99.

how could they have an inkling of beauty who saw in everything only matter? How could they exercise reason and freedom who were only either mastered or masters? How could they have hoped even for the poor immortality
in which consciousness of the individual is preserved, how could they have
wished to persist in self-subsistence who had in fact renounced the capacity to
will and even the very fact of their existence, who wished only for a continuation of the possession of their land through their posterity, a continuation
of an undeserving and inglorious name in a progeny of their own, who never
enjoyed any life or consciousness lifted above eating and drinking?[62]

In this passage Hegel illustrates the full imbrication of the opposition between
Hellenism and Hebraism in the overlapping discourses of metaphysics, aesthetics, and politics. Hegel finds the Jews lacking in beauty—the immediate
marker of Greek identity—and this lack in relation to the aesthetic sphere
finds its concomitant in a lack of freedom. Hegel constructs a powerful equation where truth, beauty, freedom, and spirituality are each seen as mutually
constitutive. The Jews are trapped in a perpetual vicious circle of their own
making. The ethical commands of the Mosaic law trap the Jews into their
position of servitude from which they will only be liberated by the advent of
a new religion.

"Over against commands which required a bare service of the Lord, a direct slavery, an obedience without joy, without pleasure or love, i.e., the commands in connection with the service of God, Jesus set the precise opposite,
a human urge, so a human need." Hegel, as we have already seen, characterizes the emergence of Christianity as a turning away from the "positivity" of
Judaism. "Against the purely objective commands Jesus set something totally
foreign to them, namely, the subjective in general." Far from tracing the continuities between Jesus and the Jews, "The Spirit of Christianity" sets Christ
in diametrical opposition to the Jewish faith. Where Abraham regards the
"whole world" "as his opposite," Jesus finds his antithesis only in Abraham:
"Jesus did not fight merely against one part of the Jewish fate; to have done
so would have implied that he was himself in the toils of another part, and he
was not; he set himself against the whole. Thus he was himself raised above
it and tried to raise his people above it too." The new conception of ethics that Jesus embodies is explicitly marked as a rejection of Kant's "moral
imperative."[63] As Bernstein argues:

> Hegel thinks there is an ethical content embedded in the emergence of Chris-
> tianity, above all in Jesus' narrative, that Kant misses and misrepresents alto-

62. Hegel 1948, 196.
63. Ibid., 205, 206, 209, 213.

gether; so fully does Kant mistake the fundamental ethical logic of Christianity that his logic is not Christian at all, but rather a rationalized version of the very Judaism biblical Christianity aimed to supplant.[64]

Judaism's only possible liberation from itself is to be found in its opposite. The imperative of raising his "people above" their Judaism is at the heart of Christ's message in the Sermon of the Mount: "This spirit of Jesus, a spirit raised above morality, is visible, directly attacking laws, in the Sermon on the Mount, which is an attempt . . . to strip the laws of their legality."[65] Christ's Sermon is not a development but rather a full repudiation of the Sinaitic Covenant.

If the object of "The Spirit of Christianity" is to set Judaism and Christianity up as irreconcilable opposites, this aim is only achieved via a sustained exploration of the incommensurability of the Greek and the Jew. The necessity of overcoming Judaism is demonstrated, on the one hand, by the characterization of Hellenic culture as proto-Christian and, on the other, by a depiction of Christianity as the culmination and completion of the Greek miracle. It is the Greek example that makes the analysis of the Jewish polity key to the condemnation of Judaism as a religion. When Hegel asserts that "the Jews have no share in anything eternal," behind his denunciation of the earthbound gaze of a religion that cannot comprehend spiritual truth lies a political condemnation of a people who have no share in the universal. As Derrida remarks: "The Jew cannot become, as such, a citizen: he cannot have any true laws of state. . . . The Jews have no political obligation because they have no concept of freedom and of political rationality."[66] But Hegel's assertion that the Jews were unable to convert a moral code into an effective practice of the political is paradoxically constructed on an analogy with the Greeks. Discussing the Jewish restrictions on property rights, Hegel finds an echo of the laws established by Solon in Athens and Lycurgus in Sparta.[67] Both Greeks had sought, like the Jews, "to put an end to the inequality of riches":[68]

> Just as here a similar consequence—release from truths—follows from opposite conditions, so, in reference to the subordination of civil rights to the

---

64. Bernstein 2003, 3.

65. Hegel 1948, 212.

66. Derrida 1986, 51, 52.

67. The analogy between Moses and the lawgivers and Solon and Lycurgus was already in circulation in antiquity and appears in the historians Hecataeus, Diodorus, Strabo, and, especially, Josephus. Josephus and Philo both argue that Moses put the achievements of the Greek legislators into the shade. See Gruen 2009.

68. Derrida 1986, 52.

law of the land, and institution of the Mosaic state has a striking resemblance to the situation created in the republic by the two famous legislators though its source is very different. In order to avert from their states the danger threatening to freedom from the inequality of wealth, Solon and Lycurgus restricted property rights in numerous ways and set barriers to freedom of choice which might have led to unequal wealth.[69]

But "once more," as Derrida sighs, "the analogy between Greek and Jew is limited to appearance." The appearance in the letter conceals a profound disparity in "spirit." The two laws may at first sight seem to signal a common concern for equality, a common desire to preserve freedom through an attempt to "neutralize" disparity. "But the same literality will have, according to Hegel, a completely different spirit in the Greeks: and first of all a spirit and nothing else, an inner sense animating the law of the inside."[70] Once more, it is the Jews' "positivity," their exteriority, which prevents them from accessing real ethical (and political) consciousness. Where the Jews have the letter, the Greeks have the spirit, where the Jews have commandments, the Greeks have freedom:

> In the Greek republics the source of these laws lay in the fact that, owing to the inequality which would otherwise have arisen, the freedom of the impoverished might have been jeopardized and they might have fallen into political annihilation; among the Jews, in the fact that they had no freedom and no rights, since they held their possessions only on loan and not as property, since as citizens they were all nothing. The Greeks were to be equal because all were free, self-subsistent; the Jews equal because all were incapable of self-subsistence.[71]

The Jews command equality because they are all equally impoverished with respect to their land. Quoting Leviticus and the practice of the "Jubilee" to support him, Hegel reveals how the Jews do not actually own their land, they have it merely as a loan from their God. As such, they have no concept of family property. "The Greek process founds right and politics, constitutes family subjects as citizens. The Jewish process, on the contrary scoffs at rights and politics."[72] The Jews are stuck in the same double bind that has marred their existence since Noah. They are incapable of being citizens because they are incapable of being a family, incapable of being a family because they lack

69. Hegel 1948, 197.
70. Derrida 1986, 52, 53.
71. Hegel 1948, 198.
72. Derrida 1986, 52.

the political rights of the citizen. In the end, for Hegel, the Jews cannot be citizens because they are not Greeks. The commands of Moses may mirror the laws of Solon and Lycurgus but the essence of politics was foreign to the Jews; it was inextricably linked to the Greek experience.[73] In denying a concept of the political to the Jews, Hegel again founds his difference from Kant on a distinction between Greeks and Jews. Kant's (albeit highly unfavorable) characterization of Judaism as politics accords the Jews a degree of consciousness that Hegel reserves exclusively for the Greeks. As Bruce Rosenstock argues:

> Kant thought that the apparent absence of any reference to an afterlife in the Hebrew Bible showed it to be a merely "political faith." Hegel went further and took the purely this worldly-rewards and punishment of the Hebrew Bible as evidence that the Jews had reduced themselves to a condition *below* the political, a condition of enslavement so profound that they "renounced the capacity of will and even the very fact of their existence."[74]

If the connection to the contemporary situation of the Jews remains implicit in Kant's discussion of Judaism in *Religion within the Limits of Reason Alone*, in Hegel's "Spirit of Christianity" it becomes increasingly explicit:

> The subsequent circumstances of the Jewish people up to the mean, abject, wretched circumstances in which they still are today, have all of them been simply consequences and elaborations of their original fate. By this fate—an infinite power which they set over against themselves and could never conquer—they have been maltreated and will be continually maltreated until they appease it by the spirit of beauty and so annul it by reconciliation.[75]

For Hegel, the model of citizenship to emerge from the political battles of the late eighteenth century may have been unique to modernity but it was a model that was forged in a sustained dialogue with the polities of democratic Athens and republican Rome. As we saw in the previous chapter, in debating the extension of citizen rights to the Jews, the revolutionaries were confronted with the question of how much like a Greek (or a Roman) can a Jew be. Hegel's answer is resolute: the Greek and the Jew are incommensurable. In his portrayal of "the subsequent circumstances of the Jewish people," Hegel at one and the same time opens the door to salvation and simultaneously

---

73. As Bourgeois (1970, 46–47) writes: "Contrary to the ancient city, the absolute centre of the life of its citizens, an end in itself . . . the Jewish state is not an end in itself, it is a means allowing the Jews to serve their values and the supreme being, their god, in other words it is their natural security. *The Jewish state is an essential instrument dictated by necessity to defend the animal egoism of the Jews.*"

74. Rosenstock 2010, 206.

75. Hegel 1948, 199–200.

shuts it. He offers the promise of "reconciliation," but it is a "reconciliation" that can only be achieved through complete self-denial. Ultimately, the Jews will never be able to survive the dialectic. In their opposition to the Greeks they cannot hope for recuperation in the synthesis. For Hegel defines Judaism as precisely incapable of synthesizing: "Moses' failure has not reached the Jews. Judaism is constituted starting from it, as the impossibility of Moses to raise his people, to educate [sic] and relieve [sic] (erheben and aufheben) his people." As Derrida surmises, "the Jew is incapable of this in his family, his politics, his religion, his rhetoric. If he became capable of it, he would no longer be Jewish. When he will become capable of it, he will have become Christian."[76]

Christianity, then, is not the fusion between the Hebraic and the Hellenic. Christianity's triumph is to liberate itself of Judaism by revealing itself as always already Greek. Just as Deucalion and Pyrrha discovered in their reaction to the flood that they were already Christians, Christ realizes that he is still a Greek. The horizon of the present makes itself felt in Hegel's essay, written only seven years after the debates in the Assemblée Generale about the extension of citizen rights to the Jews. Despite the revolutionaries' decision to grant equal rights to the Jews, at this stage in his career, for Hegel, citizenship remains a decidedly Christian privilege. To be a citizen is to be a Christian by virtue of having been Greek. To conclude with Derrida, citizenship "was first a Greek event from which Christianity would have developed an outer graft."[77]

In Hegel's early theological writings, then, the relationship between ancient Jews and their "subsequent fate" is subtly blurred. Written in the aftermath of the French Revolution, Hegel's reflections on Jewish citizenship ancient and modern are marked by their fervent hostility.[78] In "The Spirit of Christianity," Hegel's stance on contemporary Jews seems merely to be an extension of his condemnation of ancient Israel. As Amy Newman writes in the context of her discussion about Hegel: "as Protestant beliefs and values were progressively translated from dogmatic articles of faith into a revolutionary social agenda during this period, the locale of the death of Judaism was progressively transferred from the metaphysical to the socio-historical arena."[79] Yet, many years later, in the aftermath of the Napoleonic wars when certain Jews had started gaining political rights in Germany, Hegel appears to adopt a different position. In the only place in his writings where he explicitly

76. Derrida 1986, 54.

77. Ibid., 56.

78. For the classic account of Hegel's relationship to the French Revolution see Ritter 1982.

79. Newman 1993, 479.

addresses modern Jewish rights he presents himself as an advocate of Jewish emancipation. His extensive footnote from the *Philosophy of Right* (1821) deserves to be quoted at some length:

> Thus technically it may have been right to refuse a grant of even civil rights to the Jews on the ground that they should be regarded as belonging not merely to a religious sect but to a foreign race. But the fierce outcry raised against the Jews, from that point of view and others, ignores the fact that they are, above all, *men*; and manhood, so far from being a mere superficial, abstract quality (see Remark to §209), is on the contrary itself the basis of the fact that what civil rights rouse in their possessors is the feeling of oneself as counting in civil society as a person with rights, and this feeling of self-hood, infinite and free from all restrictions, is the root from which the desired similarity in disposition and ways of thinking comes into being. To exclude the Jews from rights, on the other hand, would rather be to confirm the isolation with which they have been reproached—a result for which the state refusing them rights would be blamable and reproachable, because by so refusing, it would have misunderstood its own basic principle, its nature as an objective and powerful institution (compare the end of the Remark to §268). The exclusion of the Jews from civil rights may be supposed to be a right of the highest kind and may be demanded on that ground; but experience has shown that so to exclude them is the silliest folly, and the way in which governments now treat them has proved itself to be both prudent and dignified.[80]

As James Doull summarizes: "The Jews, wrote Hegel against the anti-Semites of his time, ought to be given civil rights not only because they are men but also because they are Jews."[81] Hegel's position in *The Philosophy of Right* will become central to the formulation of Marx's response to the "Jewish question," which we will examine in chapter 4. Hegel articulates a position on civil rights that moves beyond Kant. He argues that the Jews deserve to be granted civic rights not just on the basis of an abstract principle of the rights of man but also on account of their right to an embodied individuality. Hegel thus not only accepts the Enlightenment principle of universal tolerance but also advocates a tolerance for specificity. In this acknowledgment of alternative universalisms Hegel seems to be true to the legacy of Mendelssohn rather than to Kant, who had made the abandonment of Jewish particularity a condition of emancipation.

And yet, it is difficult to reconcile Hegel's explicit statements about modern Jews in the *Philosophy of Right* to his repeated characterization of the limi-

80. Hegel 1942, 168–69n1.
81. Doull 1973, 195.

tations of Judaism as a historical religion. It is notable that with the exception of the highly negative comments he makes about the "subsequent circumstances of the Jewish people" in "The Spirit of Christianity," Hegel nowhere else addresses the contemporary situation of the Jews. As Yovel writes:

> The evaluation of ancient Jews has little bearing, for him, on their surviving modern offspring, who must be treated as they are *now*, and judged according to the new ethical consciousness of the era they are entering, rather than the religious phenomenon from which they came. Hence the gulf between Hegel's critique of historical Judaism and his support of Jewish emancipation in the present.[82]

Such a gulf even makes itself present in this passage from the *Philosophy of Right*. Should the Jews be granted rights on philosophical or on purely pragmatic grounds? The final sentence of the passage with its convoluted grammar voices Hegel's hesitation. Hegel falls short of a full philosophical endorsement of Jewish emancipation. Hegel's philosophy of history, a philosophy in which Judaism could only stand to lose, stands in the way of his ability to grant Jews an active philosophical role to play in the modern world. Despite the complexity of Hegel's evolving attitudes to Judaism, the Greek/Jew antithesis that Hegel establishes in his early theological writing subtends his later analyses of the historical evolution of Spirit. Legros concludes: "In spite of all these ruptures . . . Hegel will never renege on the opposition between the Greek spirit as the spirit of beauty, and Judaism as the spirit of separation."[83] If Hegel has difficulties articulating a philosophically convincing vindication of the rights of Jews in the present, it is because Judaism remains locked in the same historical dialectic with the Greeks which had preoccupied him from his earliest writings.

The Tragedy of Judaism

> The great tragedy of the Jewish people is no Greek tragedy; it can rouse neither terror nor pity, for both of these arise only out of the fate which follows from the inevitable slip of a beautiful character; it can arouse horror alone. The fate of the Jewish people is the fate of Macbeth who stepped out of nature itself, clung to alien Beings, and so in their service had to trample and slay everything holy in human nature, had at last to

---

82. Yovel 1998, 94. See also Avineri (1963, 47), who writes: "Hegel's view on the granting of civil rights to the Jews is thus completely divorced from his historico-philosophical attitude toward the immanent content of Judaism." Yovel (1998) and Avineri (1963) also describe the immediate historical and political circumstances of Hegel's intervention.

83. Legros 1997, 45.

be forsaken by his gods (since these were objects and he their slave) and be dashed to pieces on his faith itself.

HEGEL

It is a short journey from Antigone to Jesus.

DOMINIQUE JANICAUD

In their need to incorporate into and devise some dignity for sacrilege, they [the Greeks] invented *tragedy*—an art form and a pleasure that has remained utterly and profoundly foreign to the Jew, despite all his poetic talent and inclination towards the sublime.

NIETZSCHE

"Nearly till the moment of their decline," writes George Steiner, "the tragic forms are Hellenic. Tragedy is alien to the Judaic sense of the world."[84] Hegel would agree. "The tragedy of the Jewish people is no Greek tragedy," he concludes in "The Spirit of Christianity." It is instead "the tragedy of Macbeth." It is in Aristotle's terms that Hegel here excludes the Jews from attaining the status of true tragic heroes. Their fate, he tells us, "can arouse no terror or pity," both emotions that can only be roused by the "inevitable slip" of a "beautiful character." The Jews, we hardly need reminding, are barred from beauty. But despite the heavy reliance on Aristotle's definition of tragedy in this passage, the reader is nonetheless offered an intimation of Hegel's later and distinctive characterization of the tragic. Hegel's radical new theory of tragedy finds its exemplary formulation in the *Philosophy of Right*:

> The *tragic* destruction of figures whose ethical life is on the highest plane can interest and elevate us and reconcile us to its occurrence only in so far as they come on the scene in opposition to one another together with equally justified but different ethical powers which have come into collision through misfortune, because the result is that then these figures acquire guilt through their opposition to an ethical law. Out of this situation there arises the right and wrong of both parties and therefore the true ethical Idea, which, purified and in triumph over this one-sidedness, is thereby reconciled in *us*. . . . This it is which constitutes the true, purely ethical interest of ancient tragedy.[85]

The tragedy that conforms most perfectly to Hegel's vision is, of course, Sophocles' *Antigone* about which he famously wrote: "Among all the fine creations of the ancient and modern world—and I am acquainted with pretty nearly everything in such a class, and one aught to know it and it is quite possible—the *Antigone* of Sophocles is from this point of view in my judg-

84. Steiner 1961, 3–4.
85. Hegel 1942, 102.

ment the most excellent and satisfying work of art."[86] In his seminal analysis of the play in the *Phenomenology of Spirit* (1807), Hegel investigates precisely such a clash between "equally justified but different ethical powers." In exploring the transition from *Moralität* to *Sittlichkeit* Hegel places Greek tragedy at the heart of his account of the ethical progress of the Spirit. But as our passage makes clear, this vision of the "true," "purely ethical" ancient tragedy can be contrasted with a baser vision of the tragic. The fate of a beautiful Antigone stands in opposition to the fall of a merely horrific Macbeth. As A. C. Bradley phrased it:

> Let me attempt to test these ideas by choosing a most unfavorable instance—
> unfavourable because the play seems at first to represent a conflict simply of
> good and evil, and so according to Hegel . . . , to be no tragedy at all: I mean
> *Macbeth*. What is the conflict here? It will be agreed that it does not lie be-
> tween two ethical powers or universal ends, and that, as Hegel says, the main
> interest lies in the personalities.[87]

"The collision," Bradley argues, "is more tragic in the *Antigone* than in *Macbeth*."[88] The reason for this, as Bradley notes, is not just the hierarchy between different forms of tragedy that Hegel elaborates in his *Aesthetics* where the tragedy of character or "personalities" exists on a lower plane than the tragedy that address more universal ends. It is also because the tragedy of Macbeth originates from the outside. Hegel anticipates this later depiction of Macbeth in "The Spirit of Christianity" by highlighting how his fall comes about not through some inner flaw of a "beautiful character" but from his decision to listen to "the equivocal sisters of fate," "allowing himself to be driven to a crime by their 'double-tongued' promises and false admonitions."[89] Macbeth's downfall is the fate of man "who stepped out of nature itself, clung to alien Beings, and so in their service had to trample and slay everything holy in human nature, had at last to be forsaken by his gods (since these were objects and he their slave) and be dashed to pieces on his faith itself." The witches in *Macbeth* here are symptoms of the same lack of moral freedom that condemns Judaism to "positivity." Macbeth's tragedy, then, is no ethical tragedy. On the one hand, it simply opposes a wrong to a right and thus falls short of producing the true ethical conflict that Hegel sees as intrinsic to the tragic experience. On the other hand, the fall it traces

86. Hegel 1986, 550.
87. Bradley 1962, 382.
88. Ibid., 384.
89. Paolucci and Paolucci 1962, xxviii.

is not one brought about through the internal conflict of a complex ethical being but is rather imposed from the outside. This too, Hegel surmises, is the tragedy of the Jewish people.

As Steiner exemplifies, Hegel will not be the last figure to exclude Judaism from the spirit of tragedy. Nietzsche's *Birth of Tragedy* also characterizes the tragic as an exclusively Hellenic condition.[90] Introducing his analysis of the myth of Prometheus Nietzsche writes, "I shall now contrast the glory of passivity with the glory of activity which shines through the *Prometheus* of Aeschylus." As Jim Porter recounts, Nietzsche's choice of Prometheus is far from arbitrary. "The ethical significance of Prometheus' acts and the question of its legibility from within the Judeo-Christian framework of sin and atonement had long been debated by nineteenth century scholars."[91] In particular, in this section of *The Birth of Tragedy*, Nietzsche draws heavily on the Indo-European scholar Adalbert Kuhn and especially on Friedrich G. Weckler's *Griechische Götterlehre*, which contained a lengthy contrast between the "Aryan" myth of Prometheus and the "Hebrew" Fall of Eve.[92] It is in the terms of this new "science" that Nietzsche will construct his own Greek / Jew opposition:

> Originally, the legend of Prometheus belonged to the entire community of Aryan peoples and documented their talent for the profound and the tragic; indeed it is not unlikely that this myth is as significant for the Aryan character as the myth of the Fall is for the Semitic character, and that the relationship between the two myths is like that between a brother and a sister.[93]

Bruce Lincoln argues: "In this chapter Nietzsche's focus shifted from the opposition of Apollonian and Dionysian internal to (and constitutive of) Greek civilization to the opposition of Greeks to their antithetical other." Inheriting the Hegelian trope of conflict and opposition as constituting the essence of tragedy, Nietzsche had conducted his analysis by pitting two visions of Hellenic culture against themselves. This internally fissured identity of the Greeks is what constitutes their privileged relationship to the tragic. Like Hegel, Nietzsche sees the Greeks' capacity for internal conflict as fully constitutive of their greatness. But at this moment in *The Birth of Tragedy* Nietzsche moves away from the exploration of the competing drives of the Hellenic aes-

---

90. See Kofman 1994, 39–40, 60 on the passage from *The Gay Science* cited in the epigraph.

91. Nietzsche 1999, 49; Porter 2000, 275.

92. See Lincoln 1999; Porter 2000

93. Nietzsche 1999, 49.

thetic toward an investigation of cultural difference. "In this passage Nietzsche used mythic narratives not just to stereotype peoples but also to erect
a discriminatory structure of interlocking binary oppositions that conflated
categories of race, gender, religion and morality."[94] Despite their isolated
presence in this section of his text, Jim Porter makes the claim that "the allu-
sions to Aryanism . . . appear only in section 9 of *The Birth of Tragedy*, but . . .
profoundly color the whole of the work." Indeed, Porter sees this investment
in racial vocabulary as so pervasive that he asserts: "One consequence of these
equations is that whenever we speak about Nietzsche's prelapsarian Greeks in
The Birth of Tragedy, down to Socrates and Euripides at the end of the fifth
century, we are in fact talking, or should be talking, about *Aryans*."[95]

But beyond Nietzsche's enthusiasm for a new scientific discourse of racial difference, one of the most striking elements of this passage is the extent to which it repeats the old critique of Judaism that permeates Hegel's
early writings. For, as the opening statements about Prometheus suggests, it
is precisely in terms of an opposition between "activity" and "passivity" that
Nietzsche will contrast Greek tragedy and the fate of the Jews. Nietzsche's
definition of tragedy upholds the familiar antithesis between Greek religion
as the faith of a "free people" and Judaism, a religion characterized by the
slavish "positivity."

> Humanity achieves the best and the highest of which it is capable by commit-
> ting an offence and must in turn accept the consequences of this, namely the
> whole flood of suffering and tribulations which the offended heavenly powers
> *must* in turn visit upon the human race as its strives nobly towards higher
> things: a bitter thought but one which contrasts strangely with the Semitic
> myth of the Fall, where the origin of evil was seen to lie in curiosity, men-
> dacious pretence, openness to seduction, lasciviousness, in short: in a whole
> series of predominantly feminine attributes. What distinguishes the Aryan
> conception is the sublime view that *active sin* is the true Promethean virtue;
> thereby we have also found the ethical foundation of pessimistic tragedy, its
> *justification* of the evil in human life, both in the sense of human guilt and in
> the sense of the suffering brought about by it.[96]

The "*active sin*" of the Greeks is contrasted to the "mendacious pretence,
openness to seduction" and "lasciviousness" of the Jews. Nietzsche may have
added the peculiarly modern charge of effeminacy to his anti-Semitism, but
his condemnation of Judaism rests on the same philosophical premises that

94. Lincoln 1999, 64, 65.
95. Porter 2000, 274–75.
96. Nietzsche 1999, 49–50.

had governed Hegel's analysis. Greek metaphysics are contrasted to Jewish materialism just as the Greeks' troubled agency finds its true antithesis in the Jews' unthinking submission. For Nietzsche, just as for Hegel, the tragedy of the Jewish people cannot be a Greek tragedy. The nature of the tragic, in all its pathetic unavoidability, in all its overdetermined predetermination, necessitates a certain relationship to freedom. And with this freedom comes a certain ethical promise:

> But the most wonderful thing in that poem about Prometheus . . . is its profound, Aeschylean tendency to *justice*: the limitless suffering of the bold "individual" on the one hand, and the extreme plight of the gods, indeed a premonition of the twilight of the gods, on the other; the power of both these worlds of suffering to enforce reconciliation [*Versöhnung*], metaphysical oneness— all this recalls in the strongest possible way the centre and principal tenet of the Aeschylean view of the world, which sees *moira*, as eternal justice, throned above gods and men.[97]

Nietzsche's language here does not at first sight seem particularly Hegelian. And yet, in its search for a distinctly Nietzschean notion of "metaphysical oneness," this theory nevertheless foregrounds perhaps the most central term in Hegel's analysis of tragedy: "reconciliation." Reconciliation, *Versöhnung* as we remember from the *Philosophy of Right*, is the *telos* of tragedy. Where Aristotle posits *catharsis*, Hegel sees the "reconciliation in *us*" of two opposing forces as the ethical force of tragedy. Nietzsche's language of Versöhnung exposes the still Hegelian outcome of his own idiosyncratic dialectic of tragedy. Apollo and Dionysus may not be the family and the state, but the reconciliation of opposites in the name of "justice" has a distinctly Hegelian ring.

Moreover, Cohen claims that despite its relationship to the essence of *Greek* tragedy, the concept of reconciliation bears the mark of Christianity even in Hegel's most pagan writings. As such it is the concept of "reconciliation" that separates Greco-Christianity from Judaism. Explaining the concept of *pleroma*, which becomes central to Hegel's analysis of Jesus' Sermon on the Mount in "The Spirit of Christianity," Cohen writes:

> In truth he borrows it from the Greeks and transforms it into a Christian theme. Because the reconciliation in question is the harmony between the ideal of the beautiful Greek totality and the truth of Christianity. The beautiful Greek totality will always be too abstract and will only be able to decline into the tragic destiny of profound fragmentation. . . . Its reconciliation is achieved in and through its sublimation in the passion of Christ.[98]

97. Ibid., 48–49.
98. Cohen 2005, 76n1.

But as Cohen goes on to demonstrate, this by no means condemns the Greeks to an equal status to the Jews: "Greek thought far from confining itself to the enclave of separation, far from seeking security in infinite transcendence, confronts the whole force of its destiny and therefore confronts 'tragedy', that is to say it is always already engaged in a process of reconciliation."[99] The Greeks, because they are not Christian, are condemned to tragedy; the Jews don't even get that far. In *actively* confronting their destiny, the Greeks in the end, may still ultimately be condemned to their tragic fate but they are, nonetheless, caught up in the dynamics of reconciliation which will eventually lead to the truth of Christianity. Greek tragedy, by virtue of its implication, on the one hand, in an active confrontation with destiny and on the other, in the logic of reconciliation, is proto-Christian through and through.[100] As Janicaud puts it:

> The Jewish world is *a priori* an alienated world and will always remain so. . . .
> This absolute alienation is no doubt tragic but its origin, like that of Macbeth,
> can only arouse horror. Greek tragedy, on the other hand, arouses fear or pity:
> it is a life affirming force. The Greek destiny is therefore not static negativity, it
> is the empowerment of reconciliation. That is why the Greek world, at its best,
> is so close to Christian love: it is a short journey from Antigone to Christ.[101]

Jim Porter speculates: "Is Nietzsche's approach to ancient Greece possibly Christianizing?"[102] In his emphasis on Aryan agency and tragic reconciliation even Nietzsche's writings seem to the carry the burden of the Christian destiny of Hegel's tragic Greeks. But despite the striking persistence in Nietzsche of Hegel's Christianizing imperative, Hegel's and Nietzsche's visions of tragedy could not be predicated on more different philosophies of history. While Greeks, Jews, and Christians will figure heavily in both their respective narratives of progress, they come to take on quite distinct roles. Nietzsche's narrative of tragedy will see its ultimate corruption in the advent of Christianity foreshadowed by the dual forces of Euripides and Socrates. Nietzsche's Socrates, in *The Birth of Tragedy*, was famously the "archetype of *theoretical man*," but this figure of uncompromising rationality also embodied a decidedly Christian decadence.[103] "Socrates was a misunderstanding," he writes later in the *Twilight of the Idols*,

99. Ibid., 77n1.
100. Hodgson (2005, 97) makes it clear: for Hegel, "Christianity is the religion of *reconciliation*."
101. Janicaud 1975, 71.
102. Porter 2000, 275.
103. Nietzsche 1999, 72.

the entire morality of improvement, Christianity's included, was a misunderstanding . . . the harshest daylight, rationality at all costs, life bright, cold, cau-
tious instinct-free, instinct resistant: this itself was just an illness, a different
illness—and definitely not a way back to "virtue," "health," happiness . . . to
have to fight against the instincts—this is the formula of decadence.[104]

Nietzsche's Socrates represents at one and the same time the advent of Greek
reason and the transition from happy paganism to life-denying Christianity.
But as so often with Nietzsche, the critique of Christianity conceals a harsher
denunciation of Judaism. Socrates' rationality may augur the self-denial of
Christ, but his "jaundiced malice" is borrowed from Jews: "You choose dialectics only when you have no other means. . . . It can only be an emergency
defence when you have no other weapons left. You must *force* your being in
the right out of other people: otherwise you do not use it. That is why the
Jews were dialecticians; Reynard the Fox was one: what? and was Socrates,
one too? . . . Was Socrates," asks Nietzsche, "a Greek at all?" Sarah Kofman
concludes, "Nietzsche begins by comparing Socrates to the venerable masters
of Greek philosophy and ends up turning this figure—who never ceases to
haunt and trouble him—into a veritable monster, a hybrid creature, more
Jew than Greek."[105]

Where for the late Nietzsche Socrates had come to represent the Jew
in another guise, for Hegel, of course, Socrates is the representative of the
anti-Jew par excellence. Where Nietzsche's Socrates is Jewish by virtue of his
association with Christianity, Hegel's Socrates marks his distance from the
Jews in foreshadowing of a more perfect Christianity denuded of its Jewish
"positivity." So while the fall from tragic destiny plays a pivotal role in both
Hegel's and Nietzsche's narratives of world history, it will take on a diametrically opposed functions in their two writings. In Nietzsche it is the combined
forces of Judaism and Christianity that will cast the spell of decadence on the
tragic age of the Greeks, which is represented as the high point of European
culture. In Hegel, on the other hand, it is the tragic destiny of the Greeks that
foreshadows the promise of Christian reconciliation. It is as the bearers of a
tragic worldview that the Greeks show themselves to be the true forerunners
to Christianity. It is the Jews' exclusion from such a tragic fate that bars the
door to salvation through Christian reconciliation.

The dialectical force of tragedy, then, stands in in Hegel's writing for the
dialectics of world history. For it is precisely their inability to play a role in
the dialectical movement of history that characterizes the Jews in Hegel's later

104. Nietzsche 1998, 15.
105. Ibid., 13; Kofman 1998, 12.

accounts. Despite the striking absence of a sustained discussion of Judaism in the *Phenomenology of Spirit* (1807), one passing remark elucidates what role Hegel sees the Jews playing in his system: "It may be said of the Jewish people that it is precisely because they stand before the portal of salvation that they are, and have been, the most reprobate and rejected."[106] Yovel writes: "The Jewish people reached the gate of salvation but refused to go through it; therefore they will be locked out of the great gates of salvation forever, with no further evolution and no real hope. In other words, *they will no longer have a history*. As the most reprobate people, all that remains for the Jews is an ongoing fossilized existence."[107] In this same passage from the *Phenomenology*, Hegel goes on to imply that had the Jews been able to make the transition to Christianity they might have been able to re-enter the dynamics of world history. And yet, as Hegel knows too well, this inability is constitutive of their very identity. "Unlike Kant," Yovel continues,

> and those who recommended that the Jews convert to Christianity to facilitate their entry into European society, Hegel understood it to be impossible, because what maintains the Jews as such, is above all, their fidelity to their original refusal. The implied conclusion is that the Jews' dehistoricization is irremediable. Jewish history has not only been *aufgehoben* (sublated) by Christianity; it is also dried out and has become drained out and become frozen and drained of all spiritual content.[108]

This is why, for Hegel, the Jews' exclusion from modernity is so absolute. It also explains how Hegel has no difficulty transitioning from his analysis of Moses and ancient Judaism to his pronouncement on his contemporaries:

> The subsequent circumstances of the Jewish people up to the mean, abject, wretched circumstances in which they still are today, have all of them been simply consequences and elaborations of their original fate. By this fate—an infinite power which they set over against themselves and could never conquer—they have been maltreated and will be continually maltreated until they appease it by the spirit of beauty and so annul it by reconciliation.[109]

The Jews, then, are not just figures of history, they are not *even* figures of history. They are both always already superseded by history and have not yet entered into it. They are trapped in a perpetual vicious circle of exclusion where progress is predicated on a historical process from which the Jews have

106. Hegel 1977, 206.
107. Yovel 1998, 55.
108. Ibid.
109. Hegel 1948, 199–200.

been debarred *ab origine*. Derrida observes: "Jewish culture does indeed have something of the underdeveloped childhood. But it is nonetheless, perverse enough to have lost the deep charm of childhood. Jewish culture is neither maturity nor innocence."[110] Hellenic culture, on the other hand, has *both* maturity *and* innocence. Both the beauty of childhood and the promise of our future as adults. Once again we can see the contrast to Nietzsche. To Hegel's ahistorical Jews we could oppose Nietzsche's ahistorical Greeks. Where Hegel's exclusion of the Jews from history functions as the ultimate condemnation, Nietzsche's claim that the Greeks had no historical sense is the sincerest of compliments.[111] Moreover, tragedy plays a crucial role in this distinction. In Hegel, the dialectic movement that animates the best of Greek tragedies stands in synecdochically for the central role the Greeks play in the dialectics of world history. Indeed, Hegel elevates the clash of opposing forces, which he sees as the essence of tragedy, to a theory that accounts for the sum of historical progress. In Hegel, then, the Greeks can play a role in the analysis of modern culture because through the creation of tragedy they have provided the conceptual apparatus for the exploration of historical development. Because the Greeks are historical they are part of modernity. Or as Lévinas phrases it: "the ultimate meaning of modernity is therefore essentially Greek." Because the Jews, on the other hand, are ahistorical they are *a fortori* excluded from modernity. In Nietzsche, it is the Greeks' ahistoricity, their untimely nature, which makes them such an appealing model for the present: "I do not know what meaning classical studies could have for our time if they were not untimely—that is to say, acting counter to our time and thereby acting on our time and, let us hope, for the benefit of time to come."[112] It is precisely because it is "untimely," Nietzsche proclaims in *The Birth of Tragedy*, that Greek tragedy can offer the hope of a better future. Modernity's relationship to the historical finds itself again being written through an antithesis between the Greek and the Jew.

George Steiner's observation that "all the major philosophical systems since the French Revolution have been tragic systems" reveals the power of Greek tragedy in transforming the "opus metaphysicum" of modernity.[113] But Steiner's comments about the inability of modern philosophy to think outside the framework of the tragic should be brought into dialogue with his earlier proclamations about the exclusively Hellenic identity of the tragic vi-

110. Derrida 1986, 74.

111. See Nietzsche's arguments about the unhistorical Greeks in his essay "On the Uses and Disadvantages of History for Life" (1997).

112. Lévinas 1963, 329; Nietzsche 1997, 60.

113. Steiner 1984, 2.

sion. Steiner's assertion that "tragedy is alien to the Judaic sense of the world," I would argue, is by no means incidental to his insight that the tragic has become the privileged trope of modernity. By uncovering an uncanny mirroring of Hegel's dialectical system in his writings on tragedy, we have seen that Hegel's definition of tragedy is predicated on a particular philosophy of history. Hegel's analysis of tragedy is part and parcel of his broader elevation of Greek culture to the status of a proto-Christianity founded on the exclusion of the Jews. His philosophy of tragedy also goes hand in with his understanding of modernity as the fulfillment of a Greco-Christian promise. When we have realized that Hegel's tragic philosophy is tragic by virtue of its exclusion of the Jews we will come to understand with Joseph Cohen "that his radical condemnation of Judaism cannot simply be characterized as 'of its time,' it is rather entirely inscribed, anchored and founded in Hegel's philosophy. It is as if anti-Judaism was itself the affirmation of the Spirit, or as if it was necessary to constantly deny and efface Judaism as the 'religion of the Law' in order to open oneself onto the possibility of 'coming into the light.'"[114] Perhaps then, we will truly know why "the great tragedy of the Jewish people is no Greek tragedy."

---

114. Cohen 2005, 24. See Lyotard (1990, 85–89), who explores the legacy of Hegel's writings on the "tragedy of the Jewish people" in an attempt to make sense of the Shoah.

3

Matthew Arnold in Zion:
Hebrews, Hellenes, Aryans, and Semites

Socrates is terribly *at ease in Zion.*
MATTHEW ARNOLD

At a time of intense political turmoil in the aftermath of the 1870 Franco-Prussian War, the French intellectual Ernest Renan wrote a tract entitled *La Réforme intellectuelle et morale*—a call to national regeneration. Renan argued that France would have to undergo a profound change in political and cultural outlook if it wanted to compete with Prussia. It was only a year earlier that Matthew Arnold had published his own polemic, *Culture and Anarchy* (1869), an appeal to the intellectual and moral reform of England. Arnold, a great admirer of Renan's and a strong supporter of French culture more generally, found himself reacting with uncharacteristic discomfort to Renan's latest work:

> No one feels more than we do the harm which the exaggeration of Hebraism has done in England but this [Renan's critique of the lack of faith in science] is Hellenism in a vengeance! Considering what the natural propensions of men are, such language appears to us to be out of place anywhere, and in France simply fatal. Moral conscience, self-control, seriousness, steadfastness, are not the whole of human life certainly, but they are by far the greatest part of it; without them—and this is the very burden of the Hebrew prophets and a fact of experience as old as the world—nations cannot stand. France does not enough see their importance.[1]

While noting the deficiencies of his own countrymen, Arnold chastises the French for their overzealous Hellenism. This untrammelled enthusiasm for things Greek, Arnold suggests, could be fatal. The cure he prescribes: a good dose of Hebraism. While England, Arnold implies, feels the need to unshackle itself from the "burden of the Hebrew prophets," France could do well from

1. Arnold 1960–77, 7:44–45.

taking over the load. For Arnold, the concepts of Hellenism and Hebraism had taken on the force of a potent cultural and political prescription.

The turn to antiquity in nineteenth-century Europe, as many studies have shown, was deeply implicated in the emerging discourses of nationalism.[2] As is clear from the dialogue between Arnold and Renan, the question of a national "culture" became hotly contested precisely in terms of an antithesis between the competing ancient traditions we have been examining. "German," "French," and "British" national identities were defined and refined with reference to the two categories of Greek and Jew. Yet, significantly the age of growing nationalism and particularism coincides with the growth of a fascination in world-historical enquiry. The context of empire and what Raymond Schwab termed the "Oriental Renaissance" had already brought an interrogation of the place of European civilization in the world to the fore. But the intensification of imperial projects, coupled with the intellectual developments of Romanticism, gave a new dimension to the ever-expanding field of study. Classical Greece and ancient Israel found themselves competing with a growing number of other cultures. But the relationship of the "Hebraic" to this "Oriental Renaissance" is far from straightforward. The question of whether the "Jew" is inside or outside the "Orient" remained unresolved.[3] So while the Greek/Jew polarity is integral to the formulation of this hierarchy of cultures, the specific placing of the "Hebraic" and the "Hellenic" in this competition for cultural dominance is complex.

It is a paradox that the most enduring formulation of the Greek/Jew opposition was written not, as one might expect, in Germany, where the antithesis had by the middle of the nineteenth century already become a cliché, but in England. Matthew Arnold's famous essay "Hellenism and Hebraism" in *Culture and Anarchy* marks the moment that the terms "Hebrew" and "Hellene" enter into the vernacular. As Stefan Collini has observed, "Arnold had the shrewd controversialist's eye for ways of gaining attention for his ideas, and a talent for condensing an argument into a catch-phrase."[4] Arnold himself was well aware of the impact of his writing and, in particular, was convinced of the force of this specific intervention into social and cultural criticism. Thus he wrote of the chapters on "Hellenism and Hebraism" that they are "so true that they will form the centre for English thought and speculation on the matters treated in them."[5]

2. See Stephens and Vasunia 2010; Marchand 1996.
3. See Kirchhoff 2006; Marchand 2009.
4. Collini 1988, 82.
5. Russell 1895, 2:11.

In Arnold's first attempt to describe the Hellenism/Hebraism opposition it is notable that far from referencing the German philosophical or scholarly tradition, it is the discourse of British imperialism that is given prominence:

> And these two forces we may regard in some sense as rivals, —rivals not by the necessity of their own nature, but as exhibited in man and his history, —and rivals dividing the empire of the world between them. And to give these forces names from the two races of men who have supplied the most signal and splendid manifestations of them, we may call them respectively the forces of Hebraism and Hellenism.[6]

Where Hegel had described the Hebrew and the Hellene as antithetical manifestations of the "spirit of world history," Arnold describes them as the races that "divide the empire of the world between them." Edward Said identified Arnold as a writer "who had definite views on race and imperialism," a position that Robert Young endorses when he contends that *Culture and Anarchy* has the "dubious distinction" of having "introduced into British life not only the idea of culture as such but also the tenacious modern identification of culture with race and nation."[7] It is difficult to imagine that Arnold could have written a manifesto about the state of England in 1869, at the apex of enthusiasm for the British Raj and not long before Victoria was named the Empress of India, without empire forming a determinative context for his thinking. When Arnold chooses the word *empire* to define the expanse of global geography, then, his choice of vocabulary can hardly be seen to be innocent. Conversely, however, his contention that the whole world could be divided between Hellenism and Hebraism is all the more provocative within the context of an imperial mission that had brought the English into direct contact with cultures whose relationship to *both* Athens *and* Jerusalem was at the very most oblique.

I want to approach Arnold's essay through a series of frames that explain how the shifting discourses of language, nation, and race gave a new meaning to the confrontation between Greeks and Jews at the heart of Arnold's analysis of English culture. "Hellenism and Hebraism," I argue, is richly overdetermined. It simultaneously extends the project of German philhellenism and looks toward a new conceptualization of culture in which the specificity of language and, increasingly, race were to play determinative roles. As we have already seen, the French Semiticist Ernest Renan becomes an important interlocutor for Arnold. Within the context of this shifting framework, the

6. Arnold 1993, 126.
7. Young 1995, 62, 83.

question of religion that has been a central preoccupation of the first two chapters becomes submerged and yet is never fully eclipsed. Indeed, it is the fusion of religious preoccupations with a new discourse of Orientalism which Arnold's essay is testimony to.

History, Language, Culture

The resonance of the Greek/Jew opposition in a wide variety of contexts is startling. We have seen in the previous two chapters how this polarity finds itself lodged in philosophical discourse. Hegel's monumental philosophical narrative of world-historical progress explicitly sets the "Hebraic" and "Hellenic" worldviews in opposition. So Hegel summarizes the role of Judaism in his *History of Philosophy* : "On the whole Jewish history exhibits grand features of character; but it is disfigured by an exclusive bearing (sanctioned in its religion), toward the genius of other nations . . . by want of culture generally, and by the superstition arising from the idea of the high value of their peculiar nationality."[8] Moreover, for Hegel, the "Hebraic" and "Hellenic" are understood precisely against the background of a plurality of global traditions. The Hebraic tradition is for Hegel steeped in an Oriental spirit that must be overcome. As Suzanne Marchand and Anthony Grafton point out: "Hegel, it should be remembered, in creating a dialectics of world history, gave Greece and the Orient not just different but *antithetical* 'spirits' evident in every aspect of cultural development, from the arts to religion, politics, and social organization."[9] The influence of Hegel's philosophy on historical thinking throughout the nineteenth century was profound. Both Hegel's dialectical method and his pronouncements on the "spirit" of the Orient found their way into a very wide range of different discourses. Hegel's work, then, provided the philosophical framework for the historical study of competing cultures.

But the absorption of the Greek/Jew antithesis into a broad-scale philosophy of history that we find in Hegel had already been anticipated in the work of Johann Gottfried Herder. Although he has to some extent been assimilated to the legacy of a Hegelian philosophy of history, his distinctive role in the emergence of "historicism" has now become a subject of great interest.[10] Often seen as a precursor to the Romantics, Herder was, like Hamann, a friend of Kant and an Aufklärer whose thought foreshadowed many of the later cri-

8. Hegel 1957, 197.
9. Marchand and Grafton 1997, 14.
10. Zamitto 2009, 65.

tiques of the Enlightenment. His role in the development of a new discourse of nationalism has been well acknowledged, but his powerful writings on national culture are part of a much more complex philosophy of history that is open to widely different interpretations. Herder played a significant role in the movement of Grecophilia that swept across German intellectual life in the aftermath of the publication of Winckelmann's great works in art history, but he was also a committed scholar of Hebrew. His Hellenism certainly shares some of the flavor of the contemporary idealization of Greek culture: "From their dress, the fine proportion and the outline of their thoughts, the natural vivacity of their sentiments and lastly from the melodious rhythm of their language, which never yet found its equal, we have much to learn. In all arts of life . . . the Greeks attained almost the highest point."[11]

And yet, Herder was simultaneously developing a critique that would subject this call for cross-cultural and transhistorical emulation to the scrutiny of a new historicist outlook. In contrast to many of his contemporaries, writes Maurice Olender, Herder "celebrated the incommensurable diversity of nations and cultures." Herder was critical of misguided attempts to compare the cultural and aesthetic achievements of the past to those of more modern periods. Thus both Winckelmann's desire to hold Greek art up as a model for contemporary aesthetics and his practice of viewing Egyptian art "through Greek eyes" were considered suspect by Herder.[12] As Zamitto phrases it, "In disputing Winckelmann's effort to make Greece the eternal standard for cultural achievement, Herder emphasized the situatedness of cultural forms. This resulted in a historicism far more hermeneutically radical than any of his day." "Every nation," Herder famously proclaimed, "has its own inner centre of happiness, as every sphere its own centre of gravity."[13]

At the core of Herder's analysis of cultural difference lay a preoccupation with language. "There is no other philosopher of the eighteenth century . . . who is haunted by language in the same passionate way as Herder."[14] He may have been responsible for the introduction of "ethnicity as a principle of historical explanation," as Martin Bernal puts it, but this investment has its source in the systematic analysis of language.[15] The eighteenth century saw the emergence of the study of language as the key to uncovering the distinctive marker of national and cultural identity. Herder is thus part of a larger intellectual movement in the development of a discipline whose emergence

11. Herder 1968, 4:3
12. Olender 1992, 39, 40.
13. Zamitto 2009, 70; Herder 1968, 5:502.
14. Trabant 2009, 117.
15. Bernal 1987, 224.

Foucault has characterized as marking the "threshold of our modernity." So Foucault affirms: "Having become a dense and consistent historical reality, language forms the locus of tradition, of unspoken habits of thought, of what lies hidden in a people's spirit."[16]

Herder's historicism derives in large part from the awareness of the centrality of language as medium of cultural individuality. As we saw above, Herder places "the melodious rhythm of their language" at the core of his valorization of the Greeks. But the distinctiveness of their linguistic accomplishments differentiates them from the other peoples with whom they have been mistakenly compared. The reason, for instance, why Greek and Egyptian art cannot be intelligently measured up against one other is to an important extent because of the incommensurabilty of their languages. This same incommensurability governs the relationship between Jews and Greeks. Herder's insight into the distinctiveness of linguistic cultures is closely derived from his study of the Hebrew Bible.[17] Herder's admiration for the sublimity of the Hebrew scriptures led him to comment on the specific contribution of the Jews to the history of humanity. But the value of the scriptures, he affirms, cannot be understood without a process of cultural defamiliarization: "Be a shepherd with the shepherd," he exhorts, "a peasant in the midst of an agricultural people, an oriental among the primitive dwellers of the East, if you wish to enjoy the creations in the atmosphere of their birth." The Jews' great works were "written in ancient, simple, rustic, poetical not abstract or philosophical language."[18] There is no point, Herder argues, in expecting to find in the poetry of the Hebrews the philosophical abstraction of the Greeks. The Hebrews' contribution is distinctive, commensurate with the primitivism of their culture. In order to fully appreciate the Old Testament, the modern must first rid himself of the expectations of his age and then disinherit the enormous cultural privilege accorded to the Greeks: "You see, my friend, how holy and sublime these books are to me, and how very much a Jew I am—as in Voltaire's jest—when I read them, for must we not be Greeks and Romans when we read their books too? Every book must be read in its own spirit."[19]

Herder positions himself simultaneously against the practice of measuring the primitive Jewish writings up against the cultural achievements of the Greeks and against the easy assimilation of his contemporary German culture to the Greek experience. To read the Greeks and the Romans requires a pro-

16. Foucault 1966, 13; Foucault 1970, 297.

17. On the importance of Herder's study of the Old Testament for German Orientalism see Marchand 2009, 43–52.

18. Herder 1877–1913, 5:436, 438.

19. Herder 1790, 192.

cess of defamiliarization comparable to the decoding of the writings of Ori-
entals. Herder at one and the same time seems to call for a process of absolute
alienation and radical assimilation. All cultures are equally unintelligible but
one must make every attempt to inhabit each culture's mindset to make sense
of that group's cultural artifacts. This imperative of cultural understanding
can even lead Herder to declare "I am a Jew"! In Paul Hamilton's words:

> The philosophical point to be taken here helps specify Herder's historicism
> in two ways. First it highlights his linguistic determinism, his belief that it is
> in the use of language that we become human. . . . The humanity revealed in
> language, therefore, is a cultural manifestation bound to conventions of time
> and place, pastoral and Oriental in the case of the "Hebrew Scriptures." And
> this diverse, cultural determination of what is human is the second main as-
> pect of Herder's historicism.[20]

When Herder declares "I am a Jew" he is not only satirizing a national
climate in which the mantra "I am a Greek" had become the only universal,
he is also criticizing the whole philosophy of history that lies behind such an
identification. Herder's influence on later historical thinking is profound. As
Hamilton writes, Hegel's philosophy can be seen as its direct descendent:

> [Herder] introduced history, culture, and individuality—the particular se-
> mantics of particular languages—into the transcendental processes, which,
> therefore, ceased to be transcendental. But of course this happened a whole
> generation later with Hegel. Hegel . . . built on Herder's anthropological in-
> sights, which the immediate contemporaries and followers of Kant could not
> accept.[21]

But perhaps one of the most striking aspects of Herder's contribution is
the extent to which his uncannily modern "historicism" is allied to a profound investment in biblical culture.[22] It is a paradox that Herder's insights
into the irreducible diversity of human existence emerges from his study of
Hebrew scriptures. Moreover, when we consider that Herder would call the
historical development of mankind "God's epic," we get a sense of the immersion of his historical writings in a religious worldview.[23] "Surprising aspects
of the Romantic sage's work emerge," as Olender phrases it, "when one follows the alternation in his writings between a very secular ambition to write

20. Hamilton 2002, 33.

21. Trabant 2009, 138.

22. See Aarsleff 1982 and Olender 1992 on the connections between the developments in
philology and the search for Adamic language.

23. Herder 2004, 72.

cultural history respecting national and spiritual diversities and a very Lutheran desire to institute a providential anthropology." Or to follow Zamitto:
"Philosophy of history was for Herder always also a theodicy, the recognition
and celebration of Divine Providence in the created world and in the history
of man."[24] Herder's continued immersion in biblical scripture appears all the
more interesting when one contrasts it with the image of linguistics and its
self-identification as a secular science. As Said has written:

> The difference between the history offered internally by Christianity and the
> history offered by philology, a relatively new discipline, is precisely what made
> modern philology possible. . . . For whenever "philology" is spoken of around
> the end of the eighteenth century and the beginning of the nineteenth, we
> are to understand *new* philology, whose major successes include comparative
> grammar, the reclassification of languages into families, the final rejection of
> the divine origins of language. . . . What Foucault called the discovery of lan-
> guage was therefore a secular event that displaced a religious conception of
> how God delivered language to man in Eden.[25]

The foundation of the study of language enshrined in philology, then, had
an avowedly secular premise that distanced it from the study of scripture.
Indeed, as many scholars have noted, classical philology emerges as a discipline that explicitly sets itself up in opposition to the study of the Bible. But,
as James Porter and Anthony Grafton have argued, the new philology may
not so much have been trying to distance itself from the theological basis of
Christianity as from the study of Oriental peoples. Thus Porter demonstrates
how Friedrich August Wolf in his *Darstellung der Altertumswissenschaft* "justifies his conception of classical antiquity and his seminal definition of its
discipline as a 'self-enclosed' totality by means of a powerful exclusion":[26]

> One would very much like to comprehend all such peoples [of this place, which
> has been considered "the most beautiful region of the ancient world"] within a
> single scientific object; yet several reasons make a division necessary and per-
> mit us not to put *Aegyptians, Hebrews, Persians,* and other nations of the Orient
> on a par with *Greeks* and *Romans.* One of the most significant differences be-
> tween the latter and the former nations is that the former did not at all, or only
> barely, raised themselves above the level of cultivation that should be called
> *civil order* or *civilisation,* in contrast to the *higher genuine intellectual culture.*[27]

24. Olender 1992, 44; Zamitto 2009, 70.
25. Said 1978, 135.
26. Porter 2000, 278. On which see also Kirchhoff 2006, 107.
27. Cited and translated by Porter 2000, 278.

But such an exclusion of Oriental people from the field of study did not, as Grafton makes clear, entail a radical break with the methods of biblical scholarship. "[The] tradition of Biblical research and controversy was still very active in the eighteenth century; and Wolf had it very much in mind when he worked on Homer." Grafton demonstrates how Wolf's seminal study of Homer was significantly indebted to J. G. Eichhorn's historical scholarship on the Old and New testaments that Wolf cites in his *Prolegomena*.[28] In this sense, Wolf's project is merely an extension of the tradition of erudition that leads back to the Renaissance humanists such as Joseph Scaliger and Isaac Casaubon who were as learned in Hebrew as they had been in Greek.[29] And yet, Wolf inscribes a division between classical cultures and the Orient as the founding gesture of the new philology. Far from being separated along a religious/secular divide, historical biblical scholarship and the emerging disciplines of philology rather shared an opponent in the Jew. Where the new proponents of Altertumswissenschaft sought to guard the racial purity of the Greeks by differentiating them from the Oriental Jews, a new breed of biblical scholars worked to rid Christianity of its original Judaic sin.[30]

Looking back on a generation of progress in the field of comparative linguistics in his *Lectures on the Science of Language*, Max Müller makes the link between Christianity and the new philology clear:

> *Humanity* is a word which you would look for in vain in Plato and Aristotle; the idea of mankind as one family, as the children of God, is an idea of Christian growth; and the science of mankind, and of the languages of mankind, is a science which, without Christianity, would never have sprung into life. When people had been taught to look upon all men as brethren, then, and only then, did the variety of human speech present itself as a problem that called for a solution in the eyes of the thoughtful observers; and I, therefore, date the real beginning of the science of language from the first day of Pentecost.[31]

As Frank Manuel has argued: "The definition of Judaism in nineteenth-century Christendom was profoundly affected by the spectacular advances of comparative philology, the development of anthropological theories of race, and archaeological discoveries in the Near East."[32] But if, on the one hand, Judaism found that it had been marginalized in relation to classical culture

28. Grafton 1981, 120, 121.
29. Grafton 1999, 12.
30. See Marchand 2009; Heschel 1998, 2008.
31. Müller 1862, 123.
32. Manuel 1992, 302.

and Christian culture, on the other hand, its relationship to the broader concept of the "Orient" was being challenged from a different direction. Where
for Hegel, Judaism had manifested itself as an example of the discredited
"spirit of the Orient," the developments in linguistics increasingly marginalized Hebrew in relation to other Eastern languages. As Olender phrases it, by
the late eighteenth century "Sanskrit had supplanted Hebrew as the fashion-
able subject."[33] And the champion of this new vogue for the Indian classical
language was the English poet and jurist William Jones. Appointed a Justice
to the High Court of Bengal he set about the systematic study of Sanskrit. In
a formal address to the recently established Asiatic Society of Bengal in Feb-
ruary 1786, he was to formulate what would come to be seen as the founding
statement of Indo-European studies:

> The Sanskrit language, whatever be its antiquity, is of a wonderful structure;
> more perfect than the Greek, more copious than the Latin and more exqui-
> sitely refined than either; yet bearing to both of them a stronger affinity, both
> in roots of verbs, and in the forms of grammar, than could possibly have been
> produced by accident; so strong indeed that no philologer could examine all
> three, without believing them to have sprung from some common source,
> which, perhaps, no longer exists. There is a similar reason, though not quite
> so forcible, for supposing that both the Gothick and Celtick, though blended
> with a different idiom, had the same origin with Sanskrit; and the old Persian
> might be added to the same family, if this were the place for discussing any
> question concerning the antiquities of Persia.[34]

Jones's insight was to be given new legitimacy by Friedrich Schlegel who
established a connection between Jones's linguistic analysis and the ethnographic study of race. Looking back at these early developments, Max Müller
wrote in 1863:

> Thanks to the discovery of the ancient languages of India, Sanskrit as it is
> called . . . and thanks to the discovery of close kinship between this language
> and the idioms of the principal races of Europe, which has been established
> by the genius of Schlegel, Humboldt, Bopp and many others, a complete
> revolution has taken place in the method of studying the world's primitive
> history.[35]

The formulation of what Poliakov has called the "Aryan myth" was to
give a new dimension to the conceptual opposition between Hellenism and

33. Olender 1992, 6.
34. Jones 1788, 422–23.
35. Müller 1864, 404.

Hebraism. Where Jones and his successors had looked to Sanskrit to define the contours of the "Aryans," it was Ernest Renan who would systematize the study of "Semitic" languages and cultures. Influenced by current developments in Indo-European studies, Renan saw the world in terms of these two dominant structures of the "Aryan" and the "Semite." "His whole conceptual scheme is based on these 'two rivers' these two linguistic families, which constitute the wellspring of human civilisation."[36] He saw the Aryan and the Semite as "two poles of the movement of humanity." But Renan's two poles were far from being alternatives; they were profoundly hierarchical. He opposed the multiple dynamic dialects of Indo-European to a single static and underdeveloped Semitic family.

> The unity of the Semitic family has been noticed since antiquity, whereas at the start of this century we had not yet even suspected the links between the scattered branches of the Indo-European family. And yet, what a difference there is in the results between the application of the comparative method to these two families of languages! It only takes three or four years to unveil by analyzing Indo-European languages the most profound laws of language, whereas Semitic philology has remained to this day closed in on itself and almost alien to the general movements of science.[37]

Renan ascribes the extraordinary strides in the disciplines of philology and comparative linguistics to the object of its analysis. A symbiotic relationship between "methode" and "matière" is revealed in Renan's account. The discovery of Indo-European was perfectly suited to the emerging methodological revolution of comparative philology. In Renan's eyes a philology of Semitic languages would be a contradiction in terms. Philology can only be Indo-European. At this stage Renan will insist that it is *language* and not "physiology" that determines this distinction: "the division of Semites and Indo-Europeans was created by philology not by physiology."[38] And yet, the description of their philological incompatibility had already been mapped onto difference in "character." Renan thus continues:

> The reason for this unique phenomenon has to be found in the very character of the Semitic idioms. Languages which have virtually displayed no interior life, were incapable of revealing the organism of language and the laws of its decomposition. We will show that the ability of Indo-European languages to reproduce themselves and to be reborn from their ashes is virtually totally absent from Semitic language. They have undergone no such profound revo-

36. Olender 1992, 53.
37. Renan 1855, xi.
38. Renan 1947, 8.102.

lution, no development, no progress. . . . Semitic philology is devoid of this
fluidity of this ability to metamorphose which characterizes Indo-European
philology. Semitic philology is metallic, if I may say so, and has preserved
since high antiquity, perhaps even since the first days of the apparition of
language, a most remarkable sameness.[39]

The philological binary, then, is the expression of a much wider series of
cultural oppositions. To the metallic language of the Jews one can contrast
the sinuous fluidity of the Indo-Europeans. "The Semitic language is distinguished for its capacity to convey what is immutable. This inalterability,
regarded as an objective linguistic fact, of course matches the image of the
Hebrew people as unchangeable, allegedly impervious to history and uncompromising in their fate." In the course of his writings, as Olender demonstrates, Renan's linguistic particularities would morph into a familiar series of
cultural antitheses: "abstract metaphysics versus sensuous poetry, scientific
reason versus religious feeling, philosophy versus music, family versus tribe,
political organization versus desert nomadism."[40] Renan's characterization of
Semitic languages as "immature" and inward looking, then, had its corollary
in his understanding of Jewish monotheism. Like Hegel before him, Renan
will typify the monotheism of the Hebrews as excessive and tyrannical by
pitting the carefree polytheism of the Greeks against the punishing strictures
of the Old Testament. The timeless nature of the Semitic racial disposition
made its application to contemporary Jews seemingly unproblematic. The
"Aryan"/"Semite" debate, formulated in the scholarly context of linguistics,
came to take on the attributes of potent contemporary cultural stereotypes.
So while the Semite was endowed with the dour traits of the modern Jew, the
Aryan came to resemble the idealized conception of the joyful ancient Greek
that had been in circulation since Winckelmann.[41] Olender summarizes:

> Many specialists attributed to all Semitic groups characteristics ostensibly de-
> rived from the Hebrews of the historical period. As a corollary, Renan and
> many other nineteenth-century European scholars ascribed to the groups
> they called Aryan (or Indo-Germanic or Indo-European) characteristics they
> attributed to the Greeks. Within the Aryan universe the energy and abstract
> intellectual gifts of the Greeks prefigured the progress of the Indo-European
> world, while the Vedic pole represented the power of the primitive.[42]

39. Renan 1855, xii–xiii.
40. Olender 1992, 55, 79.
41. As we have already seen, the attribution of various different characteristics to both the
Greeks and the Jews is far from consistent and was, in fact, very malleable.
42. Olender 1992, 12.

Renan's analysis of the characteristics of Semitic languages and their in-stantiation in Judaism was to have profound consequences for the study of religion more generally. His particular hostility to Hebraic monotheism has often been seen as the product of his own complex relationship to Christian-ity. Despite his ostensible rejection of Catholicism in favor of an enlightened secularism, Renan remained committed to saving what he called a "liberal Christianity" from its Semitic ancestor. So he writes: "The Semites have nothing further to do that is essential . . . let us remain Germans and Celts; let us keep our 'eternal gospel,' Christianity . . . only Christianity has a future."[43] Renan's conviction that "fundamentally there was nothing Jewish about Je-sus" was explicitly linked by him to his linguistic analyses.[44] Although Renan's descriptions sometimes remained within a traditional theological register, "Christianity completely transcended the limits of the Semitic spirit," more often the link between his study of religious origins and his explorations of Semitic and Indo-European racial typographies was explicit: "Originally Jew-ish to the core, Christianity over time rid itself of the nearly everything it took from the race, so that those who consider Christianity the Aryan religion par excellence are in many respects correct." According to Renan, Judaism was a false start for Christianity. It was only *qua* Aryan religion that it could come to real fruition. The Jews can, thus, claim no credit for the later developments of a religion that remained antithetical to its most basic attributes. "The Bible thus bore fruits that were not its own. Judaism was the stock on which the Aryan race produced its flower."[45]

Renan's typology here transcends the more traditional narrative of his-torical development. His struggle with the Semitic character of Christian religion exemplifies the complex overlap between discourses of race and religion at this period. That Renan can transform the dichotomy between Aryan and Semitic races into a debate about the future of Christianity in Europe is just one indication of the contemporary relevance of these schol-arly disputes. Moreover, the intersection of Renan's linguistic, racial, cul-tural and religious vocabulary reveals the extent to which debates in schol-arship were fully implicated in the wider cultural discourse of the period. In Renan we find Hegel's philosophical speculations on historical progress transformed into a competition between different racial typologies. The language of "spirit" has given way to a new discourse of language, nation, and race.

43. Cited in Poliakov 1974, 207.
44. Renan's notebooks, quoted in Olender 1992, 69
45. Renan 1904, 440; Renan 1947, 5.1142, 1143.

Arnold: Between Psychomachy and Physiology

It is this background that makes sense of perhaps the most influential text of
the post-Enlightenment exploration of Athens and Jerusalem. Arnold's essay
has traditionally been read as one of the central documents of Victorian Hellenism. Thus both Turner and Jenkyns devote substantial sections to Arnold in
their studies of the "Greek heritage" in nineteenth-century English culture.[46]
And yet, despite the acknowledgment of the centrality of Arnold's writings,
few critics have situated *Culture and Anarchy* in the context of contemporary
writings on Hellenism. Indeed the consensus remains that Arnold was out of
touch with the findings of modern scholarship and classical scholarship in
particular. Most attribute to Arnold an outdated and watered down importa-
tion of the German philhellenism of the late eighteenth century. They see his
Greeks infused with a Winckelmannian calm that had long been superseded
by the academic study of Greek culture. Collini highlights how Arnold's famous praise of Sophocles, his ability "to see life steadily and see it whole," was
in marked contrast to Nietzsche's near-contemporary focus on the Dionysiac qualities of Greek tragedy. Arnold's Apolline Greeks (in contrast to those
of Walter Pater, for instance) have been seen as a diverting anachronism.[47]
Indeed, Turner argues that his subsequent readers were willfully complicit
with Arnold's backward-looking gaze: "Later it was to Arnold's image of the
Greeks that numerous intellectuals wished to return when anthropologists
and archaeologists had revealed a very different version of Greek life."[48]

   This accusation of derivativeness has been central to the critique of Arnold's Hellenism. Arnold's investment in Greek culture has been seen as
nothing more than a transposition of a German cultural obsession to an English context. But Arnold's relationship to the German tradition of philhellenism is rather more complex than this version may suggest. Arnold's Hellenism functions as much as a critique of German thought as a straightforward
cultural borrowing. Indeed the relationship to the Greeks becomes a central
plank of national identification in Arnold's writing. It is precisely in the context of the search for the distinctiveness of national characteristics that the
term *Hellenism* comes into force. The German and French wholehearted espousal of Greco-Roman culture is for Arnold a source of worry rather than
a straightforward model worthy of emulation. Philhellenism poses an ethical

   46. Turner 1984; Jenkyns 1981.
   47. See Evangelista (2009), who argues that Pater's different characterization of Hellenism is
also an implicit critique of Arnold's Christianized Hebraism. Evangelista also mentions Pater's
juxtaposition of Dionysus and Christ, which strongly echoes Nietzsche (see next chapter).
   48. Turner 1984, 18.

challenge for Arnold. Just as the desired return to a Greek "totality" had been a way of dealing with the moral and political shortcomings of the late eighteenth century for German Grecophiles, Arnold's re-evaluation of German Hellenism is at the core of his own exploration of a contemporary cultural malaise.

But it is not just that Arnold's ancient Greeks turn out to be modern Germans, but that their translocation to English shores has further distanced them from any "true" classical referent. Indeed, in Arnold's hands the conversion from historical reality to expedient cultural metaphor has become complete. The term *Hellene* bears no relationship to the historical inhabitants of Athens. *Hellene* has rather become a buzzword of English social criticism. And just as *Hellene* stands in for a category of Arnold's contemporary society, its antitype *Hebrew* is also divested of a relationship to the history of ancient Judaism. Turner concludes:

> Arnold's Hebrews were not Jews but rather contemporary English Protestant Nonconformists. His Greeks were not ancient Hellenes but a version of humanity largely conjured up in the late eighteenth-century German literary and aesthetic imagination. Hellenism for Arnold was not the experience or thought of ancient Greece, but a set of more or less traditional English humanist values long employed to oppose commercialism, excessive religious zeal, dissent from Anglicanism, philosophical mechanism, political radicalism, subjective morality, and social individualism.[49]

In fact, far from being a debate about Athens and Jerusalem, most critics have domesticated Arnold's intervention, arguing that the "real" referents of his provocative terms are the different understandings of Christianity and its role in English culture. The debate is not so much between secular Greek and religious Jew as between "Non-Conformist" and "Catholic."

The transposition of the opposition between Hellenism and Hebraism into a localized discussion of the future of Christianity recalls the preoccupations of Renan. We have seen how Renan's scholarly contributions to the Aryan/ Semite debate were intimately related to his own negotiation of Christianity. For Renan, the historical opposition between Indo-European and Semitic forces was still being played out in nineteenth-century discussions about the role of Christianity in modern secular society. But for Renan, "Aryan" and "Semite" were no mere metaphors; they referred to both a very real historical tradition and a congenital racial disposition. Arnold's debt to Renan has been underplayed in the discussions of his Hellenism. Despite Frederic Faverty's

---

49. Ibid., 21.

assertion that "no contemporary writer exercised more influence on Mat-thew Arnold's thinking," recent analyses of Arnold have tended to marginal-ize Renan's contribution to Arnold's writings about the Greeks.[50] What seems to be at the heart of this neglect is a desire to dissociate Arnold's investment in Greek culture from the racializing tendencies of Renan's philosophy. "The extent," Robert Young affirms, "of the academic silence on the racial centre of *Culture and Anarchy* is quite remarkable."[51] David De Laura, for instance, has written the classic full-length study of *Hebrew and Hellene in Victorian England* without at any stage mentioning the racial basis of the distinction. Arnold's critics have been complicit in their failure to expose the racial un-derpinnings of his analysis of English culture.

And yet, what is so interesting about Arnold's prose is the extent to which it both distances and fully implicates itself in the racial schema of Renan. Renan's articulation of "two poles of the movement of humanity" undoubt-edly looms large behind Arnold's central formulation of his problematic: "Hellenism and Hebraism, —between these points of influence moves the world. At one time it feels more powerfully the attraction of one of them, at another time of the other; it ought to be, though it never is, evenly and hap-pily balanced between them."[52] But as Arnold himself notes, he had inherited the crucial terms "Hellenism"/"Hebraism" not from Renan, but rather from the German poet and writer Heinrich Heine.[53] Arnold's reference to Heine is significant from a number of perspectives. On the one hand, as a promi-nent figure of post-Romantic Germany, Heine's writing acted as vehicle of the German philhellenism in which Arnold was steeped. On the other hand, Heine's own distinctive identity as a baptized Jew gave him a particular in-vestment in Hellenism that could not simply be reduced to a national pre-occupation. Heine's particular conceptualization of the Greek/Jew antithesis was formulated at the precarious intersection of German and Jewish philhel-lenism. Arnold's appropriation of his terms bears the mark of Heine's com-plex self-positioning.

By the time he wrote the essay on "Hellenism and Hebraism," Heine had already been an important influence on Arnold, who had written a long and influential essay on Heine's work. Arnold's fascination with Heine was closely related to his wider exploration of European thought and its contrast with the narrow cultural horizons of England. In Heine Arnold found an arche-

50. Faverty 1951, 167.

51. Young 1995, 62.

52. Arnold 1993, 126.

53. The exact nature of Arnold's debt to Heine is disputed by his various readers. For most extensive study of the relationship between the two writers see Tesdorpf 1971.

type of cosmopolitan intellectualism and a stern critic of the "philistinism" that he had identified as the most stultifying aspect of his native country. In fact, as much as the Hebrew/Hellene distinction, Arnold owes the cultural vocabulary of philistinism to Heine. Commenting on Arnold's earlier poetic tribute "Heine's Grave," T. S. Eliot remarks, "Heine is one of the *personae*, the masks behind which Arnold is able to go through his performance."[54] In Eliot's eyes, Arnold's identification with this German-Jewish poet is a mere pretext "for his sermon to the English public." While it is true that Arnold's poem reduces Heine's critical stance to his unfavorable view of England, his later essay pays much greater attention to the distinctiveness of Heine's voice. Indeed, far from minimizing the specificity of Heine's Jewish identity, Arnold makes a point of foregrounding it:

> No account of Heine is complete which does not notice the Jewish element in him. His race he treated with the same freedom with which he treated everything else, but he derived great force from it, and no one knew this better than he himself. He has excellently pointed out how in the sixteenth century there was a double renascence, —a Hellenic renascence and a Hebrew renascence—and how both have been great powers since. He himself had in him both the spirit of Greece and the spirit of Judaea; both these spirits reach the infinite, which is the true goal of poetry and art, —the Greek spirit by beauty, the Hebrew spirit by sublimity. By his perfection of the literary form, by his love of clearness, by his love of beauty, Heine is Greek; by his intensity, by his untamableness, by his "longing which cannot be uttered," he is Hebrew. Yet what Hebrew ever treated the things of the Hebrews like this?[55]

Arnold uses strikingly Hegelian terms in contrasting the "Greek spirit" of "beauty" to the "Hebrew spirit" of "sublimity." But Arnold's residual Hegelianism in his depiction of Heine as a happy fusion of the Hebraic and the Hellenic remains at odds with the rather more tortured relationship that Heine depicts in his own work. Heine had formulated the opposition between Hebrew and Hellene that Arnold draws upon, in the course of his polemical attack on his counterpart Ludwig Börne.

> Börne betrays the narrowness of mind of the Nazarene. I say "Nazarene," in order to use neither the term "Jewish" nor the term "Christian," although the two terms are synonymous for me and are used by me to designate not a faith but a natural disposition. "Jews" and "Christians" are for me closely related in opposition to "Hellenes," by which I likewise do not mean a particular

54. Eliot 1968, 112.
55. Arnold 1962, 127–28.

people, but a turn of mind and an outlook, both inborn and acquired. From
that point of view, I could say that all men are either Jews or Hellenes, men
motivated by asceticism, hostility to graven images, and a deep desire for the
spiritual, or men whose essential being is delight in life, pride in the development of their capacities, and realism. In this sense, there have been Hellenes
among German pastors who come from families of pastors and Jews born in
Athens and perhaps descended from Theseus.[56]

"Alle Menschen sind entweder Juden oder Hellenen [All men are either Jewish or Hellenes]."[57] For Heine the Hellenic and the Hebraic described character types that each one of us could inhabit at different points in our lives.
His typologies were, in fact, explicitly not racialized and rather functioned
as a kind of psychological taxonomy. Writing out of the context of German
philhellenism, Heine's spiritual identification with his inner Hellene at the
expense of his Hebraic heritage was an expression of his complex relationship
to German culture.[58] Heine's own Jewishness and his conversion to Christianity form an important background. Indeed, Heine's antithetical terms take
on a particular resonance in the context of the debates about the necessity of
conversion confronting most Jews at this period. Heine's self-identification
as a Hellene at this point in time could be seen as a retrospective legitima-
tion of his conversion. Moreover, his synthesis of the Jew and the Christian
into the category of the "Nazarene" stands in direct contrast to the efforts to
separate Christianity from its Judaic heritage. In his opposition of Hellenism
to a synthesized category of Judeo-Christianity, Heine departs from both Hegel and Renan and marks himself out as a precursor to Marx and Nietzsche.
Heine makes a distinctive and radical contribution to the shifting allegiances
between Athens, Rome, and Jerusalem.

Despite his overt identification as a Hellene in the Börne essay, Heine had
earlier given voice to a much more ambivalent relationship to both Judeo-
Christian and Hellenic culture. His poem "Die Götter Griechenlands" starts
with melancholic lament on the passing of the great polytheistic religion:

> Those are they themselves, the gods of Hellas,
> Who once so joyfully ruled the world.
> But now, driven out and wasted in death,
> As huge apparitions wander away
> In the midnight heaven.

56. Heine 1968–76, 11:18–19; cited in English in Carroll 1982, 242.
57. Heine 1968–76, 11:18–19.
58. On which see Goetschel 2004.

This vision of the "Gods in Exile" anticipates Heine's later essay, which envisions the Greek gods scattered throughout the German landscape in the wake of the triumph of Christianity. Christianity had forced the pagan gods and in all their sensuality into exile but their presence still haunts the German countryside. But from this depiction of desolation the poem takes an unexpected turn:

> You I have never loved, you gods!
> For contrary to me are the Greeks,
> And even the Romans to me are hateful;
> Yet holy compassion and shuddering pity
> Stream through my heart
> As I watch you now, up there,
> Abandoned gods,
> Dead, night-wandering shadows,
> Mist-frail, that the wind in terror scatters,
> And when I consider how cowardly and windy
> Are the gods that conquered you,
> The new, ruling, wistful gods,
> The malicious ones in humility's sheepskin—
> Oh, then a gloomy resentment seizes me,
> And I could break the new temples,
> And fight for *you*, you ancient gods,
> For you and your good, ambrosial right,
> And before your lofty altars,
> All built again, all smoky with sacrifice,
> I myself could kneel and pray
> And lift up my arms beseeching.[59]

Heine's proclamation of aversion to the Greeks and hatred of the Roman stands in contrast to the tradition of German philhellenism from which his poem seemingly emerges. In fact, Heine's poem sets itself up in curious dialogue with Schiller's poem of the same name. Schiller's "Die Götter Griechenlands" is a lament for the passing of the Greek gods in all their beauty and humanity and an attack on the forces of modernity: science, materialism, and, implicitly, Christianity. Heine's contempt for the "new gods" is much less implicit. For Heine the return to Greek paganism is a strategic venture placed at the service of a strident critique of Christianity. Heine's Hellenism, then, was never, as Arnold tends to imply, an easy identification with the

59. Heine 1982a, 15, 17; translated by Vernon Watkins.

ancient Greeks, but rather a conflicted response to the competing forces of modernity. Heine sees a modern culture riven by an "unresolved and perhaps never to be resolved duel between Jewish spiritualism and Hellenic glorification of life."[60]

Heine's own identity as a Hellene, as Robert Holub makes clear, came under increasing strain in the later years of his life when illness confined him to what he would call his "mattress grave."[61] In fact, it is precisely to the Hellene/Hebrew opposition that Heine will return to express his growing regrets about his earlier rejection of Judaism: "a great change has come over me. . . . I am no longer a joyful Hellene. . . . I am only a poor Jew sick unto death."[62] In "Für die Mouche," generally considered to be his last poem, Heine describes and then recognizes his own coffin adorned with the competing imagery of the Hellenic and biblical traditions. But this is no vision of harmonious reconciliation, only one of perpetual conflict:

> Does the old superstition haunt my bier,
>> And are the marble phantoms still debating?
> Is sylvan Pan, with his loud cry of fear,
>> The anathemas of Moses emulating?
>
> Oh, well I know they never will agree;
>> Beauty and truth will always be at variance.
> The army of mankind will always be
>> Split in two camps: the Hellenes and the Barbarians.

Arnold's attempt to capture Heine's fissured identity seems to be a willful domestication: "By his perfection of literary form, by his love of clearness, by his love of beauty, Heine was Greek; by his intensity, by his untameableness, by his longing which cannot be uttered, he is Hebrew."[63]

Heine's experience as a troubled philhellene can be interestingly contrasted with that of the "orthodox Jewish philologist Jacob Bernays." In Arnaldo Momigliano's affectionate portrait, he connects Bernays's upbringing in Hamburg specifically to Heine and his circle. So he writes:

The Jewish community of Hamburg was then mainly made up of moderately affluent shopkeepers, who fought for their civic rights and wanted a modernization of their educational institutions. The destitute and the very rich were on the fringe of the congregation, and among the very rich the dominant figure was the banker Solomon Heine. His nephew and protégé Heinrich had

60. Heine cited in Gossman 1994, 17.
61. Holub 1981, 174–89.
62. Beiber 1956, 421.
63. Arnold 1962, 128.

abandoned Hamburg two years before, in 1819, after failing both in business and in love, but the shadow of Heinrich Heine—the poet and the apostate—lingered on in Hamburg and especially in the Bernays' family, which was somehow related to him.[64]

Unlike Heine, Jacob Bernays refused conversion, and his academic career was forever marked by this decision. For most of his life he taught at the Jewish seminary in Breslau and it was only much later that he was admitted to the Prussian academy (and even then, only partially). Bernays's dual training as a classical philologist and as a rabbinical scholar was paralleled by his lifelong desire to "unite" as he put it "the Bible with Greco-Roman *Bildung*." His refusal to sever his interest in Greece and Rome from a wider investigation of the Near East made Bernays what Suzanne Marchand and Anthony Grafton call "a lonely figure" in contemporary classical studies.[65] The example of Bernays somewhat complicates the image of an increasingly balkanized scholarly community. Bernays's polymathic scope, as well as his rejection of the Hebrew/Hellene or Aryan/Semite distinction, mark him out as an exceptional figure in the history of classical scholarship. He stands both against the increasing specialization of the field as well as the movement toward separating the study of the Greco-Roman world from its Oriental and Semitic neighbors so controversially charted by Martin Bernal. So while Hamburg's renegade son Heinrich Heine formalized the distinction between Hebrew and Hellene, Jacob Bernays, the respected classical philologist, resisted the lures of both conversion and the exclusionary polarity of Hellenism and Hebraism alike. While Heine's Hellenism is testimony to his failed attempt at assimilation, Bernays's refusal to assimilate went hand in hand with his scholarly refusal to endorse the growing currency of the "Aryan myth" in classical scholarship.

Arnold's essay professes to share Bernays's desire to reverse the climate of anti-Hebraism that had left its mark even on Heine. Lionel Gossman makes the claim that Arnold's reappropriation of Heine's Hebrew/Hellene distinction underplays the extent to which the opposition had been steeped in a German cultural landscape marked by anti-Semitism. As Gossman writes: "By the middle of the nineteenth century . . . the antithesis of 'Hellenes and Jews' was part of a repertory of anti-Semitism among the educated classes in Germany."[66] Heine's vision of the eternal struggle between these two

64. Momigliano 1994a, 124–25.

65. Marchand and Grafton 1997, 21 (citing Bernays), 22. For the wider context of Jewish intellectuals and the disciplines of philology in the late nineteenth century see Barner and König 2001. See also Marchand 2009, 112–13, and especially Bollack 1998 and Glucker and Laks 1996.

66. Gossman 1994, 3.

forces was fully implicated in a dialectical scheme that could only be resolved through a Hegelian Aufhebung. But despite the superficial nod to dialectical thought in Arnold's essay, his vision resolutely refuses the movement of the Hegelian dialectic:

> For *the days of Israel are innumerable*; and in its blame of Hebraising too, and in its praise of Hellenising, culture must not fail to keep its flexibility, and to give to its judgments that passing and provisional character which we have seen it impose on its preferences and rejections of machinery. Now, and for us, it is time to Hellenise, and to praise knowing; for we have Hebraised too much, and have overvalued doing. But the habits and discipline received from the Hebraism remain for our race an eternal possession; and as humanity is constituted, one must never assign to them the second rank to-day, without being prepared to restore them to the first rank tomorrow.[67]

As Gossman concludes: "The provocative tensions of Hegel, Heine and later Nietzsche are relaxed in what the last would almost certainly have characterized as an insipid optimism."[68] In Arnold's vision, far from a violent clash that results in a mutual cancellation, Hellenism and Hebraism are involved in a constant interplay from which both emerge unscathed. While the urgency of the present demands a turn to Hellenism, Hebraism remains an "eternal possession" that cannot and must not be annihilated. In her analysis of Arnold's encounter with Heine, Ilse-Maria Tesdorpf argues that Arnold takes over Heine's philosophy of history while giving the Hebrew and the Hellene a different content. But Arnold's analysis appears to be at odds with both the philosophy and the content of Heine's antithesis. Where Heine associates the Hellenic with the sensual, Arnold associates his Hellenes with "knowing." Indeed, Heine's characterization of the Hellenes as sensualists is a complete reversal of the repeated association of the Jews with the body we have been tracing in the previous chapters of this book. In restoring the Greeks to the realm of "knowing," Arnold returns the Hellene/Hebrew opposition to the hierarchy we found in Hegel. The identity of Heine's Hebrews may be less clearly defined but they hardly seem to have much in common with Arnold's "doers." Heine's Greeks and Jews anticipate Nietzsche's and Freud's far more obviously than they do Arnold's. Moreover, while Heine's philosophy of history seems to be governed by the Hegelian dialectic, as we shall see below, Arnold's historical outlook may have its source much closer to home.

---

67. Arnold 1993, 210.
68. Gossman 1994, 27.

What Arnold's exploration does share with Heine is the explicit psychologization of their respective categories. Where in Hegel, Greeks and Jews functioned both as historical actors and as manifestations of different stages of the progress of consciousness, in Arnold and Heine they have become descriptions of internal psychological predispositions. As Gossman comments on Arnold's wider schema in *Culture and Anarchy*: "The terms 'Barbarians,' 'Philistines,' 'Populace' transform a concrete historical struggle into a psychomachy, an allegory of 'eternal' conflict in human history of competing forces."[69] So Arnold turns to a new vocabulary:

> Both Hellenism and Hebraism arise out of the wants of human nature, address themselves to satisfying those wants. But their methods are so different, they lay stress on such different points, and call into being by their respective disciplines such different activities, that the face which human nature presents when it passes from the hands of one to those of the other, is no longer the same.[70]

In Arnold's "psychomachy" history falls away. Hebraism and Hellenism no longer exist as different historical stages of the development of man but are just opposing attributes of a transhistorical "human nature." Arnold continues:

> To rid oneself of one's ignorance, to see things as they are, and by seeing them as they are to see them in their beauty, is the simple and attractive ideal which Hellenism holds out before human nature; and from the simplicity and charm of this ideal, Hellenism, and human life in the hands of Hellenism, is invested with a kind of aerial ease, clearness, and radiancy: they are full of what we call sweetness and light.[71]

Hellenism is a way of seeing and, what is more, a way of being. "Sweetness and light" are attributes of a psychological disposition rather than the description of a historical legacy to humanity. And just as "life in the hands of Hellenism" has given rise to a distinctive aesthetics of existence, so Hebraism has manifested itself and continues to manifest itself in a very different psychological legacy:

> There is a saying which I have heard attributed to Mr Carlyle about Socrates, —a very happy saying, whether it is really Mr Carlyle or not, —which excellently marks the essential point in which Hebraism differs from Hellenism. "Socrates," this saying goes, "is terribly *at ease in Zion*." Hebraism, —and here is the source of its wonderful strength, —has always been severely pre-

69. Ibid., 24.
70. Arnold 1993, 130.
71. Ibid.

occupied with an awful sense of impossibility of being at ease in Zion; of the
difficulties which oppose themselves to man's pursuit or the attainment of that
perfection of which Socrates talks so hopefully.[72]

The inability to "feel at ease" is the dubious gift of Hebraism to human nature. "At ease" was a term of praise in this period. To be "at ease" was an
aspiration of many a protagonist in Victorian novels and a quality that met
with appreciation in etiquette handbooks. To be "at ease" was having the ability to fit in. The wandering Jew was the archetype of the figure who fails to
fit in, who fails to be at ease in Zion or anywhere else. If the failure to be at
ease has political consequences for the Jews, it also has a psychological legacy.
With Arnold's comments here, we are surely not far from the stereotype of
the neurotic Jew. Arnold's insight into Socrates in Zion may prefigure future
discussions of Freud and the identification of psychoanalysis as the quintessentially Jewish science. So in Arnold's analysis Hellenism and Hebraism are
quite capable of coexisting historically; indeed, as Heine had suggested, they
could even coexist in the same person.

But just as Arnold appears to remove history from the frame of reference
it seems to re-emerge in another more pernicious guise: "Science has now
made visible to everybody," he writes, "the great and pregnant elements of
difference which lie in race, and in how single a manner they make the genius
and history of an Indo-European people vary from those of a Semitic people. Hellenism is of Indo-European growth, Hebraism is of Semitic growth;
and we English, a nation of Indo-European stock, seem to belong naturally
to the movement of Hellenism."[73] Arnold's reference to the term "Indo-
European" situates him at the very heart of the debates within linguistics and
ethnology.[74] His discussion of Indo-European appears to be a direct reference back to Renan and his racialization of the Greek/Jew antithesis. But
Arnold's perhaps most explicit expression of racial preoccupation is framed
by a series of hesitations. So he immediately follows this statement with the
concession:

> But nothing more strongly marks the essential unity of man, than the affini-
> ties we can perceive, in this point or that, between members of one family of
> peoples and members of another. And no affinity of this kind is more strongly
> marked than that likeness in the strength and prominence of the moral fibre,

72. Ibid.
73. Ibid., 135.
74. On which see Poliakov 1974, Bernal 1987, Olender 1992, and Marchand 2003, 2009.

which, notwithstanding immense elements of difference, knits in some special sort the genius and history of us English, and our American descendants
across the Atlantic, to the genius and history of the Hebrew people.[75]

While not disavowing these "immense elements of difference," Arnold pur-
ports to reconcile the two distinct "geniuses and histories" into some sort of
synthesis. Arnold's most forthright adoption of the "Aryan myth" gives way
to a reflection on the hybrid identity of the English nation. So he continues:
"Eminently Indo-European by its *humour*, by the power it shows, through
this gift, of imaginatively acknowledging the multiform aspects of the problem of life, and thus getting itself unfixed from its own certainty, of smiling
at its own over-tenacity, our race has yet (and a great part of its strengths
lies here), in matters of practical life and moral conduct, a strong share of
the assuredness, the tenacity, the intensity of the Hebrews."[76] While Arnold
clings to the vocabulary of race, his narrative here has none of the emphasis
on the exclusionary character of cultural progress. His "Indo-Europeans," in
other words, have no difficulty borrowing from their Semitic counterparts.
Arnold's espousal of Aryanism by no means precludes his identification of
Semitic traits in his eminently Indo-European countrymen. But Arnold's
identification of the English with a misplaced strain of "Hebraism" is ultimately invoked to show up the limitations of his compatriots. Thus he concludes his essay with an unequivocal denunciation of the false consciousness
of English Semitism:

> For more than two hundred years the main stream of man's advance has moved
> towards knowing himself and the world, seeing things as they are, spontaneity
> of consciousness; the main impulse of a great part, and that strongest part,
> of our nation has been towards strictness of conscience. They have made the
> secondary the principal at the wrong moment, and the principal they have at
> the wrong moment treated as secondary. This contravention of the natural
> order has produced, as such a contravention must always produce, a certain
> confusion and a false movement, of which we are now beginning to feel, in
> almost every direction, the inconvenience.[77]

For Arnold, Hebraism will always be not only a false start, but a "contraven-
tion" of nature. Arnold's formulation in his closing peroration of the "false"
movement of Hebraism contrasts markedly with his opening statements

75. Arnold 1993, 136.
76. Ibid.
77. Ibid., 137.

about the balance he wished to achieve. His juxtaposition of Hellenism and
Hebraism may disavow the dialectical framework of its Germanic counterparts but it still seems to take over its implicit hierarchy. When Hegel had
sought to contrast Greek and Jew in "The Spirit of Christianity and Its Fate,"
the "balance" between Hebraism and Hellenism that Arnold so ardently
strives for is revealed in all its elusiveness. In the Hegelian dialectic the Jew
must always represent a stage to be overcome on the inexorable march of
progress. Arnold's discussion may not be the heir to a Hegelian philosophy
of history but his immersion in language of racial typology implicates him in
a historical discourse that is no less marked by a narrative of progress. The
historicist outlook that had gone hand in hand with the developments in
comparative philology and ethnology since Herder returns to haunt Arnold's
avowedly dehistoricized analysis.

But the conception of history in Arnold has another striking intertext.
Arnold's narrative of the alternating "movements" of "Hellenism" and "Hebraism," "Indo-European" and "Semitic" recalls the cyclical conception of
history that had been so important to his father, Thomas Arnold.[78] As Momigliano recounts, Thomas Arnold had formulated his vision of history at his
inaugural lecture as Regius Professor of Modern History at Oxford:

> We are living in the latest period of the world's history. No other races remain
> to perform what we have neglected or to restore what we have ruined. . . . [It
> follows] that the interest of modern history does become intense, and the im-
> portance of not wasting time still left to us may well be called incalculable. Our
> existing nations are the last reserve of the world; its fate may be said to be in
> their hands—God's work on earth will be left undone if they do not do it.[79]

The apocalyptic tone of his pronouncements went hand in hand with a
particular conception of race: "I say nothing of the prospects and influence
of the German race in Africa and in India: it is enough to say that half of
Europe, and all America and Australia, are German more or less completely
in race, in language, or in institutions, or in all." Profoundly influenced by
the classicist Christian Karl Bunsen, Arnold senior became convinced by the
superiority of the Germanic races, a superiority in which England as a Germanic nation shared.[80] But this Germano-centric view of history was allied

78. On which see also Turner 1984, 26–32.
79. Arnold 1842, 39
80. Bunsen is an interesting figure: as well as being a scholar of classical and biblical culture, Bunsen was a Prussian envoy to the Court of St. James and a strong advocate of Christian
Zionism.

to Thomas Arnold's wider philosophy, a new movement of historicism that suggested that all nations developed through a series of organic stages that resembled the development of the individual human. History was, then, a "record of the cycle of nations," with each nation developing to its full maturation at different times. It was thus possible to compare two historically distanced nations by reference to their analogous stage in development and maturation.

Momigliano traces the influence of Thomas Arnold's influence on the younger classical scholar Edward Augustus Freeman. Freeman had voiced his debt to Arnold at his own inaugural lecture to the same post nearly half a century later: "It was from Arnold that I first learned the truth which ought to be the centre and life of all historic studies, the truth of the unity of history." But this unity is given a special dimension: "It was ruled by the Teutoburg wood that there should be a free Germany to plant a free England, and a free England to plant a free America."[81] Freeman developed Arnold's interest in race and the cyclic nature of history into a new vision of comparativism. His enthusiasm for the comparative method was given voice in his important work "Comparative Politics," in which he applied the methods previously developed in philology to Aryan institutions. Here Freeman attempted to understand a plurality of manifestations of political organization with reference to their shared Aryan origin. Momigliano traces how Freeman's adoption of the Arnoldian "unity of history" quickly takes on the attributes of racial discourse: "But notice that at that point what seemed to be a vindication of the unity of mankind becomes a celebration of the Aryan tribe or race." As Freeman writes: "Looking then at the history of man, at all events at the history of Aryan man in Europe, as one unbroken whole, no part of which can be safely looked at without reference to other parts." As Momigliano comments wryly, "All that is needed is a turn of phrase, a mere 'at all events' to move from the history of man to the history of Aryan man."[82]

For all his love of German culture, Matthew Arnold vocally disavowed his father's "Teutonism" and his championing of Celtic and French culture was in marked opposition to his father's views. Nor did the younger Arnold share his father's more explicit racial prejudices. Thomas Arnold's antagonism to contemporary Jews came to the fore in his resistance to the admission of Jews into parliament: "Jews are strangers in England, and have no more claim to legislate for it than a lodger has to share with a landlord in

81. Freeman 1884, 9.
82. Momigliano 1994a, 206.

the management of his house . . . for England is the land of Englishmen not Jews."[83] The younger Arnold fell well short of his father's anti-Semitism.[84] But in his analysis of the historical development of England, Matthew Arnold takes over Thomas's historiographic framework; his work is also suffused by the "scientific" Aryanism of his father's disciple, E. A. Freeman. What is interesting about Arnold's essay is the extent to which it finds itself negotiating the poles of nature and culture. "While Arnold intended to privilege 'culture' over 'race,'" writes Bryan Cheyette, "he is no less scathing about an untransfigured or unhellenized Jewish particularity than Dr Arnold about non-Christianized Jews." Arnold's "racial exclusivism" clearly undermined his "cultural inclusivism." One gets a sense of Arnold struggling against the very racial determinism that he himself mobilizes within his own essay. So he wrote to his mother: "we are none better for trying to make ourselves Semitic, when nature has made us Indo-European."[85] As Amanda Anderson phrases it: "Arnold is drawn to and wants to believe in the possibility of transformative and critical relations to what he construes as natural racial forces, but he is also haunted by the fact that such forces are starkly determining."[86] For Robert Young, despite Arnold's attempts to prise apart the realms of "culture" and "race," there is no doubt which holds the privileged status in his work. Arnold's very conception of "culture" was marked to the core by "race":

> So *Culture and Anarchy*, the highly influential, virtual founding document of English culture, locates the culture's energy and history as a product of racial difference. It thus neatly relocates and displaces the class conflict that is so clearly apparent in the turbulent social scenarios that it describes. The struggles between what for Arnold are in effect four classes (the aristocracy, the gentrified middle class, the radical dissenting middle class and the working class) are subsumed into the struggles of racial history.[87]

83. Quoted in Cheyette 1993, 19.

84. It is possible to find more direct anti-Semitic passages in Matthew Arnold's writings; see for instance this passage: "This does truly constitute for Israel a most extraordinary distinction. In spite of all which in them and in their character is unattractive, nay repellent, —in spite of their shortcomings even in righteousness itself and their insignificance in everything else, —this petty, unsuccessful, unamiable people, without politics, without science, without art, without charm, deserve a great place in the world's regard, and are likely to have it more and more, as the world goes on rather than less" (1960–77, 6:51).

85. Cheyette 1993, 19, 21 (quoting Arnold).

86. Anderson 2001, 101.

87. Young 1995, 60

The Philological Laboratory and the Jewish Question

Despite the consensus to the contrary, Arnold's essay is a powerful intervention in the up-to-the-minute debates of its age. Far from representing a self-consciously anachronistic and idealized "Hellenism," Arnold manages to provide a synthesis of disparate strands in the modern contests about Greece. An embodiment of the very kind of culture he is advocating, Arnold looks beyond England to draw on the writings of French and German writers such as Renan and Heine. Arnold's "Hellenism" was also fully conversant with the prevailing debates within contemporary classical scholarship. For all its tone of gentlemanly amateurism, "Hebraism and Hellenism" should be read as a contribution to the central debates within philosophical, theological, historiographical, ethnological, and philological studies of his day. Arnold's essay shows how the nineteenth-century scholarly community, what Edward Said calls the "philological laboratory," was fully part of wider cultural and social controversies that had real effects in the world. As Said writes about Renan:

> Indeed, it is not too much to say that Renan's philological laboratory was the actual locale of his European ethnocentrism: but what needs emphasis here is that the philological laboratory has no existence outside the discourse, the writing by which it is constantly produced and experienced. Thus even the culture he calls organic and alive—Europe's—is also a *creature being created* in the laboratory by philology.[88]

Said's comment about the uncanny mirroring of the form and content in the nineteenth century's scholarly obsession with philology has a particular currency in our modern understanding of the history of classical scholarship. The narrative of increasing institutional specialization that has been the preoccupation of many recent studies finds its parallel in the narrowing of the object of study.[89] The story of growing professionalism within the classical academy has also been one in which, as Suzanne Marchand has demonstrated, the history of Greece is increasingly detached from a universal history.[90] Judaism finds itself playing a key role in this detachment and realignment. Figures like Jacob Bernays and, later, Eduard Meyer may continue to study both Greek and Hebrew cultures concurrently but they did so against a scholarly back-

88. Said 1978, 146.
89. See Stray 1998; Marchand 1996, 2009.
90. See Marchand 2003.

ground that was increasingly hostile to such a juxtaposition.[91] At the same
time the Jew and the Hebrew continued to occupy a particularly ambivalent
role in relation to these wider debates about Greece and the Orient. As we
have been seeing, the Hebraism/Hellenism, Aryan/Semite opposition cuts
across the debate about philology and Orientalism. Judaism's relationship
to Christian monotheism would endow the "Jew" with a distinctive identity
that was not easily assimilated into an undifferentiated concept of the Orient.
The Jews ancient and modern always occupied an ambivalent position both
within and without the European nation.

But while the "Semite" may be "a creature being created in the laboratory," the existence of his living contemporary descendants within European
culture adds another dimension to the problem. Just as Said sees Oriental
philology as the laboratory of the wider European imperial project, the debates about "Hellenism" and "Hebraism" and "Aryan" and "Semite" can be
seen as the ersatz scholarly intervention into the "Jewish question" that was
beginning to have such currency in contemporary politics. Critics of Said
have long noted that the German case seems to offer an obvious exception
to his reflections on the relationship between power and knowledge. "By
1830, the Germans had emerged as the preeminent Orientalist scholars in
Europe—the leading Semiticists, biblical critics and Indologists—and they
did so in the absence of any colonial holdings in the Near East, or anywhere
else for that matter."[92] But as Jonathan Hess and others have contended,

> Orientalism in Germany often tended to be directed inwards as well as out-
> wards, and the case of the Jews offers in many ways the perfect arena for test-
> ing this hypothesis. Judaism was not just an object of Orientalist scholarship
> alongside Islam and the East in the nineteenth century. Both the academic
> study of Arabic and the field of comparative Semitic languages trace their
> origins to eighteenth-century innovations in historical approaches to the
> Bible.[93]

91. On Meyer and this trend cf. Marchand and Grafton 1997, 22. "The disciplines of philology took a long time, and put up some strong resistance, before they were finally torn definitively from one another's sticky embrace and embodied in separate institutes, journals and,
editions. At the end of the century, after all, Eduard Meyer was able to compose a monumental
Geschichte des Altertums (1884–1902), covering the ancient world from the Babylonians to the
Romans, and based on original sources in all the oriental and classical languages. Meyer was indeed an exceptional, inimitable, linguistic and historical genius; by the fin de siècle, it is exceed-
ingly difficult to find another academically important classicist or orientalist whose expertise
extended beyond his most favoured nation."

92. Hess 2002, 13.

93. Ibid., 14.

Marchand's own meticulous study of German Oriental scholarship seems to come to a similar conclusion. She thus launches her book with a lengthy quotation from the Indologist and oriental popularizer Herman Brunnhofer, who argued that

> The Bible is the book through which the world of the West, even in times of the most melancholy isolation, remains persistently tied to the Orient. Even when one ignores its character as a sacred book of revelation, and examines it from a historical and geographical standpoint, the Bible can be seen as a world-historical book of wonders, as the book which ever again reawakens in the Aryans of the West, who have deserted their homeland, that longing for the Orient which binds people together.[94]

The question of the Bible and, in particular, as Marchand demonstrates in her book, the question of protestant Germany's relationship to Judaism were motivating forces in the production of Oriental scholarship in the nineteenth century. "In Germany, Orientalist discourse," as Hess concludes, "was neither an apolitical body of scholarship nor an abstract colonial fantasy. . . . At key junctures, it . . . helped set the terms for the emancipation of Germany's Jewish minority, a group whose regeneration was often discussed with reference to experiments undertaken with subject peoples of French and British colonialism."[95]

To what extent does Arnold's essay, indebted as it is to a whole series of German preoccupations, inherit an anxiety about Jewish emancipation? The date of Arnold's essay is of particular interest. The essays that were published in *Culture and Anarchy* first appeared in print in 1867–68. During the course of the 1850s and 1860s a number of important laws were passed that contributed to the political emancipation of the Jews in Britain.[96] In 1858 following the Oath Bill, Jews were finally allowed to take their seats in Parliament and by 1868 Disraeli (a baptized Jew) had become prime minister.[97] While, as we have seen, Thomas Arnold was a stern opponent of Jewish emancipation, Matthew was in favor of granting civic rights to the Jews. *Culture and Anarchy*, rather than being a direct intervention into political debates about Jewish emancipation, could be seen as an attempt to deal with the cultural

94. Marchand 2009, xvii.

95. Hess 2002, 14.

96. As Salbstein (1982, 57) remarks, there were "no less than fourteen attempts to remove parliamentary disabilities [from the Jews]. One bill was presented in each of the years 1830, 1833, 1834, 1836, 1847–1848, 1849, 1851, 1853, 1854, and 1856 and four further measures were considered in 1857 and 1858."

97. On which see Salbstein 1982, Feldman 1994, and Bar-Yosef and Valman 2009.

consequences of the admission of Jews into political life. Unlike his father, Matthew Arnold had no desire to exclude Jews politically from the nation, but his ambivalence about English Semitism betrays his worries about the cultural force of Judaism in modern England.[98]

Arnold's "culturalization" of the Jewish question, then, is part of a wider intellectual context where live political debates were transposed into oblique scholarly interventions. The abstract philological constructs worked hard to obscure their referent in the Jews who inhabited the European cities that housed the very philological laboratories that produced them. As we have seen, even outside the laboratory from Heine to Arnold the willful meta-phorization of Jewish experience has been equally widespread. As Galchinsky writes: "At various times, Jewishness was abstracted and figuratively identi-fied with every aspect of the nation from its legal system to its outbreaks of socialism to its stock exchange to its monarchy to its journalism. By 1869 in *Culture and Anarchy*, Matthew Arnold was able to express this abstraction of Jewishness in an extreme form without any sense of impropriety." Or as Jean-Francois Lyotard phrases it: "What is most real about real Jews is that Europe, in any case, does not know what to do with them."[99] Of course, there is a strong motivation to be complicit in this metaphorization. As we have seen, Arnold's "Hebrews" and "Hellenes" are much more attractive as con-ceptual movements in cultural history or psychological dispositions than as vehicles of racial typology. It is precisely the literalization of "Hellenism" and "Hebraism" into "Aryan" and "Semite" from which the twentieth-century reader is bound to recoil. Poliakov opens his study of the development of the *Aryan Myth* with the following statement: "From about 1940 to 1944, the most important differentiation between the inhabitants of Europe was that between Aryans and Semites: the former was permitted to live, the latter were condemned to die."[100] The strong teleology of Poliakov's account is both what must ultimately lie behind our persistent interest in a Greek/Jew polarity, but at the same time make any study of it so problematic. "Hellenism" and "Hebraism" occupy that ambivalent position between the real and the meta-phorical that is what has ultimately made them such powerful expressions of the contested relationship, a relationship both real and metaphorical, be-tween antiquity and modernity.

This ambivalence was central to the mobilization of competing antiqui-

---

98. For the broader political context of Matthew Arnold's position on Jewish emancipation, see Cheyette 1993, 13–23.

99. Galchinksy 2004, 51; Lyotard 1990, 3.

100. Poliakov 1974, 1.

ties in the development of modern nationalism.[101] Greece and Rome played a crucial role in the emerging discourse of national identity from the French Revolution to the Greek War of Independence. The centrality of Greece to the foundation of a German national culture has been particularly well studied. German philhellenism was predicated on a notion of the continuity between Greek culture and the modern German spirit. This notion may have been formalized in Humboldtian ideal of Bildung but the ideology that lay behind it was pervasive. "The name of Greece," writes Hegel, "strikes home to the hearts of men of education in Europe, and more particularly is this so with us Germans." For, "among the Greeks," he asserts "we feel ourselves immediately at home for we are in the region of Spirit."[102] Writings about Greece in nineteenth-century Germany, then, were implicated in a debate about national identity. It is no surprise, then, to find Renan looking for a German prescription to the cultural malaise of France in the aftermath of the Franco-Prussian War. It is Renan's search for a new Bildung for France that Arnold correctly sees as being inextricably linked to a new Hellenism. But if the presence of the ideals and vocabulary of Hellenism in Renan's and Arnold's respective discourses of national identity should come as no surprise, the appearance of "Hebraism" as an axis of national identification is perhaps more striking.

And yet, as Cheyette and Valman have demonstrated, the Jews occupied an increasingly important space in European anxieties about national culture in the latter half of the nineteenth century:

> Arnolds' synthesis of Renan's racial discourse . . . and Heine's efficacious distinction between "Hebrew and Hellene" give a strong sense of how French, German and English understandings of "culture" or *Bildung* were brought together in relation to the cosmopolitan or extraterritorial construction of the Jew. The anxiety, especially in the second half of the nineteenth century, concerning whether culture or *Bildung* was to be linked with the nation-state, or was, in a more humanistic definition to transcend mere national characteristics, was often embodied in the figure of the Jew.[103]

Just as the Greeks had been chosen as the origin of a pan-European identity in the ideology of Philhellenism, the Jews had been singled out as a pan-European problem in the ideology of anti-Semitism. The Jews' presence in

101. For an influential twentieth-century account of the role of "Israel" and "Hellas" in the creation of modern nationalism see Kohn 1945.

102. Hegel 1974, 149; Hegel 1902, 300.

103. Cheyette and Valman 2004, 8.

a number of European countries made them a common source of debate across national boundaries. If the notion of Bildung since Humboldt had been linked to Hellenism, debates about culture in the second half of the nineteenth century repeatedly returned to the "question" of the Jews. Hebraism and Hellenism, then, cannot escape the discourse of nationalism in which they had become respectively embedded. Moreover, there is a striking mirroring of the discourses of Hellenism and Hebraism as they appear in the rhetorics of nineteenth-century nationalism. The historical confusion that marked the struggle for Greek independence, where philhellenes took arms in the struggle for the foundation of a modern nation wholly inspired by a frustrated identification with the ancient Greeks,[104] is paralleled in a vocabulary of Hebraism that both did and did not have anything to do with contemporary Jews.

Although I have been laying emphasis on the extent to which Arnold's essay engages in a willful abstraction of the political question of Jewish emancipation, one could make a parallel argument about the expressly depoliticized concept of "Hellenism" in his work. Not only does Arnold eschew the kind of overt politicization of classical Athens that was central to his fellow Victorian George Grote's program of political reform, he also (in common with many of the other figures in this book) makes no reference to contemporary Greeks and their political struggle for independence. This is all the more striking as many of his fellow philhellenic compatriots had openly supported the cause of Greek independence. Moreover, at the time that Arnold was writing this essay, England was still embroiled in a political debate about the Greek nation through the on-going debate about the "Eastern question." For Arnold, just as for Hegel and for Nietzsche, both "Greeks" and "Jews" inhabited a precarious middle ground between the historical and the ahistorical.

It is no coincidence that key figures in the development of comparative linguistics in the nineteenth century are also champions in the development of the modern theory of the nation. Both Herder and Renan are part of an essential canon of nationalist thought. Arnold's debt to their writings extends beyond the insights they offered into the distinctiveness of individual cultures. Instead, Arnold recognizes the extent to which their pronouncements on the nation were predicated on their wider explorations of linguistic and racial typology. For Arnold the question of England had become unthinkable outside the context of an opposition between Aryans and Semites. To be a modern nation one had to take sides in the conflict between the Greeks and Jews.

104. On which see Gourgouris 1996; Güthenke 2008.

4

Greeks, Jews, and the Death of God:
Feuerbach, Marx, Nietzsche

From Moses Mendelssohn to Matthew Arnold, discussions about the antithesis between Greeks and Jews have been haunted by the specter of Christianity. Lavater was able to see Mendelssohn's assumption of a Socratic identity as an indication that he would one day "recognize and worship the crucified Lord of Glory!" When Matthew Arnold, for his part, diagnosed a conflict between Hellenism and Hebraism as the pathology of English cultural life his commentators identified a raging debate between nonconformism and Catholicism as the true referents of Arnold's innovate terms. Hegel, in the wake of Kant, would examine Judaism's relationship to freedom and ethical consciousness and find it lacking where Christianity excelled. Hegel's Hellenism is a form of proto-Christianity that fashioned itself as the "precise opposite" of Judaic thought. Where we might have expected to find the Hellenic providing a standpoint from which to critique the dominant religion, instead we find pagan, polytheistic Greece repeatedly aligned with Christianity in the service of a critique of Judaism. The modern Athens/Jerusalem polarity has more in common with its ancient counterpart than one might have imagined: Tertullian still lurks behind the modern project of reconciling philosophy to Christianity.

But the age of the radical critique of religion that would follow the philosophies of Kant and Hegel would not abandon the antithesis between Greeks and Jews. When the so-called Young Hegelians began to formulate their assaults on established religion the conflict would take on a different flavor. The Hegelian leftists may primarily have been interested in political reform but they found themselves compelled to address the issue of religion that was at the core of the Hegelian scheme. The critique of Christianity and religion in general became a central plank of their radical outlook. Indeed, it was the

furious reaction to David Strauss's *Life of Jesus* that first gave a shared identity to the group of writers who came to be known as the Young Hegelians.[1]
Strauss's excavation of the Gospels was strongly influenced by Hegel but was
equally the product of the growing dominance of historical Wissenschaft.
In his highly controversial work, Strauss argued that the account of the life
of Jesus in the Gospels should not be treated as history but as myth. Drawing on Schelling's writings on myth, which were developed in part through a
dialogue with Mendelssohn's *Jerusalem*, Strauss aimed to expose the mythical
structure not just of the Old but of the New Testament, too. Strauss's assault
was conducted in the new language of historical scholarship.[2] But despite
its grounding in historical method, Strauss's work would provide the impetus for a much broader philosophical and political critique of religion that
formed the basis of revolutionary thinking in the mid-nineteenth century.

This chapter will explore how the opposition between Greeks and Jews
provided a crucial context for the formulation of three of the most influential
atheist writers in the nineteenth century: Feuerbach, Marx, and Nietzsche.
Their radical reevaluation of religion, I argue, has important continuities
with the philosophical explorations of Judaism and Hellenism I have been
tracing but also orients the discussion toward a new secular discourse. The
chapter will compare the role that religion (specifically Judeo-Christian religion) played in their respective writings on Greek culture. While each writer
champions Hellenism in the name of his critique of contemporary religion,
the "Greek" and the "Jew" take on very specific identities in their works. Nevertheless, while these figures have been instrumental in moving away from
the Christian worldview, they share a much contested and ambivalent role in
the development of modern anti-Semitism. This chapter will trace how the
conflict between Athens and Jerusalem played a crucial part in the shift from
Christian anti-Judaism to secular anti-Semitism.

Greek Nature and Jewish Appetites: Ludwig Feuerbach's *The Essence of Christianity*

In *The Essence of Christianity*, Ludwig Feuerbach morphs Strauss's historical insights into a philosophical meditation on the nature of religion. Published in 1841, the book was a sensation, immediately translated into English
by none other than the novelist George Eliot (whose first published work

---

1. See Massey 1983.

2. On Strauss and his relationship to the Greco-Roman conception of myth see Williamson
2004.

had been a translation of David Strauss' *Life of Jesus*). Revealing the influence of his master, Hegel, Feuerbach considered the publication of his book to have been "a world-historical event." Although he is mainly read today as the figure who explains the transition from Hegel to Marx, Van Harvey among others has suggested that Feuerbach deserves to be considered as a "master of suspicion" in his own right.[3] When Feuerbach set about formulating his script of evangelical atheism, he would return to the question of Judaism that had preoccupied Germany philosophy since Kant.

> The Doctrine of the Creation sprung out of Judaism; indeed, it is the characteristic, the fundamental doctrine of the Jewish religion. The principle which lies at its foundation is, however, not so much the principle of subjectivity as of egoism. The doctrine of the Creation in its characteristic significance arises only on that stand-point where man makes Nature only a servant of his will and needs, and hence in thought also degrades it to a mere machine, a product of will.[4]

Feuerbach's diagnosis of religion as the "principle of egoism" marks a profound development in the critique of Hegelian philosophy. Feuerbach would seek to invert Hegel's philosophy of Spirit by showing ideas to be the product of subjects rather than the other way round. As Harvey phrases it: "instead of construing 'thinking' as an entity, one simply transforms the equation and asserts that thinking is the activity of existing individuals. . . . If Hegel had argued that the cosmos is the 'objectification' of the Absolute Spirit, then Feuerbach and his friends could argue that God could be shown to be an objectification of the human spirit."[5] Although the Young Hegelians would themselves become the object of Marx's critique, it is not difficult to see in Feuerbach's method an anticipation of Marx's later polemic in *The German Ideology*: "In contrast to German philosophy, which descends from heaven to earth, here we ascend from earth to heaven. That is to say, we do not set out from what men imagine, but from real active men. Life is not determined by consciousness, but consciousness by life."[6] When Feuerbach asserts that "man makes Nature only a servant of his will and needs," he argues that God is the product of the activity of human thinking rather than the other way around. The story of Creation ascends from earth to heaven.

But Feuerbach's argument in the *Essence of Christianity* is also central be-

---

3. Harvey 1995, 3ff.
4. Feuerbach 2008, 93.
5. Harvey 1995, 10–11.
6. Marx and Engels 2004, 47.

cause it inaugurates the intellectual tradition of the psychologization of religion that will play such a profound role in the thought of Ricoeur's established
masters of suspicion: Marx, Nietzsche, and Freud. By exposing religious doctrine as a product of the will and necessity of the Jews, Feuerbach establishes
the origin of religion as a compensation for some internal psychological lack.
We have already seen in the previous chapter one dimension of this transformation of religious identity into the description of psychological disposition
in the very different writings of Heine and Arnold. Here Feuerbach places his
insight at the service of a systematic critique of religion. Diagnosing "egoism"
as the principle of Judaism, Feuerbach deduces the fundamental principles of
Judaism from the shortcomings of the Jewish people. The egoism of Judaism
is the projection of the egoism of the Jews.

And yet, despite the striking innovation of Feuerbach's method, his characterization of Judaism owes a great deal to former accounts. By uncovering the principle of "egoism" as the core of the Jewish religion, Feuerbach
showed himself to be fully in line with the persistent association of the Jews
with materialism. The spiritual sterility of the Jews had long been associated
to their miring in the here and now of the material world. Lacking a concept
of immortality, they had no share, as Hegel would claim, in eternity:

> Truth is beauty intellectually represented. . . . But how could they have an
> inkling of beauty who saw in everything only matter? How could they exercise
> reason and freedom who were only either mastered or masters? How could
> they have hoped even for the poor immortality in which consciousness of the
> individual is preserved, how could they have wished to persist in self-subsis-
> tence who had in fact renounced the capacity to will and even the very fact of
> their existence, who wished only for a continuation of the possession of their
> land through their posterity, a continuation of an undeserving and inglorious
> name in a progeny of their own, who never enjoyed any life or consciousness
> lifted above eating and drinking?[7]

And like Hegel, Feuerbach finds his other to the bodily orientated Jews in the
spiritually directed Greeks:

> The Greeks looked at Nature with the theoretic sense; they heard heavenly
> music in the harmonious course of the stars; they saw Nature rise from the
> foam of the all-producing ocean as Venus Anadyomene. The Israelites on the
> contrary, opened to Nature only the gastric sense; their taste for Nature lay
> only in the palate; their consciousness of God in eating manna. The Greek

7. Hegel 1948, 196.

addicted himself to polite studies, to fine arts, to philosophy; the Israelite did not rise above the alimentary view of theology.[8]

At the center of Feuerbach's opposition is not only the Greeks' addiction to philosophy versus the Jewish addiction to food, but also a diametrically opposed attitude to nature. As Bruce Lincoln argues: "Feuerbach developed a sharp structural contrast between Jewish and Greek mentalities and traced this to different myths of creation. Thus, where Jewish scripture had God create nature as an object for man's use, the Greeks identified nature with the gods, and contemplated both with reverence."[9] As we have seen, Hegel also saw the relationship to nature as playing a fundamental role in the incommensurability of Greeks and Jews. For Hegel, the reaction to the flood in the time of Noah played an instrumental role in the development of Jews' despotic mastery of the natural world. Like Feuerbach, Hegel sees the exercise of Jewish "will" as characteristic of Judaism's desire to enslave natural forces.

But where Hegel founds the Greek/Jew opposition on a binary of freedom and enslavement, Feuerbach goes much further in contrasting the theoretical attributes of the Greeks to the instrumentalism of Jewish theology. To be sure, Feuerbach builds on earlier depictions of Judaism, and, in particular Hegel's writings, which emphasized the extent to which the Jews subordinated the world to their particular theological worldview. Feuerbach's sentiments are certainly foreshadowed when Hegel writes: "the whole world Abraham regarded simply as his opposite; if he did not take it to be a nullity, he looked on it as sustained by the God who was alien to it. Nothing in nature was supposed to have any part in God; everything was simply under God's mastery."[10]

But despite the undoubted continuities, a fundamental difference of method underpins their analyses. In the Hegelian version, it is the Jewish devotion to a tyrannical God that explains the inability of individual Jews to form social relationships and a bond with the natural world. For Feuerbach, it is the individual Jews' egoism that gives rise to their "utilitarian" religion:

> The Jews maintained their peculiarity to this day. Their principle, their God, is the most practical principle in the world, —namely, egoism; and moreover egoism in the form of religion. Egoism is the God who will not let his servants come to shame. Egoism is essentially monotheistic, for it has only one, only self, as its end. Egoism strengthens cohesion, concentrates man on himself, gives him a consistent principle of life; but it makes him theoretically narrow,

8. Feuerbach 2008, 95.
9. Lincoln 1999, 57.
10. Hegel 1948, 187.

because indifferent to all which does not relate to the well-being of the self. Hence science, like art, arises only out of polytheism, for polytheism is the frank, open, unenvying sense of all that is good and beautiful without distinction, the sense of the world, of the universe. The Greeks looked abroad into the wide world that they might extend their vision; the Jews to this day pray with their faces turned towards Jerusalem.[11]

As Andrée Lerousseau argues: "the term of 'utilitarian' as used by Feuerbach translates the intimate link between so-called Jewish materialism and a collective egoism. The Jew is impervious to his neighbour, the non-Jew, other than when he is useful to him."[12] Feuerbach transforms a long-held theological condemnation of Judaism's materialism into a sociological analysis of contemporary Jews. Moreover, his analysis links historical Judaism's most defining characteristic—its particularism—to his psychological analysis of the individual Jew. The Jews' collective status as chosen people is seen in continuity with the indifference of the contemporary Jew "to all which does not relate to the well-being of the self." In contrasting this egoistic predisposition to the Greeks, Feuerbach returns his analysis to some of the more familiar tropes of the Jew/Greek binary: where the Jews are narrow, the Greeks are expansive; where the Jews have utility, the Greeks have beauty; the Jews have political cohesion, the Greeks freedom and openness; the Jews are mired in practicality, the Greeks invent the arts and philosophy. But despite the predictability of this distribution of attributes, one cannot help but be struck by the innovation of Feuerbach's vocabulary. Feuerbach has made a conceptual leap beyond the historical schema of a Hegel. In his proclamation that "In the Israelites, monotheistic egoism excluded the free theoretic tendency. . . . The polytheistic sentiment, I repeat, is the foundation of art and science," we hear the echoes not just of Herder but of a much broader investment in historical *Wissenschaft*.[13]

Israel is the historical definition of the specific nature of the religious consciousness, save only that here this consciousness was circumscribed by the limits of a particular, national interest. Hence, we need only let these limits fall, and we have the Christian religion. Judaism is worldly Christianity; Christianity, spiritual Judaism. The Christian religion is the Jewish religion purified from national egoism, and yet, it is certainly another, a new religion.[14]

11. Feuerbach 2008, 95–96.
12. Lerousseau 2001, 199.
13. Feuerbach 2008, 96.
14. Ibid., 100.

It was this vision of Israel as a "historical definition" that enabled Feuerbach, moreover, to differentiate Judaism from Christianity. In Hegel the break between Judaism and Christianity is absolute: "Jesus did not fight merely against one part of the Jewish fate; to have done so would have implied that he was himself in the toils of another part, and he was not; het set himself against the whole. Thus he was himself raised above it and tried to raise his people above it too."[15] The philosophical premise of Christianity is so alien to the Judaic principle that it must oppose it in all its forms. Indeed, as the movement of Hegel's analysis makes clear, it is to the Greek rather than the Jew that the Christian will turn to ground his philosophical outlook. In Feuerbach, by contrast, the splitting of Judaism is a historical accident. Christianity is Judaism minus the nation. Christianity, in other words, does not presuppose a doctrinal split from Judaism but rather represents a movement away from the collective national interest of the Jews to the individual spiritual needs of the Christian. By defining Judaism as "worldly Christianity" and Christianity as spiritual Judaism, Feuerbach appears merely to be rehearsing a traditional opposition. Indeed when he goes on to contrast Judaism as the religion of law to Christianity as a theology of love, his tropes could not seem more familiar: "The highest idea, the God of a political community, of a people whose political system expresses itself in the form of religion, is Law, the consciousness of the law as an absolute divine power; the highest idea, the God of unpolitical, unworldly feeling is Love."[16]

Feuerbach seems to be drawing wholesale on previous philosophical explorations, from Kant's characterization of Judaism as a politics through Hegel's critique of the legalism of Judaism to his affirmation of Christianity as the religion of love. And yet, as Harvey has suggested, the premise of Feuerbach's analysis remains the profound continuity between Jewish and Christian theology: "Unlike Schleiermacher or Hegel, he was not making an invidious comparison of Judaism with Christianity but, on the contrary, was making the point, quite unrepresentative at the time, that Christianity as a religion has simply radicalized and individualized the egoism already present in Judaism."[17] In fact, as Harvey goes on to argue, the critique of Judaism has the function of revealing the common tendency of monotheisms and their doctrines of creation *ex nihilo* to treat nature as the instrument of human will and need. "Whereas some cultures tend to think of nature as an end in itself or, as in Greece, an object of theoretical reflection, Judaism

15. Hegel 1948, 205.
16. Feuerbach 2008, 101.
17. Harvey 1995, 86.

made the world of nature the vassal of self-interest."[18] Judaic and Christian doctrine, then, are both condemned for their self-interest but Judaism nevertheless remains the exemplary case. While, in stark contrast to Hegel, in Feuerbach Christianity is no longer functioning as a covert Hellenism, it is still to Judaism that he will turn to provide his antithesis to the noble Greeks. Judeo-Christianity may come in for criticism as an entity in its contrast to pagan polytheism but it is still *qua* Judaism that Christianity will ultimately be denounced.

When Feuerbach uncovered "egoism" as the essence of Judaism, then, he was both drawing on an established philosophical tradition and steering the analysis in a new direction. On the one hand, Carlebach claims, "Feuerbach's 'egoism' was partly derived from Kantian ethical theory."[19] On the other hand, Feuerbach metamorphosed the tropes of the philosophical critique of Judaism into a new antitheological vocabulary. Following in the footsteps of the rationalist historicism of David Strauss, Feuerbach transformed the old debates *within* the philosophy of religion into a rejection of the philosophy of religion itself. In Feuerbach, concepts that had previously been the preoccupation of Kant and Hegel are almost imperceptibly altered so that they come to take on contrary meanings. Carlebach gives a good sense of Feuerbach's role in the philosophical treatment of Judaism when he analyzes the evolution of the concept of Jewish servitude: "We might say that there is here a notion of the continuity of Jewish self-imposed slavery first to the law (Kant), then to God (Hegel), to egoism (Feuerbach) and then to money (Marx)."[20]

That Feuerbach's contribution was vital to the development of Karl Marx's thought is well known. In Carlebach's comprehensive genealogy of Marx's writings about Judaism, Feuerbach's vision is so close to that of Marx that, he maintains, "all that Marx had to do was to strip the Feuerbachian thesis of its religious context to produce his 'real' image of the 'worldly' Jew."[21] But if Marx's analysis of Judaism can be characterized as Feuerbach without the theology, the role that Hellenism played in this progression still needs to be explored. As we have seen, the Greek/Jew opposition was central to Feuerbach's formulation of Jewish egoism. The pivotal role he ascribes to this antithesis both helps locate Feuerbach's contribution in a much longer debate and also represents an important stage in shifting the discourse of Hellenism from a theological to a secular order. While many scholars have identified

18. Ibid., 84.
19. Carlebach 1978, 108.
20. Ibid., 153.
21. Ibid., 109.

Feuerbach's critique as exerting a powerful influence over Marx and have, in particular, insisted that his analysis of nature is central to understanding Marx's developing theories of alienation and the species-being, the opposition between Hellenic and the Hebraic conceptions of nature that lies at the foundation of the Feuerbachian analysis is ignored by scholars of Marx. This remains true despite an increasing interest and acknowledgment of the role that the Greeks played in the formulation of Marx's thought, from his dependence on Aristotle for his development of a theory of value to his conception of the unity of the Greek state, which he shared with Schiller and Hegel.[22]

But while Marx's depictions of ancient societies are compulsively drawn back to eighteenth-century German philhellenism, he also creates a vision of the Greeks that goes well beyond even Feuerbach in its commitment to radical secularism. Marx places the Greeks in an entirely new philosophy of history. While elements of the Greek/Jew opposition extending as far back as Mendelssohn seem to pervade Feuerbach's analysis in *Essence of Christianity*, what role will this tradition play in Marx's writings about Judaism? I want to try to make sense of Marx's early essay "On the Jewish Question" by reexamining the presence of Greece and Rome in his thought and exploring the role they play in defining the contours both of the modern secular state and its relationship to the Jews. Marx's conception of the Jewish question, I will suggest, cannot stand outside a history of the opposition between Athens and Jerusalem.

Prometheus and the Pentateuch: Karl Marx "On the Jewish Question"

To democracy all other forms of state stand as its Old Testament.
KARL MARX

Marx famously said that "the criticism of religion is the premise of all criticism."[23] It comes as no surprise, then, to find among Marx's most prominent early writings an exploration of the relationship between the church and the state. What is perhaps more surprising is that the particular religion that finds itself at the heart of Marx's critique is not the dominant religion of the state—Christianity—but Judaism. Marx's controversial essay "On the Jewish Question" occupies an ambivalent place both in Marx's oeuvre in general and his writings about religion more specifically. Indeed it has given rise to diametrically opposed interpretations. Not only is the nature of its

22. See McCarthy 1992; Kain 1982.
23. Marx 1992, 243.

criticism of the Jews and Judaism subject to a huge divergence of opinion, its centrality to the development of Marxist thought has repeatedly come into question. Thus Robert Misrahi's book-length study, which contrary to some others does not shy away from identifying the "implicit and manifest anti-Semitism" of the essay, nevertheless argues that Marx's anti-Semitism is non-Marxist, it is extraneous to the content of Marxism: "Marx's anti-Semitism is nothing but a crisis point, it is a momentary explosion of a contradiction in Marxist doctrine and more generally in Marx's overall project."[24] Misrahi identifies Marx's anti-Semitism as a personal failing of Marx "the man" independent of the future development of his "objective," "rationalist" philosophy. Misrahi thus examines the philosophical and social context of Marx's essay purely as an elucidation of his "subjective" proclivities rather than providing any elucidation of the genealogy of Marxist thought. André Lerousseau takes Misrahi to task, arguing that the representation of Judaism was not only intrinsic to Marx's thought, but it also played a foundational role in the creation of a whole tradition of German philosophy. According to Lerousseau, the development of idealist and rationalist philosophy in Germany from the mid-eighteenth century was constituted through a dialectical relationship to the figure of the "Jew."

Paul Rose for his part claims that "On the Jewish Question" is so central to Marx's thought that it "marks the first real step on the road to *The Communist Manifesto*." "Nevertheless" he argues, the essay "has been persistently undervalued as a crucial step in the evolution of Marx's thought. Marx himself suppressed any mention of it when he reconstructed his intellectual biography in 1858. Many later commentators have been too embarrassed by its ferocious Jew-hatred to recognize the genesis of humane Marxism in such a repellent essay."[25] The debates about the significance of Marx's writings on Judaism to his wider project reflect a wider anxiety about the centrality of the critique of Judaism not just to nineteenth-century German thought broadly conceived but more specifically to the emergence of the radical and revolutionary movements in the middle of the century.

Despite its obvious break with the political and philosophical premises of Moses Mendelssohn's *Jerusalem*, Marx's "On the Jewish Question" can be seen to inherit many of its basic preoccupations. Both essays are divided into two parts. The first section of Marx's essay, like Mendelssohn's, addresses the more general issue of the separation of church and state; the second section deals with the distinctive relationship of Judaism to the political sphere.

24. Misrahi 1972, 136.
25. Rose 1990, 298.

Marx's starting point was a radicalization of the argument made by his fellow Young Hegelian, Bruno Bauer, in his own essay on the Jewish question. Bauer argued that Jews would never achieve true emancipation in a Christian state unless both the state and the Jews emancipate themselves from their religion. Freedom would not be achieved through the state's granting of political rights to the Jews because they would still be enslaved to their own religion. Moreover the Christian state could not emancipate the Jews because it wasn't itself emancipated. "Jews must give up Judaism, Christians Christianity."[26] But despite its semblance of balance, as Carlebach makes clear, Bauer reserves his harshest criticism for the Jews.

Marx takes Bauer's arguments about the limits of Jewish emancipation and extends his scope to a discussion of political and social emancipation more generally. But central to Marx's analysis will be the observation that Bauer fails to move beyond his criticism of the Christian state to a denunciation of the state as such and his consequent failure to explore the relationship between political emancipation and human emancipation.

> The German Jews seek emancipation. What sort of emancipation do they want? Civil, political emancipation. Bruno Bauer answers them: No one in Germany is politically emancipated. We ourselves are not free. How then could we liberate you? You Jews are egoists if you demand a special emancipation for yourselves as Jews. You ought to work as Germans for the political emancipation of Germany, and as men for the emancipation of mankind, and consider your particular sort of oppression and ignominy not as an exception to the rule but rather as a confirmation of it.[27]

From the very start Marx opens up the question of emancipation by pluralizing its potential referents. Bauer's claim that no one in Germany is politically emancipated calls for a recognition of a communality of purpose beyond the narrow distinctions of religious identification. Indeed, Marx explicitly relates the Jews' call for emancipation to the charge of "egoism" so resonant of Feuerbach's analysis. But Marx turns a debate about exceptionalism, which had for so long preoccupied the philosophical and theological discussion of Judaism, into a purely political question. For Feuerbach the diagnosis of the Jews' egoism results from his analysis of their theology. Hegel's exegesis in "The Spirit of Christianity and Its Fate" proceeds from an exemplification of the theological limitations of Judaism to an assertion of the Jews' incapacity to play a role in political life. Kant uncovers Judaism's true identity as a

26. Carlebach 1978, 129.
27. Marx 2000, 46–47.

politics as a symptom of its moral and spiritual poverty as a religion. If the theological debate about Judaism seems to have been compulsively drawn to a debate about the political realm, it had nonetheless been founded on a critique of the religious identity of the Jews. Even Mendelssohn, whose politicized account of the Jews had inadvertently led the way to Kant's critique, had used the theological particularity of the Jews as the basis for his call for political emancipation in his *Jerusalem*. For Marx, the current political debate about the Jews is inextricably linked to this inescapable theological frame of reference. The specificity of the German "Jewish question" owes its identity to a theologized conception of the political.

> The Jewish question always presents itself differently according to the state in which the Jew lives. In Germany, where there is no political state, no state as such, the Jewish question is a purely theological one. The Jew finds himself in religious opposition to the state which recognizes Christianity as its foundation. This state is a professed theologian. Criticism is here criticism of theology, a two-sided criticism of Christian and Jewish theology. But we are still always moving inside theology however critically we may be moving.[28]

The German state is in need of political emancipation. Unlike its French or American counterparts, which have succeeded in attaining the basis of political emancipation through the emancipation of the state from theology, the German state remains "a professed theologian." Marx saw the strong necessity of achieving this form of political emancipation. "Political emancipation is of course a great progress. Although it is not the final form of human emancipation in general, it is nevertheless the final form of emancipation inside the present world order." The American Revolution, as Marx says, is an example of a political emancipation that succeeded in exiling religion from the public to the private sphere. But far from real emancipation, what they achieve is: "The decomposition of man into Jew and citizen, protestant and citizen, religious man and citizen, this decomposition is no trick played upon political citizenship, no avoidance of political emancipation. It is political emancipation itself. The political way of emancipating oneself from religion."[29] The French Revolution with its violent anticlerical stance may provide Marx with a more radical example. And indeed, it was the French Revolution that first established political emancipation for the Jews in Europe.

> Of course, in times when the political state is born violently as such out of civil society, when man's self-liberation tries to complete itself in the form of politi-

28. Ibid., 50.
29. Ibid., 53, 54.

cal self-liberation, the state must go as far as abolishing, destroying religion, but only in the same way as it goes as far as abolishing private property, at the most, by declaring a maximum, by confiscation or a progressive tax, or in the same way as it abolished life by the guillotine.[30]

Religion, like the monarch's head, may have been sacrificed in the initial moment of revolutionary fervor, but such emancipation is ultimately short-lived:

> In moments of particular self-consciousness political life tries to suppress its presuppositions, civil society and its elements, and to constitute itself as the real, harmonious life of man. However, this is only possible through violent opposition to its own conditions, by declaring the revolution to be permanent. The political drama therefore ends necessarily with the restoration of religion, private property, and all the elements of civil society, just as war ends with peace.[31]

Marx's remarks here strongly anticipate his striking characterization of the French Revolution in his analysis of the Eighteenth Brumaire. In this later context, Marx's analysis of the failure of the French Revolution as a bourgeois revolution is formulated through sustained analogy with the Roman Republic. The *Eighteenth Brumaire* famously formulates the role of the Rome in the French Revolution as an instance of history repeating itself.

> Men make their own history but they do not make it as they please; they do not make it under self-selected circumstances but under circumstances existing, given from the past. Tradition from all the dead generations weighs like a nightmare on the brain of the living. And it is just when they appear to be revolutionising themselves and their circumstances, in creating something unprecedented, it is in just such epochs of revolutionary crisis, that they nervously summon up the spirits of the past, borrowing from them their names, marching orders, uniforms, in order to enact new scenes in world history.[32]

Marx's earlier comments in "On the Jewish Question" about the illusion of the permanent revolution are here transformed into an analysis of the illusion of an unprecedented revolution. There can never be such a thing as an "unprecedented" event. Marx seems to be claiming the French Revolution was an event not despite but because of the fact that it had a precedent. On the other hand, it could be argued that Marx is proclaiming that the very innovation of the event is predicated on the return of some "spirit of the past."

30. Ibid., 55.
31. Ibid.
32. Ibid., 19–20.

The "newness" of the French Revolution consists in its untimely reenaction of the "very ancient" in the "very modern."[33] Marx writes: "The heroes as well as the parties and the masses of the old French Revolution, achieved in Roman costumes and with Roman phrases the task of their time." The active agents of the French revolution achieve the "task of their time." "Men," as Marx says, "make their *own* history" (emphasis added). This is no regressive, nostalgic backward gaze, but rather a progressive and active mobilization of the past in the present.

In fact, it is this very moment identified by Marx that Walter Benjamin elected as the archetypal instance of what he called the *Jetztzeit*: "History is the subject of a structure whose site is not homogeneous, empty time, but time filled by the presence of the now. Thus, to Robespierre ancient Rome was a past charged with the time of the now which he blasts out of the continuum of history. The French Revolution saw itself as Rome reincarnate."[34] In his analysis of revolution Marx reveals how "agents in the present are compelled and yet simultaneously restricted, by the imagery and symbols of the past when they come to fulfill some historic task":[35]

> Once the new social formation was established, the antediluvian colossi, and along with them the resurrected Romans—the Brutuses, the Gracchuses, the Publicolas, the tribunes, the senators, Caesar himself—all vanished. . . . Wholly absorbed in the production of wealth and peaceful competitive struggle, it could no longer comprehend that the spectres of Roman times had kept watch over its cradle.[36]

As Derrida phrases it, "One has to forget the spectre and the parody, Marx seems to be saying, for history to continue. But if one contents oneself with forgetting, this becomes bourgeois platitude, life as usual. One must therefore not forget, one must remember while forgetting enough, in this very memory, to 'recover the spirit of revolution not to relaunch its spectre.'"[37] Marx seems to be suggesting that the seeds of bourgeois self-satisfaction are both intrinsic and completely external to Rome. He implies that the reception of Rome is compelled to reinscribe itself in an inexorable history of bourgeois ascendancy. And yet, it is precisely by *forgetting* Rome that the French have precipitated this impasse. "In the strict classical traditions of the Roman re-

33. To quote Derrida see Kearney 1984, 112.
34. Benjamin 1973, 263.
35. Cowling and Martin 2002, 5.
36. Marx 2002, 20.
37. Derrida 1994, 110.

public its gladiators found the ideals and art forms, the self-deceptions that they needed, in order to hide from themselves the constrained, bourgeois character of their struggles, and to keep themselves emotionally at level of high historical tragedy."[38] For Marx, Rome is both the promise of an ideal and ultimately a "self-deception." But the responsibility of this self-deception rests ultimately with its receivers. Marx leaves open the possibility that Rome could be an ideal which precisely prevents a return to the same. In fact, if anything could save the revolutionaries from this false consciousness it is the spectre of Rome "watching over their cradle."

To use Marx's language from "On the Jewish Question," the French Revolution "failed to constitute itself as the real, harmonious life of man."[39] The role of Rome, however, in this incomplete revolution remains ambivalent. In terms of the development of Marx's argument about the necessity of political emancipation, the Jews, just like everyone else, clearly need Rome, but "the real, harmonious life of man" needs more than Rome.

Republican Rome, in other words, may provide a model for the kind of political emancipation that Bauer had in mind but for Marx the paradigm it provides is necessarily incomplete. So although, ironically in contrast to Hegel, Marx cannot be viewed as a straightforward advocate of political rights for the Jews, there is no doubt that the purpose of Marx's rebuke of Bauer was to show up the limitations of the concept of political emancipation as such. As Marx puts it:

> We do not change secular questions into theological ones. We change theological questions into secular ones. History has for long enough been resolved into superstition: we now resolve superstition into history. The question of the relationship of political emancipation to religion becomes for us a question of the relationship of political emancipation to human emancipation.[40]

Indeed, as Rose and others have argued, "On the Jewish Question" represents Marx's earliest formulation of his crucial insight that not only could political emancipation exist side by side with economic enslavement, but also that the political emancipation afforded by the capitalist state actually *requires* economic enslavement.[41] "Now he repudiated the self-interest of civil society and, claiming that man was essentially a 'species being,' preached an ethic of social love that would destroy the egoism and self-interest on which

---

38. Marx 2002, 20.
39. Marx 2000, 55.
40. Ibid., 51.
41. My thanks to Elizabeth Wingrove for helping me with this formulation.

the 'state'—whether 'rational,' 'free,' or not—was founded."[42] As Carlebach argues, "It is clear, therefore, that the essay contains in rudimentary, but unmistakable, form some of the most fundamental concepts in the Marxian system, namely: the criticism of civil i.e. bourgeois society; a materialist approach to history; the analysis of the 'rights of man' as inadequate; the call for a revolution more profound than the earlier ones; the vision of a perfect society."[43] But if "On the Jewish Question" has proved crucial in the development of Marx's critique of the liberal concepts of political rights, why is it specifically Judaism that stands in the way of the real revolution? Or to put it another way, how does one make sense of the much contested disjunction between the first and the second half of the essay?

The progression from the first to the second half has variously been characterized as the movement from the theological to the secular, from the critique of state religion to the critique of the Jews, from political to human emancipation. It could equally be seen as the progression from Rome to Athens. Where we have seen that Marx viewed the Roman republic as an exemplar of political emancipation, he inherits from Schiller and Hegel a conception of classical Athens as the ideal of an unalienated society in which human emancipation was the necessary precondition of political freedom.[44]

> Freedom, the feeling of one's dignity, will have to be awakened again in these men. Only this feeling, which disappeared from the world with the Greeks and with Christianity vanished into the blue mist of heaven, can again transform society into a community of men to achieve their highest purposes, a democratic state.[45]

As George McCarthy puts it: "For Marx, the realization of human possibilities as a universal being demands a more radical critique and a more structural transformation of society."[46] Where the French revolutionaries had looked to Rome as a source of political rights, Marx would look to democratic Athens as a source of human freedom. Kain argues, building on the models of Hegel and Schiller,

> Marx's perfected state overcomes opposition between man and state, overcomes the opposition between public and private interest, through democracy, the self-determination of the people. The constitution appears as the

42. Rose 1990, 297.
43. Carlebach 1978, 165.
44. See Kain 1982; McCarthy 1990, 175–89; Morley 2009; Yack 1986.
45. Marx 1967, 206.
46. McCarthy 1990, 188–89.

free product of man. The citizens determine the whole. This is not the rational but the aesthetic state. Its goal is to regain the substantial unity of the ancient Greek state.[47]

And yet, despite Marx's debt to Hegel and Schiller in his early writings, his vision of Greece is predicated on a revolutionary philosophy of history. In Marx's new philosophy of history, Athens and Jerusalem will occupy radically altered positions.

> We attempt to break the theological conception of the problem. The question of the Jews' capacity for emancipation is changed into the question what particular social element needs to be overcome in order to abolish Judaism? For the fitness of the present-day Jew for emancipation is bound up with the relationship of Judaism to the emancipation of the contemporary world.
>
>   . . . Let us discuss the actual secular Jew, not the Sabbath Jew as Bauer does, but the everyday Jew.
>
>   Let us look for the secret of the Jew not in his religion, but let us look for the secret of religion in the actual Jew.
>
>   What is the secular basis of Judaism? Practical need, selfishness.
>
>   What is the secular cult of the Jew? Haggling. What is his secular god? Money.
>
>   Well then, an emancipation from haggling and money, from practical, real Judaism would be the self-emancipation of our age.[48]

Rose writes that in his project of exposing the myth of emancipation in bourgeois civic society, "Judaism was uniquely suited to Marx's purpose, *Judentum* might designate the religion of the Jews and at the same time represent their existence as a socio-economic community. Furthermore, *Judentum* was an especially apt way of characterizing the consciousness of a bourgeois society based on money and self-interest."[49] "For" if "the fitness of the present-day Jew for emancipation is bound up with the relationship of Judaism to the emancipation of the contemporary world" this is because the condition of being a Jew shares a great deal with the more generalized condition of the contemporary. Turning on its head the pervasive stereotype in the German Enlightenment and post-Enlightenment critique of Judaism as a religion stuck in history, Marx represents Judaism as the ultimate modernity. For Hegel, "it may be said of the Jewish people that it is precisely because they stand before the portal of salvation that they are, and have been, the most reprobate

47. Kain 1982, 103.

48. Marx 2000, 65–66.

49. Rose 1990, 297–98.

and rejected."[50] Hegel's Jews stand before the portal of salvation, but more important they are also locked out of the dialectic of historical progress. In Hegel's opposition between Greeks and Jews it is the Greeks' foundational role in the dynamics of world-historical progress that is constantly opposed to the Jews' inability to enter the realm of history. As Lévinas argues, it is the Greeks' privileged participation in the historical, which means that for Hegel "the ultimate meaning of modernity will be . . . essentially Greek."[51] Where for Hegel, modernity is essentially Greek, for Marx it is irredeemably Jewish.

At the core of Marx's reversal of the Hegelian conception of Greeks and Jews is a reversal of his historical method. Marx not only topples a deeply held conviction about Judaism's incompatibility with the modern world, he does this by reversing the premises of previous historical accounts.

> The method by which Marx achieved the final reduction of the Jew, to expose his "real social significance," is the same . . . which had enabled Marx to turn Hegelianism, which was standing on its head, back on its feet. This was accomplished by reversing subject and predicate, so that if, according to Hegel, reality is the appearance of the idea, then to Marx the idea is the appearance of reality. If for Hermes, religion makes man, then for Marx, man makes religion. If for Bruno Bauer, the secret of the Jew is his religion, then for Marx, the secret of religion is the Jew. Finally, then, if for Kant (and indeed most of Christian Western Europe) the Jew is a trader, then for Marx, *the trader is the Jew.*[52]

The project of revealing the "real social significance of the Jew" for Marx involves developing a new understanding of history that moves beyond the theologized conception of the Hegelian dialectic. The reversal of the positions of the Greeks and the Jews in the account of world history can be directly mapped onto the overturning of the Hegelian dialectic by dialectical materialism. It is only by privileging the idea over the real that Hegel could claim that modernity was Greek and not Jewish. The Greek conception of freedom that Hegel valorized has nothing in common with the Jewish call for emancipation:

> The Jew has emancipated himself in a Jewish manner, not only by acquiring financial power, but also because both through him and without him, *money* has become a world-power and the practical Jewish spirit has become the practical spirit of the Christian peoples. . . .

50. Hegel 1977, 206.
51. Lévinas 1963, 329.
52. Carlebach 1978, 153.

> We therefore recognize in Judaism the presence of the universal and the *contemporary anti-social* element whose historical evolution—eagerly nurtured by the Jews in its harmful aspects—has arrived at its present peak.[53]

As Marx insists, "Judaism has maintained itself not in spite of, but because of history."[54] The progress of Judaism is the historical progress of capitalism.

> It is not only in the Pentateuch and the Talmud that we find the essence of the contemporary Jew: we find it in contemporary society, not as an abstract but as a very empirical essence, not as a limitation of the Jew but as the Jewish limitations of society.[55]

But despite Marx's emphasis on the role of the real in his conception of history, Rose comments,

> Marx fluctuates constantly between *Judentum* as a purely allegorical depiction of civil society and as a term of actual Jewry. On one page he can emphasize first that *Judentum* is the essence of civil society and then smoothly shift to the claim that the actual Jew's real essence is economic. The distinction between the Jew as a real person and the Jew as a metaphor is hazed over intentionally throughout the essay.[56]

The metaphorization of the Jewish experience, as we have seen in the previous chapters, is not new to Marx. The abstraction of the Jewish experience into a convenient sound bite of social criticism may only reach its culmination some twenty-five years after the publication of "On the Jewish Question" in Matthew Arnold's essay "Hellenism and Hebraism" but, as we saw in the previous chapter, Arnold's metaphors have their roots in a current of German thought that extends backwards through Marx's contemporary Heine to the end of the eighteenth century.

The analysis of Judaism may sit uneasily with a purely materialist analysis of the history of modernity, but its absent other, the promise of the idealized society, has an even more precarious relationship to the historical. If Marx's Jerusalem aspires to be both "real" and "contemporary," what becomes of his Athens? We have seen how the origins of Feuerbach's critique of religion lie in his praise of the Greek conception of nature. Marx can be seen to have developed his own critique through an analysis of Greek culture. It is well known that Marx started off his academic career as a classicist writing his doctoral

---

53. Marx 2000, 66.
54. Ibid., 67.
55. Ibid., 69.
56. Rose 1990, 301.

thesis on the difference between Epicurus's and Democritus's conceptions of nature. Critics have traced the outline of the development of Marx's historical materialism in his discussion of the difference between Epicurean and Democritean atomism. Moreover, in Marx's exegesis of Epicurus's controversial introduction of the concept of the atomic swerve, we can uncover the origins of a debate about the role of free will and determinism in Marx's writings that has polarized his readers.

> Philosophy makes no secret of it. The confession of Prometheus: "In simple words, I hate the pack of gods" (Aeschylus, *Prometheus Bound*) is its own confession, its own aphorism against all heavenly and earthly gods who do not acknowledge human self-consciousness as the highest divinity. It will have none other beside.[57]

For Sannwald the implications of Marx's doctoral thesis for the later development of his critique of religion are clear:

> Marx placed Epicurus, the greatest philosopher of the Greek Enlightenment, in the line with Prometheus, the opponent of Zeus. It is the battle against the gods and faith in the autonomy of human self-consciousness, which unites both. Also Marx's atheism lives genuinely from the ideal of the completely independent man, who at last wants no other master but himself.[58]

And yet, despite Marx's immersion at the beginning of his career in the materialist philosophy of the Greeks, his own analyses of Greek culture often straddle the divide between materialism and a nostalgic idealism more reminiscent of an earlier tradition of German philhellenism. As such, his analyses of Greek culture often raise the question of the very validity of his own materialist philosophy. Frederic Jameson has recently commented:

> One . . . remembers Marx's own feelings for antiquity: Prometheus and Aristotle's theory of value, Epicurus and Hegel's thoughts on Homer. And then there is the question with which the great 1857 draft introduction to the *Grundrisse* breaks off. . . . Marx was anything but nostalgic, and he understood that the polis was a limited and thereby contradictory social formation to which one could scarcely return. And that any future socialism would be far more complex than capitalism itself."[59]

But despite Jameson's assurance that Marx has moved beyond nostalgia, the same paradoxical relationship to the classical past seems to haunt Marx's

---

57. Marx 1975, 30.
58. Sannwald 1957, 70; translated in McCarthy 1990, 21.
59. Jameson 2009, 116.

writings about Greece as had characterized his discussion of the Roman spirit of the French Revolution. Such an ambivalent perspective, for instance, subtends his well-known discussion of Greek art in the draft general introduction to the *Grundrisse*. Marx is confronted with a problem for the materialist conception of art:

> It is well known that certain periods of the highest development of art stand in no direct connection to the general development of society, or to the material basis and skeleton structure of its organization. Witness the examples of the Greeks as compared with the modern nations, or even Shakespeare.[60]

In contrasting the "arsenal of Greek art" to that of our own time, Marx can sketch out the necessary relations between the "conditions of production" and the aesthetic forms of the ancients:

> Let us take for instance the relation of Greek art, and that of Shakespeare's time, to our own. It is a well-known fact that Greek mythology was not only the arsenal of Greek art, but also the very ground from which it had sprung. Is the view of nature and social relations which shaped Greek imagination and Greek art possible in the age of automatic machinery and railways and locomotives and telegraphs? Where does Vulcan come in against Roberts & Co.? Jupiter, as against a lightening conductor? and Hermes, as against the *Crédit Mobilier*? All mythology masters and dominates and shapes the forces of nature in and through the imagination: hence it disappears as soon as man gains mastery over nature.[61]

For Marx the relationship between Greek art and Greek mythology is indissoluble. At the core of the mythology of the Greeks was a different attitude to nature. Feuerbach grounds his opposition between pagan polytheism and monotheistic Judaism on a contrast between the Greeks' and the Jews' conception of nature. Where for Feuerbach the Jew makes "Nature only a servant of his will and needs, and hence in thought also degrades [it] to a mere machine, a product of will," the Greek makes of his worship of nature a religion. So Feuerbach concludes "science, like art, arises only out of polytheism, for polytheism is the frank, open, unenvying sense of all that is good and beautiful without distinction, the sense of the world, of the universe."[62]

Feuerbach's arguments about the essential relationship between art and polytheism appear to lie behind Marx's pronouncements about Greek my-

---

60. Marx 2000, 394.
61. Ibid.
62. Feuerbach 2008, 93, 95–96.

thology. Marx draws his dividing line between the Greeks and the moderns by contrasting the ancient reverence for nature to its instrumentalization in "the age of automatic machinery." "In no event," he claims, "could Greek art originate in a society which excludes any mythological explanation of nature."[63] Marx's modernity inherits the traits of Feuerbach's Judaism, just as his antiquity is imbued with the ideological nostalgia of a century-long German Grecophilia.

> Looking at it from another side: is Achilles possible side by side with powder and lead? Or is the *Iliad* compatible with the printing press and even printing machines? Do not singing and reciting and the muses necessarily go out of existence with the appearance of the printer's bar, and do not, therefore, the prerequisites of epic poetry disappear?[64]

Neither mythology nor epic, neither Achilles nor the *Iliad* is conceivable in a world that has created the printing press. "Greek art was epoch-making and unsurpassable," Neville Morley remarks, "not because the Greeks were superior to the moderns but because they were, in material terms, far inferior. Modern progress made the classical world view unsustainable."[65] And yet, although Marx's analysis of Greek art remains consistent with the premises of his materialist analysis, a lingering worry remains:

> But the difficulty is not in grasping the idea that Greek art and epos are bound up with certain forms of social development. It rather lies in understanding why they still constitute for us a source of aesthetic enjoyment and in certain respects prevail as the standard and model beyond attainment.[66]

Although Greek mythology *had* to be surpassed, although material progress is a necessity for the advent of the new and real revolution, it is the past, the classical past, which must in the interim act as the "standard and the model." "A man cannot become a child again unless he becomes childish." Marx affirms, concluding his discussion of Greek art in the *Grundrisse*, "but does he not enjoy the artless ways of the child, and must he not strive to reproduce its truth on a higher plain?"[67] Like the spirit of Republican Rome, "the recourse to the ancient example is recognized by Marx as potentially

---

63. Marx 2000, 394.

64. Ibid.

65. Morley 2009, 99.

66. Marx 2000, 394.

67. Marx 2000, 394–95. The ambivalence of Marx's attitude to ancient art in these passages is reflected in the different interpretations of various critics see Kain 1982, 132–35; Lifshitz 1938, 82–89; and Musto 2008, 23–26.

liberating . . . , a means of legitimizing revolution."[68] Ultimately, revolution, the real revolution will have to, in Marx's terms, learn to use its own language. But in the meantime the model of classical antiquity certainly has a strategic role to play in blasting out "the continuum of modernity."[69] It is no doubt with this Benjaminian model in mind that Jameson can conclude: "The category of classical antiquity may not be the least productive framework in which a global left reinvents an energizing past for itself."[70]

George McCarthy may overstate his claim when he says that "the Greeks were at the emotional and intellectual heart of Marx's critique of modernity, science, positivism, and the false objectivity of the capitalist social relations that undermine the possibilities for individual freedom and self-consciousness."[71] Nevertheless, I have been arguing that Marx's plea for an emancipation from the ills of modernity is inextricably bound up with an idealized conception of classical antiquity. Conversely, by turning the Jews into figures of history, by allowing them not only to enter modernity but in fact to stand in synecdochally for contemporary society, Marx paradoxically removes the Greeks from history and turns them into a timeless ideal. The Jews have become agents of historical progress by harnessing themselves to the forces of capital; the Greeks can only act as a "standard and model" that remains, however, "beyond attainment."

Marx is aware, of course, that we must ultimately move beyond both Athens and Jerusalem. "The three major traditions influencing Marx's intellectual development are German Idealism, British political economy and French socialism. There are, however," McCarthy asserts, "two deeper and older cultural traditions that underlie his thought—Greek philosophy and the Hebrew prophetic tradition."[72] But where for McCarthy both traditions, the Hebraic and the Hellenic, act as profound cultural markers that subtend Marx's vision of modernity, I have been arguing that he assigns strikingly different temporalities to these opposing historical cultures. This is why Marx is able to write: "Thus it is not only in the Pentateuch or the Talmud that we find the essence of the contemporary Jew: we find it in contemporary society, not as an abstract but as a very empirical essence, not as the limitation of the Jew but as the Jewish limitations of society." The role of the Pentateuch and that of the *Iliad* in his work can hardly be equated. It is because Marx has

68. Morley 2009, 130.
69. Benjamin 1973, 263
70. Jameson 2009, 177.
71. McCarthy 1990, 20.
72. McCarthy 1994, 125.

divested Judaism of its role as timeless historical model that he can proclaim that "the social emancipation of the Jew implies the emancipation of society from Judaism."[73]

Although I have been laying emphasis on the rather traditional premises of Marx's conception of Greek culture that emerge from its dialectic with Judaic thought, I do not want to deny the innovativeness of his vision of antiquity. Although Marx is able to draw on a long history of German appropriations that pitted the Greek ideal against the failures of the modern condition, although we hear echoes of both Goethe's "Prometheus" and Schiller's "Die Götter Griechenlands," in his own Prometheus and his broader discussions of Greek mythology, Marx still offers a new and unique characterization of antiquity—it is the Greece of Epicurus and Democritus, of Aristotle's theory of value, of masters and slaves and proto-bourgeois Roman republics. Still more radical (although it owes a great deal to Feuerbach) is Marx's wholly secular identification with the cultures of Greece and Rome. Where for Hegel in "The Spirit of Christianity" the Greek is seen in his infinite superiority to the Jew in his prefiguring of Christianity, Marx, like Heine, will oppose the pagan societies of Greece and Rome to a unified conception of Judeo-Christianity. As such, just as Marx's antiquity is able to unshackle itself from the bonds of the Christian worldview to emerge as a secular ideal, so Marx's critique of Judaism in "On the Jewish Question" becomes one of the first avowedly secular pronouncements of anti-Semitism. The debate about Athens and Jerusalem no longer has Christian Rome as its ultimate reference point.

"Dionysus against the Crucified": Nietzsche's Genealogy of Christianity

Nietzsche's diagnosis of the sickness of modernity also finds its cure in a return to the Greeks. Like Marx, his despair at the decadence of the modern world is linked to an analysis of Judaism and its relationship to Christianity. In his attempt to understand the shortcomings of modernity, Nietzsche returns to the nexus of Greece, Rome, and Jerusalem. He will follow Marx in constructing Judeo-Christianity as an antithesis to pagan Greece. In the process, like Marx, he appears to substitute a secular Hellenic anti-Semitism for an earlier Christian anti-Judaism. And yet Nietzsche's investments remain ultimately more ambivalent.[74] So where Marx straightforwardly singles out Ju-

73. Marx 2000, 69.

74. See Kofman 1994 for an excellent analysis of the complexity of Nietzsche's Jews and his Greek/Jew antithesis, in particular, 55–62. Kofman concentrates especially on *The Gay Sci-*

daism as the disease of modernity, Nietzsche instead identifies anti-Semitism as a symptom of modern decadence—an anti-Semitism that has a tortured genealogy in the relationship of Christianity to Judaism. Moreover, Nietzsche and Marx operate with distinct temporalities—where it is the modern Jews who bear the brunt of Marx's attacks, it is ancient Judaism that is the object of Nietzsche's most searing critique.

Whereas Marx complained in "On the Jewish Question" that the German "state is a professed theologian," Nietzsche, by contrast, identifies German philosophy as the domain of the pastor: "The Germans understand me immediately when I say that philosophy has been contaminated by theologian blood. The Protestant minister is the grandfather of German philosophy, Protestantism itself is its *peccatum originale*. . . . You need only say 'Tübingen Seminary' to understand just *what* German philosophy really is: underhanded theology."[75] The origins of Marx's critique of religion lie, as we have seen, in the Young Hegelians' reaction to the publication of David Strauss's *Life of Jesus*. Strauss will play a similarly decisive role in the formulation of Nietzsche's analysis of Christianity. Nietzsche had read Strauss's *Jesus* when he was a schoolboy at Pforta. "Indeed," as Daniel Breazeale recounts in his introduction to *Untimely Meditations*, "some interpreters believe Strauss' book was an important contributing factor in Nietzsche's own abandonment of Christianity only a year later, during his first year at college (1865)." And yet, by the time Nietzsche devoted an essay to David Strauss in his *Untimely Meditations*, he had turned his back on his former master. The first essay of the book does not address the detail of Strauss's work but rather uses Strauss as an emblem of a radical who finds an accommodation with the status quo. Strauss had forgotten his former Young Hegelian fervor and become a social conservative. As Breazeale writes: "the real subject of the first *Untimely Meditation* is not David Strauss at all, but the smug and false complacency of the 'cultivated' German bourgeoisie in the aftermath of Prussia's victory over France in the Franco-Prussian War and the subsequent establishment of the second German *Reich*."[76]

If the theological content of Strauss's work receives scant attention in the early essay that takes his name, it will, nevertheless, become the focus of some of Nietzsche's most important later work. From *Beyond Good and Evil* to *On*

ence and *Twilight of the Idols* and (thus) depicts a more positive characterization of the Jews in Nietzsche. See also Rose (1993, 89–110), who argues against attempts of rationalize Nietzsche's contrarian representation of Judaism in his different works. On the interesting reception of Nietzsche's ambivalence by Jewish thinkers see Stegmaier and Krochmalnik 1997.

75. Nietzsche 2005, 9.
76. Ibid., xii, xiii.

the Genealogy of Morals to *The Anti-Christ*, the question of the origins and development of Christianity would emerge as an obsession for Nietzsche. In the course of his investigation of the moral underpinnings of both ancient and modern religion, the relationship between Greece, Rome, and Judea takes center stage. As we have already seen in our analysis of the *Birth of Tragedy* in chapter 2, Nietzsche was motivated by a desire to uncover the false consciousness of his age. In the *Birth of Tragedy*, Nietzsche pins his hopes on an aesthetic revival of Greek tragedy as a means of counteracting the life-denying tyranny of contemporary German (Christian) culture. But although Nietzsche fervently hopes for a return to the aesthetic ideals of Greece, he already locates the seeds of its own demise within Greek culture itself. Nietzsche's narrative of tragedy will see its ultimate corruption in the advent of Christianity foreshadowed by the dual forces of Euripides and Socrates. The Socrates of the *Birth of Tragedy* is both the "archetype of *theoretical man*"[77] and the embodiment of a decidedly Christian decadence, an association that, as we have seen, Nietzsche would later make all the more explicit in *Twilight of the Idols*:

> Socrates was a misunderstanding: the entire morality of improvement, Christianity's included, was a misunderstanding . . . the harshest daylight, rationality at all costs, life bright, cold, cautious instinct-free, instinct resistant: this itself was just an illness, a different illness—and definitely not a way back to "virtue," "health," happiness . . . to have to fight against the instincts—this is the formula of decadence.[78]

In the figure of Socrates, then, Nietzsche had begun to uncover a genealogy of moral thought that would account for our fall from Hellenic grace—a fall from which modern society had yet to recover. *Beyond Good and Evil* traces the narrative of Christianity's triumph over the Greek ideal in a more systematic way:

> What astonishes one about the religiosity of the ancient Greeks is the tremendous amount of gratitude that emanates from it—the kind of man who stands *thus* before nature and before life is a very noble one!—Later, when the rabble came to predominate Greece, *fear* also overran religion; and Christianity was preparing itself.[79]

Like Hegel, Feuerbach, and Marx before him, we find Nietzsche locating the power of Greek religion in its reverential attitude to nature. The noble

---

77. Nietzsche 1999, 72.
78. Nietzsche 1998, 15.
79. Nietzsche 1993, 78.

GREEKS, JEWS, AND THE DEATH OF GOD

Greeks stand before nature in grateful worship. In a passage that echoes Hegel's analysis of Noah's reaction to the flood, Nietzsche argues that it is "fear"
that announces the inexorable march toward an impoverished monotheism.
Nietzsche's broader project in *Beyond Good and Evil*, and even more explicitly in *On the Genealogy of Morals*, is to understand the inversion of moral
vocabulary brought about by the transition from "master" to "slave morality." The complex relationship between Greek and Christian culture that he
had already begun to delineate in his earlier works now becomes the focus of
his later writings. In the *Birth of Tragedy* it is with the figure of Socrates that
we see the first intimations of Christian decadence; in Nietzsche's later work,
however, a different genealogy takes precedence:

> The Jews—a people "born for slavery" as Tacitus and the whole ancient
> world says, "the chosen people" as they themselves say and believe—The Jews
> achieved that miracle of inversion of values thanks to which life on earth has
> for a couple of millennia acquired a new and dangerous fascination—their
> prophets fused "rich," "godless," "evil," "violent," "sensual" into one and
> were the first to coin the word "world" as a term of infamy. It is in the inver-
> sion of values (with which is involved the employment of the word for "poor"
> as a synonym of "holy" and "friend") that the significance of the Jewish people
> resides: with *them* there begins the *slave revolt in morals*.[80]

It is the Jews and not Socrates who in this account are the pivotal figures in
the development of moral thought. Indeed, in the *Genealogy*, in language that
unmistakably mocks Hegel, Nietzsche writes: "Let us stick to the facts: the
people have won—or the 'slaves' or 'the mob' or 'the herd' or whatever you
like to call them—if this has happened through the Jews, very well!!! in that
case no people have ever had a more world-historic mission."[81] Locked out of
the dialectic of history in Hegel, the Jews become *the* world-historical figures
in Nietzsche. But unlike for Marx, where it is contemporary Jews who become the agents of historical progress by harnessing themselves to the forces
of capital, for Nietzsche it is ancient Jews who bear the responsibility for the
"inversion of values" that continues to plague the modern world. More specifically, as Nietzsche establishes in the *Genealogy* it is "the priestly Jews" who
brought about this transition:

> All that has been done on earth against "the noble," "the powerful," "the mas-
> ters," "the rulers," fades into nothing compared with what the *Jews* have done

80. Ibid., 118.
81. Nietzsche 1969, 35–36.

against them; the Jews, that priestly people, who in opposing their enemies and conquerors were ultimately satisfied with nothing less than a radical revaluation of their enemies' values, that is to say, an act of the *most spiritual revenge*. For this alone was appropriate to a priestly people, the people embodying the most deeply repressed priestly vengefulness. It was the Jews who, with awe-inspiring consistency, dared to invert the aristocratic value-equation (good = noble = powerful = beautiful = happy = beloved of God) and to hang on to this inversion with their teeth, the teeth of the most abysmal hatred.[82]

Although Nietzsche is lavish in his praise for the Old Testament and even for the Jewish people and culture both in *Beyond Good and Evil* and in the *Genealogy*, the power of his characterization of the Jews as a people of vicious hatred and vengeance cannot be denied. Despite the qualification "priestly," it is of *Jews* as an all-too-familiar ahistorical collective that he chooses to write. And yet, Nietzsche's account of the Jews' contribution to morality stands directly opposed to previous anti-Judaic polemics. Unlike the tradition of thought that finds its culmination in Feuerbach's depiction of Judaism as a religion of egoism and Marx's equation of Judaism with capitalism, Nietzsche represents Jews as the ultimate unworldly people: "they were the first to coin the word 'world' as a term of infamy." Nietzsche is to some extent anticipated by Hegel who railed against Abraham for seeing the "whole world as his opposite." But Hegel would simultaneously damn Abraham for his uncompromising attitude to the world around him and lay against the Jewish people as a whole the age-old charge of materialism and lack of spirituality. Nietzsche's Jews, by contrast, are all too spiritual. They are so spiritual that they have turned "spirituality" into an act of vengeance on the much healthier world of wealth, strength, beauty, and sensuality that surrounded them.

It is no coincidence that the archetype of nobility against whom the Jews launch their campaign of hatred is represented by Nietzsche as Greek. Indeed in a passage that combines a display of philological mastery with a firm grasp of up-to-the-minute linguistic and racial theory, Nietzsche writes:

> It is of no small interest to ascertain that through those words and roots which designate "good" there frequently still shines the most important nuance by virtue of which the noble felt themselves to be men of higher rank. Granted that, in the majority of cases, they designate themselves simply by their superiority in power (as "the powerful," "the masters," "the commanders") or by the most clearly visible signs of this superiority, example, as "the rich," "the possessors" (this is the meaning of *arya*; and of corresponding words in Iranian and Slavic). But they also do it by a *typical character trait*. . . . They

82. Ibid., 33–34.

call themselves, for instance, "the truthful"; this is so above all of the Greek nobility.[83]

For Nietzsche, the culture in which the equation "good = noble = powerful = beautiful = happy = beloved of God" is unmistakably a Greek one. And the inversion of values that the advent of the Jews brought about was clearly directed against this Greek ideal. It required a prodigious linguistic manipulation by the Jews to change forever the meaning of the term *good*. In mustering the vocabulary of the burgeoning field of comparative philology, Nietzsche also seems to be suggesting that there is an ethnic or racial basis to the process of inversion. By insidiously perverting the meaning of the word *good* away from its association with nobility—an association that Nietzsche claims is inscribed in the word *arya*—the Jews waged war not only on language but on a people, too. The advent of Judaism represents a slave revolt against Aryanism. In Nietzsche's genealogical method, then, we find a potent mixture of philological rigor, racial theory, and class analysis. Moreover, he is simultaneously also steeped in a philosophical discussion of Judaism that extends back to the Enlightenment and the developing historicist accounts of early Christianity that explored its relationship to both Judaism and Greco-Roman culture.

"One knows *who* inherited this Jewish revaluation," Nietzsche announces. For from the the "trunk of the tree of Jewish hatred" a "*new* love" would grow:

> This Jesus of Nazareth, the incarnate gospel of love, this "Redeemer" who brought blessedness and victory to the poor, the sick and the sinners—was he not this seduction in its most uncanny irresistible form, a seduction and a bypass to precisely those *Jewish* values and new ideals. Did Israel not attain the ultimate goal of its sublime vengefulness precisely through the bypass of this ostensible opponent and disintegrator of Israel? Was it not part of the secret black art of truly *grand* politics of revenge, of a farseeing, subterranean, slowly advancing, and premeditated revenge, that Israel must itself deny the real instrument of its revenge before all the world as a mortal enemy and nail it to the cross, so that "all the world," namely all the opponents of Israel, could unhesitatingly swallow the bait?[84]

"The Jewish people," writes Yovel, "bequeathed Christianity to the world as an act of spiritual revenge against the Gentiles. . . . Whereas anti-Semites accuse the Jews of having killed Jesus, Nietzsche accuses them of having *begot-*

83. Ibid., 28–29.
84. Ibid., 35.

ten Jesus."[85] A profound continuity between Judaism and Christianity is as central to Nietzsche as it had been to both Feuerbach and Marx. Nietzsche's anti-Judaism is secular through and through. But like Marx and Feuerbach before him, it is interesting that Nietzsche's critique of a unified conception of Judeo-Christianity still finds its most potent expression in an invective against "the Jews." It is as an outgrowth of Judaism that Christianity is attacked by Nietzsche. Christianity is, after all, only the outward bait for the essential "poison" that is Judaism.

The flow of that poison once released cannot be stemmed: "The 'redemption' of the human race (from 'the master,' that is) is going forward: everything is visibly becoming Judaized, Christianized, mob-ized (what do words matter)."[86] Despite Nietzsche's genealogical project, "Judaism" is far from acting as a mere historical phenomenon in his writings; it remains an active malevolent force in modernity. The logic of Nietzsche's genealogy would suggest that as Christianity superseded and triumphed over Judaism, it would bear the responsibility for the modern world's continuing enslavement to its morality. Nietzsche, however, seems to share with Marx a paradoxical desire to single out Judaism as a metaphor for the ills of modernity. Despite their statistical insignificance, the practitioners of Judaism are asked by Marx and Nietzsche to shoulder the symbolic burden of the corruption of the Christian nation: its state, its morality, and its culture.

Nietzsche's analysis does not share Marx's explicit political agenda but it is significant that the trio "Judaized, Christianized, mob-ized" appear so frequently juxtaposed in his texts. This quotation is immediately preceded by the following statement: "'The masters have been disposed of; the morality of the common man has won. One may conceive of this victory at the same time as a blood-poisoning (it has mixed races together)."[87] Nietzsche exists at the other end of the political spectrum from Marx. His unabashed elitism and vilification of the "mob" stands in direct contrast to Marx's revolutionary program. Indeed, Nietzsche would characterize socialism as yet another manifestation of slave morality imposed on contemporary society by its Judeo-Christian legacy. As we saw in the previous chapter, the association of revolutionary socialism with Jews had become widespread in the latter half of the nineteenth century. Marx's attack on his fellow Jews in "On the Jewish Question" could be seen in part as a reaction to the anti-Semitic attacks on socialism as a project of Jewish supremacy. In the French Revolution it was

85. Yovel 1998, 140.
86. Nietzsche 1969, 36.
87. Ibid., 36.

inescapably to classical models that political thinkers would turn to formulate a contemporary political vocabulary. By the mid-nineteenth century, however, Judaism seems to have given rise to a political lexicon of its own. It is the Jews who take center stage when Marx addresses the problems of political and human emancipation. In Nietzsche the projects of "Judaizing" and "mobizing" can be equated just as the slave morality of Judaism, of Christianity and of Socialism are seen to be interchangeable: "Whom do I hate most among the rabble of today?" he asks in the *Anti-Christ.* "The socialist rabble, the chandala apostles, who undermine the instinct, the pleasure, the worker's sense of satisfaction with his small existence—who make him envious, who teach him revenge. The source of wrong is never unequal rights but the claim of "equal" rights."[88]

We are a long way from Hegel and his denial of political agency to the Jews! But we are also in a quite different discourse from Kant who asserted that Judaism was a covert politics masquerading under the guise of a moral religion. When Nietzsche juxtaposes "Judaized" with "mob-ized" and talks about "blood poisoning" and the mixing of races, he mobilizes almost a century of ethnic and racial science to bolster his political vocabulary. Marx's ethnographic description of capitalism as a quintessentially Jewish pursuit is also, albeit in a very distinct way, a conflation of racial, religious, and political categories. But it is perhaps Matthew Arnold who Nietzsche most resembles here. As we saw in the previous chapter, in describing the class structure of English society Arnold ends up subsuming his economic and social categories to a racial history. Nietzsche also, to some extent, shares the respective characterizations of "Hellenism" and "Hebraism" in Arnold's work.[89] His own carefree, sensuous Hellenes are contrasted with self-denying moralizing Hebrews. Indeed, the penultimate section of the first essay of *On the Genealogy of Morals* offers a striking rewriting of Arnold's analysis of Hellenism and Hebraism: "Let us conclude. The two *opposing* values 'good and bad,' 'good and evil' have been engaged in a fearful struggle on earth for thousands of years; and though the latter value has certainly been on top for a long time, there are still places where the struggle is as yet undecided."[90]

One recalls Arnold: "Hellenism and Hebraism, —between these points of influence moves the world. At one time it feels more powerfully the attraction of one of them, at another time of the other; it ought to be, though it never is,

88. Nietzsche 2005, 60.
89. Cohen (1994) makes a similar association between Nietzsche and the Arnoldian terms "Hellenism" and "Hebraism" without explicitly mentioning Arnold. The connection to Heine also seems evident.
90. Nietzsche 1969, 52.

evenly and happily balanced between them."[91] But for Nietzsche, "good and bad" find their cultural referents not in Athens and Jerusalem but in their near analogues: Rome and Judea.

> The symbol of this struggle, inscribed in letters legible across all human history, is "Rome against Judea, Judea against Rome": —there has hitherto been no greater event than *this* struggle, *this* question, *this* deadly contradiction. Rome felt the Jew to be something like anti-nature itself, its antipodal monstrosity as it were: in Rome the Jew stood "*convicted* of hatred for the whole human race"; and rightly, provided one has a right to link the salvation and future of the human race with the unconditional dominance of aristocratic values, Roman values.[92]

For Nietzsche, like Arnold, the world "moves" between "these two points of influence." Nietzsche will even implicitly follow Arnold in his attempt to map distinct moments of history when one force would triumph over the other. So for both Nietzsche and Arnold the Renaissance represents "an uncanny and glittering reawakening of the classical ideal." However, this Renaissance of classicism was short-lived: "Judea immediately triumphed again, thanks to the thoroughly plebian (German and English) *ressentiment* movement called the Reformation."[93] Nietzsche continues to trace this alternating historical narrative through the French Revolution right up to the triumph of Napoleon. His genealogy here resembles nothing so much as Arnold's and Renan's macrohistorical ethnologies. Nietzsche's Rome and Judea are Renan's "two poles of the movement of humanity."

In choosing Rome as the counterpart to Judea, Nietzsche knocks Arnold's and Renan's polarity slightly off kilter. By locating his binary in the more historically accurate setting of Rome where "real" Jews came into contact with "real" Romans, Nietzsche also literalizes Arnold's unashamedly metaphorical analysis of historical progress. Nietzsche's previous concentration on Greek nobility is now transferred to Rome. Given his vocal contempt for Romans expressed elsewhere in his writing, it is striking to see Rome become coterminous with the classical ideal. Despite what he says about Socrates, despite his claim in *Beyond Good and Evil* that Greek society prefigured aspects of Christianity, it is as if Nietzsche cannot bear to place the Greek and the Jew in naked confrontation with one another. Nietzsche in his genealogical mode cannot imagine Greece as the matrix of Judeo-Christianity.

91. Arnold 1993, 126.
92. Nietzsche 1969, 53.
93. Ibid., 54, 55.

But if Nietzsche relocates his Hellenism in Rome, he also manages to complicate the conception of Hebraism: "Which of them has won *for the present*, Rome or Judea?":

> But there can be no doubt: consider to whom one bows down in Rome itself today, as if they were the epitome of all the highest values—and not only in Rome but over almost half the earth, everywhere that man has become tame or desires to become tame: *three Jews*, as is known, and *one Jewess* (Jesus of Nazareth, the fisherman Peter, the rug weaver Paul, and the mother of the aforementioned Jesus, named Mary). This is very remarkable: Rome has been defeated beyond all doubt.[94]

We have already seen in the previous chapter how the referents of Arnold's signifiers remain infuriatingly indeterminate. Whereas at times Arnold seems to fix his Hellenes and Hebrews in a racial taxonomy of Aryan and Semite, at other moments they seem merely to represent an internal split within Christianity. Nietzsche is also involved in a deliberate blurring of categories here. There is no mistaking the provocation of Nietzsche's assertion that more than half the world bows its head before "three Jews and one Jewess." Where Arnold may have been comfortable talking about some modern Christians as "Hebrews," Renan, as we have seen, was driven throughout his career by a desire to mark out the fundamental distinction between Judaism and Christianity. Nietzsche's "Judaizing" of Christianity here represents a polemic against the attempts to sever Christianity from its origins in Judaism.

But Nietzsche does not just Judaize Christianity, he also Christianizes Judaism. Nietzsche's Judaism bears all the hallmarks of a recognizable Christianity. Where Hegel had represented Judaism as the "complete opposite" of Christianity, Nietzsche represents their doctrines as completely indistinguishable. In the process he not only transforms the Christian anti-Semitic critique of Judaism into his version of orthodox Christianity, he also denies Judaism a distinctive theological legacy. Nietzsche employs the tropes of Christian anti-Semitism to subject Christianity to its own critique. But the force of his condemnation of Christianity, is in the last analysis, predicated on the incontrovertible truth of anti-Semitism.

> For the Romans were the strong and noble, and nobody stronger and nobler has yet existed on earth and even been dreamed of: every remnant of them, every inscription gives delight, if only one divines *what* it was that was there at work. The Jews, on the contrary, were the priestly nation of *ressentiment par excellence*, in whom dwelt an unequaled popular-moral genius: one only

94. Ibid., 53.

has to compare similarly gifted nations—the Chinese or the Germans, for instance—with the Jews, to sense which is of the first and which is of the fifth rank.[95]

The Nietzschean concept of "ressentiment" is central to the analysis of both Judaism and Christianity. *Ressentiment* is the modality of slave morality, the psychological force that underpins the triumph of Judaism and Christianity. But as this passage makes clear, despite the unrelentingly negative connotations of the word, Nietzsche here seems awed by the "genius" of a people who turn such a decadent psychology to their advantage. Kaufmann writes: "Having said things that can easily be misconstrued as grist to the mill of German anti-Semites, Nietzsche goes out of his way, as usual, to express his admiration for the Jews and disdain for the Germans."[96] I do not share Kaufmann's certainty that associating Nietzsche's critique with anti-Semitism would be a straightforward misconstrual, but there is no doubt that he delights in adopting a paradoxical position here. Nietzsche's admiration for the Jews, just like his opprobrium for Judaism, is couched in the familiar language of anti-Semitism. And yet, the concept of *ressentiment* returns in the *Genealogy* with an unexpected referent.

> This hoarse indignant barking of sick dogs and rage of "noble" Pharisees, penetrates even the hallowed halls of science (I again remind readers who have ears for such things of that Berlin apostle of revenge, Eugen Dühring, who employs moral mumbo-jumbo more indecently and repulsively than anyone else in Germany today—unexcelled even among his own ilk, anti-Semites). They are all men of *ressentiment*, physiologically unfortunate and worm-eaten, a whole tremulous realm of subterranean revenge.[97]

If the priestly Jews of antiquity had been identified by Nietzsche as the "nation of *ressentiment par excellence*," it is the contemporary German anti-Semites who turn out to be their most direct descendants. "Thus in an ironic turn of events," writes Yovel, "the anti-Semite becomes the legitimate heir to the ancient Jewish priest, from whom he took over as a modern paradigm of the psychology of *ressentiment*."[98] Vulgar, "worm-eaten" German anti-Semitism represents to Nietzsche the new slave revolt.

It is in the *Anti-Christ* that Nietzsche gives further definition to the *mauvaise foi* of the Christian anti-Semite: "This is precisely why the Jews are the

---

95. Ibid.
96. Kaufmann, in ibid., 53n2.
97. Nietzsche 1969, 124.
98. Yovel 1998, 137.

most disastrous people in world history: they have left such a falsified humanity in their wake that even today Christians can think of themselves as
anti-Jewish without understanding that they are the *ultimate conclusion of
Judaism.*"[99] But while it is the German anti-Semites who come under attack
in the *Genealogy,* Nietzsche has a different antagonist in the *Anti-Christ:* "his
main target is the anti-Semitic French theologian Renan and includes the
'insidious theology' of the Tübingen seminary."[100] For as Santaniello argues,

> Nietzsche's two main concerns in the *Antichrist* are identical to those which
> generally preoccupied nineteenth-century liberal Protestantism as a whole:
> the relationship between Christianity and Judaism, and the historical quest
> of Jesus in relation to his Jewish roots. Consequently the *Anti-Christ* marks
> Nietzsche's brief attempt at a biographical / historical portrait of Jesus as a psy-
> chological type, of which Strauss and Renan were pioneers in their respective
> works of the same title.[101]

But Nietzsche's *Anti-Christ* self-consciously stands as the antithesis to the
two lives of Christ written by David Strauss and Ernest Renan.

> My difficulties are different from those demonstrated by the scholarly curios-
> ity of the German spirit in one of its most unforgettable triumphs. The days
> are long gone when, like every young scholar, I took great pleasure in the work
> of the inimitable Strauss, read at the shrewd and plodding pace of a refined
> philologist. I was twenty then: now I am too serious for this. What do I care
> about the contradictions in the "tradition"![102]

Strauss, who caused a scandal in his time, who was still in Marx's youth a figure whose work would inspire a thirst for revolution, has become for Nietzsche the archetype of the fusty philologist. What mystery can 'contradictions
in the tradition' hold for an Anti-Christ? Philologically inspired historicism
no longer has to the power to make waves in an age which has conspired to
murder God.

If Strauss's quaint methodology is ridiculed, "Mr Renan," the man whom
Nietzsche calls "this buffoon *in psychologicis,*" is subjected to a far more direct
attack. Nietzsche not only pours scorn on Renan's psychological characterization of Jesus, he also, and more fundamentally, aims to undermine the very
premise of Renan's account of Christianity's emancipation from Judaism: "I
will only touch on the problem of the *origin* of Christianity. The *first* proposi-

99. Nietzsche 2005, 21.
100. Santaniello 1994, 124.
101. Ibid., 127.
102. Nietzsche 2005, 26.

tion for solving this problem is: Christianity can only be understood on the soil where it grew, — it is *not* a counter-movement to the Jewish instinct, it is its natural consequence, a further conclusion drawn by its terrifying logic."[103] Renan, according to Nietzsche, has got his first proposition essentially wrong. "Renan located the origin of Christianity with the prophet Isaiah, discarded original Israel, and held nineteenth-century Jews, Israel's remnants, responsible for the death of Jesus. Nietzsche's position is the exact reverse."[104]

Rather than find an antidote to ancient Judaism in modern Christianity, Nietzsche seeks a cure to the combined sicknesses of Judaism and Christianity (ancient and modern) in a return to a different antiquity: "Christianity *needs* sickness, more or less as Greece needed a surplus of health."[105] "Let us look ourselves in the face," he exhorts in the opening passage to the *Anti-Christ*:

> We are Hyperboreans, we are well aware of how far off the beaten track we live. "Neither by land or by sea will you find the way to the Hyperboreans": Pindar had already known about us. . . . *This* modernity made us ill—this indolent peace, this cowardly compromise, the whole virtuous filth of the modern yes and no.[106]

We are, as Nietzsche suggests, Greeks who have lost our way, "Hyperboreans" who have become sick with the "cowardly compromise" of the "modern yes and no." For Nietzsche, modern anti-Semitism, which motivates the Christianity of a figure like Renan, is just the "terrifying conclusion" of the first originary compromise that the ancient world made with the slave morality of Judaism in the guise of Christianity. Indeed Hubert Cancik and Hildegard Cancik-Lindemaier claim: "In Nietzsche the positive pole which opposes his anti-Semitism is not, as it is in the circle of Wagner, a German Christianity purified of its Judaism, but a philhellenism reduced to the Dionysiac, to tragedy and to heroism."[107] Nietzsche's task in the *Anti-Christ* is to shake us out of our existential bad faith and to lead us "Hyperboreans" back on the path which we abandoned millennia ago.

> The entire work of the ancient world *in vain*: I do not have words to express my feelings at something so enormous.—And given that the work was preparatory, just laying the foundations with granite self-consciousness for a work that would take millennia, the entire *meaning* of the ancient world has been

103. Ibid., 20, 26.
104. Santaniello 1994, 129. See also Shapiro 1982 on "Nietzsche *contra* Renan."
105. Nietzsche 2005, 49.
106. Ibid.
107. Cancik and Cancik-Lindemaier 1991, 44.

in vain! . . . What was the point of the Greeks? What was the point of the Romans?[108]

How can modern man reconcile himself to the destruction of the whole project of antiquity? The ancients had prepared us for a different future that we seem stubbornly to have refused.

> *All of this in vain*! Turned overnight into just a memory!—Greeks! Romans! The nobility of the instinct and of taste, methodical research, genius in organization and administration, the belief, the *will* to a future for humanity, the great yes to all things made visible as the *imperium Romanum*, made visible to all the senses, the great style no longer just as art, but turned into reality, truth, *life*.[109]

In saying "no" to the Greeks and the Romans we have said "no" "to a future for humanity."

> —And not buried overnight by some natural event! Not buried by Germans and other clodhoppers! But instead defiled by sly, secretive, invisible, anaemic vampires! Not defeated, just sucked dry! . . . The hidden need for revenge, petty jealousy come to *power*! Everything miserable, suffering from itself, plagued by bad feelings, the whole *ghetto world* of the soul risen *to the top* in a single stroke![110]

But Nietzsche is not just concerned with the devastation of the Greco-Roman legacy, he is also exercised by the manner of its demise. "Christianity cheated us out of the fruits of ancient culture."[111] It was no natural disaster, no brutal and open confrontation, but a surreptitious "cheating" that denied modernity the future that antiquity had so lovingly prepared for it. Christianity overcame the Roman empire in the mode of the Jew. In "sly," "secretive," and "vampiric" fashion, the "*ghetto world* of the soul" rose up in revolt against the nobility, taste, and genius of the Hellenic world. We "Hyperboreans" against the "ghetto" of the soul: there could be no better formulation of Nietzsche's philhellenic anti-Semitism.

But Nietzsche, like Marx, is no straightforward continuation of an idealized German philhellenism. "If we do not get rid of Christianity," he riles on the next page, "it will be the fault of the Germans."[112] Despite Nietzsche's fervent hopes, the Germans are no natural heirs to the legacy of Greece. The

---

108. Nietzsche 2005, 62.
109. Ibid., 63.
110. Ibid.
111. Ibid., 60.
112. Ibid., 65.

"blond beast" can barely recognize his Hellenic origins through the haze of the German Reformation and other crimes of Hebraism. Figures like Strauss, in their adoption of rationalist historicism, appeared to shine the Hellenic light of reason onto the Old and New testaments. But for Nietzsche, this was only Hebraism in another guise. Strauss was merely the continuation of a liberal Protestantism that Nietzsche saw as the *peccatum originale* of German thought. The false Hellenism of German philosophy thus finds a parallel in the false Hellenism of the German state. Where Nietzsche sees liberal Protestantism as an insidious inversion of Hellenic ideal, Marx sees the liberal state as a betrayal of the Athenian democratic polity.

Like Marx, Nietzsche longs for a revival of Greece in modern Germany. When he turns his gaze on contemporary Christian society, however, he can only see the legacy of a "Judaizing" of Europe. Where for Hegel the Jews are incapable of historical progress, Judaism, for Marx and for Nietzsche, is an active force in modernity. Despite their many political differences, one can imagine Nietzsche agreeing with Marx's conclusion that "the social emancipation of the Jew implies the emancipation of society from Judaism."[113] If Christianity is for both Marx and Nietzsche the Jewish sickness of modernity, Greece would be its most potent antidote. Feuerbach, Marx, and Nietzsche all mark a fundamental break with an earlier tradition which attempted to rescue Christianity from its Judaism by associating it with Hellenism. By creating a unified conception of Judeo-Christianity they simultaneously discovered a distinctively secular vision of Greece. After Marx's Prometheus and Nietzsche's Anti-Christ, Athens, Rome, and Jerusalem would ever look the same again, so Nietzsche signs off *Ecce Homo*: "Have I been understood? *Dionysus versus the crucified . . .*"[114]

113. Marx 2000, 69.
114. Nietzsche 2005, 151.

5

Moses on the Acropolis: Sigmund Freud

The Disturbance of Philology

In his essay "Prayer on the Acropolis," which forms part of his autobiography, *Recollections of My Youth*, Ernest Renan reflects on the question of recollection itself: "It was not until I was well advanced in life that I began to have any souvenirs [memories]. The imperious necessity which compelled me during my early years to solve for myself, not with the leisurely deliberation of a thinker, but with the feverish ardour of one who has to struggle for life, the loftiest problems of philosophy and religion never left me a quarter of an hour's leisure to look behind me."[1] For Renan, the activity of scholarship, the white heat of intellectual inquiry, would get in the way of the leisurely activity of remembrance. Renan may have spent his waking hours trying to uncover the historical memory of past civilizations, trying to piece together, for instance, the life of Jesus or the history of the people of Israel, but the practice of history was for Renan a bar to the enjoyment of personal recollection.

"Strangely enough," he writes, "it was in Athens, in 1865, that I first felt a strong backward impulse, the effect being that of a fresh and bracing breeze coming from afar."[2] Although, by the time Renan made it to Athens in 1865, he had already been elected as the first professor of Hebrew at the Collège de France and had moreover already spent many years working among the archaeological sites of the Middle East, it was only on his arrival in Athens that he was able to link the experience of the material remains of the past to the sensation of a personal memory. "The fresh and bracing breeze coming from afar" gave a different meaning to the "backward impulse" so familiar to the scholar of ancient cultures. In this account, it is almost as if the breeze from

1. Renan 1929, 49.
2. Ibid.

afar rather than bearing testimony to the history of Athens speaks instead of
the history of Renan. As Pierre Vidal-Naquet argues, one of the many interesting features of this text is the fact that it combines historical with personal
memory. "The entire *Prayer* is presented as not only an invocation to the goddess but also a recollection of his clerical Breton childhood."[3] "I am born,"
Renan starts his prayer,

> O goddess of the blue eyes, of barbarian parents, among the good and virtu-
> ous Cimmerians who dwell by the shore of a melancholy sea, bristling with
> rocks ever lashed by the storm. The sun is scarcely known in this country, its
> flowers are seaweed, marine plants, and the coloured shells which are gathered
> in the recesses of lonely bays. . . . Priests of a strange creed, handed down from
> the Syrians of Palestine, brought me up.[4]

But, for Renan, the power of Athens over his personal memory was inextricably linked to the quality of the civilization. For he writes:

> The impression which Athens made upon me was the strongest which I have
> ever felt. There is one and only one place in which perfection exists, and that is
> Athens, which outdid anything I had ever imagined. I had before my eyes the
> ideal of beauty crystallized in the marble of Pentelicus. I had hitherto thought
> that perfection was not to be found in the world.[5]

"Prayer on the Acropolis" is not the first place that Renan would coin the
phrase "le miracle grec," but the essay is certainly its most memorable formulation.[6] Indeed, the "Prayer" became so profoundly resonant that Vidal-
Naquet writes: "Mine was probably the last generation in France to be made,
in early childhood, to read this text as a prime model of great French prose."[7]
The concept of the "Greek miracle" may have conjured up for Vidal-Naquet
and several generations of French schoolboys a peculiarly French brand of
nineteenth-century philhellenism, but the full irony of Renan's usage may not
have been appreciated by all. The notion of the "miracle" had played a very
charged role in Renan's academic career. Indeed, it was precisely his denial of
miracles in Christian theology which had led Renan to be dismissed from his
position at the Collège de France, only to be later reinstated. In his revolutionary *Life of Jesus*, Renan had baldly proclaimed: "miracles never happen."[8]
In the "Prayer," Renan contextualizes his appreciation of Greek worldly

---

3. Vidal-Naquet 1995, 179.
4. Renan 1929, 53.
5. Ibid.
6. See Psichari 1956; Peyre 1973; Fraisse 1979.
7. Vidal-Naquet 1995, 179.
8. Renan 1904, 22

"perfection" against the context of his own struggle with Judeo-Christian revelation:

> For some time past I had ceased to believe in miracles strictly so called, though the singular destiny of the Jewish people, leading up to Jesus and to Christianity, appeared to me to stand alone. And now suddenly there arose by the side of the Jewish miracle the Greek miracle, a thing which only existed once, which had never been seen before, which will never be seen again, but the effect of which will last for ever, an eternal type of beauty, without a single blemish, local or national.[9]

The rationalist historian Renan would reject "miracles" "strictly so called," but this would not stop him from figuratively identifying them with narratives in human history. Renan may have called Jesus' divinity into question but he self-consciously reanimates the theological framework of his historical vocabulary. Moreover, in extending the language of revelation to the avowedly secular history of the Greeks, Renan reverses the premises of historicist scholarship. In developing a method of rationalist approaches to the biblical texts it was to the model of Altertumswissenschaft that figures such as David Strauss would turn. In his own *Life of Jesus* published some twenty years before Renan's, Strauss, as we have seen, exposes the mythical structure of both the Old and New testaments. It would be the methodological insights that arose from the study of Greco-Roman myth that he would redeploy in the service of biblical scholarship. In this sense, scholars in the middle of the nineteenth century would return to the debate that animated Friedrich August Wolf in his development of a philological method appropriate to classical antiquity. As we saw earlier, however, Wolf's seminal study of Homer was significantly indebted to J. G. Eichhorn's historical scholarship on the Old and New testaments. Although Wolf's classical scholarship has often been seen as providing a break with previous traditions of biblical exegesis, classical and biblical scholarship seem to coexist in a dialectical relationship well into the nineteenth century. For all the irony that surrounds the use of the term *miracle*, Renan's decision to place the "Greek miracle" side by side with the "Jewish miracle" is as much evidence of the theologizing of the secular classics as of the secularization of theology. "The sight of the Acropolis was like a revelation of the Divine, such as that which I experienced when, gazing down upon the valley of the Jordan from the heights of Casyoun, I first felt the living reality of the Gospel."[10]

9. Renan 1929, 51.
10. Ibid.

In introducing the language of revelation to the encounter with classical Athens, Renan seems to elevate pagan Greece to the status of the timeless appeal of biblical culture. Far from being the dry object of intellectual and scholarly analysis, Athens had become a "living reality" that one could feel. But despite the analogy between biblical and classical culture that he constructs here, Renan ultimately presents the two cultures as irreconcilable.

> The whole world then appeared to me barbarian. The East repelled me by its pomp, its ostentation, and its impostures. The Romans were merely rough soldiers; the majesty of the noblest Roman of them all, of an Augustus and a Trajan, was but attitudinizing compared to the ease and simple nobility of these proud and peaceful citizens. Celts, Germans, and Slavs appeared as conscientious but scarcely civilized Scythians.[11]

The espousal of Greek culture cannot leave Renan's previous intellectual identifications intact. To "feel" Greece is to realize the infinite superiority of its civilization. Standing on the Acropolis, Renan adopts the same stance as his ancient Athenian counterparts—he comes to regard all other civilizations as equally crude and barbarian. But despite his focus on a number of rival peoples in this quotation, Renan has a much more specific antithesis in mind. As Vidal-Naquet writes: "To whom does the Athena of the *Prayer* stand in contrast? The fundamental opposition is clearly between Greece, symbolized by Athens, and Judaea."[12] When Renan turns in prayer to Athena on the Acropolis, there was a very particular "barbarian" he believed himself ready to renounce.

> The hours which I passed on the sacred eminence were hours of prayer. My whole life unfolded itself, as in a general confession, before my eyes. But the most singular thing was that in confessing my sins I got to like them, and my resolve to become classical eventually drove me in the opposite direction. An old document which I have lighted upon among my memoranda of travel contains the following: —
>   *Prayer which I said on the Acropolis when I had succeeded in understanding the perfect beauty of it.*[13]

Despite its notable Winckelmannian overtones, Renan's prayer is no aestheticist manifesto. "Becoming classical" for Renan does not merely involve an espousal of the beauty of Greek culture. The sin that Renan is led to confess has a far greater personal resonance. "'Oh! Nobility! Oh! True and simple

11. Ibid.
12. Vidal-Naquet 1995, 181.
13. Renan 1929, 52–53.

beauty! Goddess, the worship of whom signifies reason and wisdom, thou whose temple is an eternal lesson of conscience and truth, I come late to the threshold of thy mysteries; I bring to the foot of thy altar much remorse."[14]

Renan confronts in Athena a figure of science as well as one of beauty. The reason she embodies contrasts starkly with the mystical texts which had been the object of Renan's scholarly analysis. He may have adopted a stance of high rationalism in regard to biblical texts that he studied, but confronted with Greek reason in all its gleaming purity, Renan seems to want to achieve a more perfect Enlightenment. Renan demonstrates a strong ambivalence to his previous scholarly endeavors. It is an ambivalence that permeates the very language of Renan's prayer. Renan, as we have seen, devoted a great deal of his life to exploring the relationship between languages and cultures and in this essay he is determined to find a culturally appropriate mode of address for his ancient patron. Vidal-Naquet observes: "The text of the *Prayer* is written in a Franco-Romano-Greek dialect designed to be intelligible to the ancient deity to whom it is addressed." But Renan's entreaty to this pagan goddess, "Late in life have I known thee, O perfect Beauty," is actually articulated through a direct translation from Augustine's *Confessions*: "Sero te amavi pulchritudo tam antique et tam nova" (10:27).[15]

In the "Prayer," Renan seems to find in the Christian Latin of Augustine a bridge across the irreconcilable linguistic chasm between Athens and Jerusalem. For, as we saw in chapter 3, Renan was the first scholar to systematize the study of "Semitic" languages and cultures. Influenced by current developments in Indo-European studies, Renan saw the world in terms of these two dominant structures of the "Aryan" and the "Semite." In Renan's writing, the "Aryan"/"Semite" debate, formulated in the scholarly context of linguistics, came to take on the attributes of potent contemporary cultural stereotypes. For Vidal-Naquet, Renan's background in comparative philology cannot help but permeate the cultural message of his prayer:

> When Renan invoked his own "blue-eyed goddess," there is no knowing whether he was inspired by Homer's *glaukopis*, the statue of Athena with 'blue-green' eyes mentioned by Pausanias . . . or the "proud woman with golden hair, blue eyes and white arms" described by [the racial theorist] Gobineau. It is hard for us today to credit that the greatest minds of the nineteenth century, whether or not they used the criterion of race consciously, were all—or almost all—convinced of the fundamental inequality of different peoples.[16]

14. Ibid., 53.
15. Vidal-Naquet 1995, 180; Renan 1929, 59.
16. Vidal-Naquet 1995, 188.

Standing on the Acropolis, Renan looks again at these two great "rivers" that constitute the wellspring of human civilization. But his gaze across the wide horizon of human history ultimately brings him back to his own personal history. Outside what Edward Said has called Renan's "philological laboratory," he is confronted with an existential choice. The breeze from afar is no abstract "backward impulse" toward the scholarly enterprise of historical enquiry; it demands insistently that we confront our own identities in the present. When Renan stands on the Acropolis he has to come to terms with his autobiography in all its tortured ambivalence. And yet, despite the idiosyncrasy of Renan's encounter with his "blue-eyed" goddess, it is difficult not to read in his ascent to the Acropolis a description of a more collective memory. It is not just that Renan's paean to Greek culture is formulated in a shared language of European philhellenism that extends back at least as far as Winckelmann, it is also that Renan draws self-consciously on an established contrast between Hellenism and Hebraism. Renan's personal experience of "becoming classical" but remaining Hebrew speaks to the much wider context of nineteenth-century religious and racial politics we have been exploring in this book.

Some forty years later the Acropolis would become the scene of another encounter between Hellenism and Hebraism. Moreover, it would also be the trigger for an intensely personal memory that would bring into crisis another nineteenth-century career devoted to the pursuit of science. On September 4, 1904, Sigmund Freud and his brother Alexander spent the morning visiting the Acropolis. We know from a postcard that Freud wrote to his wife Martha that the visit made a great impression on Freud: "it surpasses everything that we've ever seen and that one can imagine," he enthused. But it would take Freud nearly thirty-two years to come to terms with the full significance of this trip. For it was not until 1936 that he would write about the experience extensively in an open letter to honor his friend the French writer Romain Rolland on the occasion of his seventieth birthday. The text of this letter is now known as the essay entitled "A Disturbance of Memory on the Acropolis." Like Renan's essay, Freud's account of his experience on the Acropolis is structured around a double experience of memory. Just as Renan's essay is a retrospective account framed by an explicit meditation on the processes of recollection, so Freud's essay is a description of a "disturbance of memory" written in recollection decades after the initial event. For Freud this delay in processing the meaning of the original encounter is far from incidental. Instead, the temporal disjunction between initial experience and recollection goes to the core of his practice as an analyst. Indeed, Freud presents his letter as a programmatic account of his *modus operandi*:

> You know that the aim of my scientific work was to throw light upon unusual, abnormal or pathological manifestations of the mind—that is to say, to trace them back to the psychical forces operating behind them and to indicate the mechanisms at work. I began by attempting this upon myself and then went on to apply it to other people and finally, by a bold extension, to the human race as a whole. During the last few years, a phenomenon of this sort, which I myself had experienced a generation ago, in 1904, and which I had never understood, has kept on recurring to my mind.[17]

By presenting his letter as an example of self-analysis, Freud seems to be returning psychoanalysis to its own origin, to be tracing it back to its beginnings in Freud's enquiries into his own mind. The trajectory that Freud maps out for psychoanalysis from its beginnings in self-analysis to its *telos* by "bold extension" to the analysis of "the human race as whole" is a familiar one. But Freud's letter, written just three years before his death, seems to reverse this chronology. Freud confesses rather sheepishly to Rolland: "In the process, I shall have, of course, to ask you to give more attention to some events in my private life than they would otherwise deserve."[18] Freud's uncharacteristic inhibition speaks of a science that has outgrown the "private life" of its originator and extended it ambitions to the life of humanity writ large. Like Renan's before it, Freud's experience on the Acropolis straddles the divide between personal and collective memory, between individual idiosyncrasy and universal truth.

But although the framing of the letter has made "The Disturbance of Memory" what Richard Armstrong has called "a classic example of Freud's 'genetic style' of discourse, a procedure that 'can be said to demand that the writer expose his own investigative past to the reader,'"[19] it is in the body of the letter that Freud describes the disturbance of memory that will come to preoccupy him later in life. For if Renan was confronted in Athens with a "fresh and bracing breeze coming from afar," which would lead him back to his own childhood, Freud experiences a "backward impulse" of a more troubling nature:

> When, finally, on the afternoon after our arrival, I stood on the Acropolis and cast my eyes around upon the landscape, a surprising thought suddenly entered my mind: "So all this really does exist, just as we learnt at school!" To describe the situation more accurately, the person who gave expression to the remark was divided, far more sharply than was usually noticeable, from an-

17. Freud, *SE* 22:239.
18. Ibid.
19. Armstrong 2001, 94, quoting Mahoney 1989, 14.

other person who took cognizance of the remark; and both were astonished, though not by the same thing. The first behaved as though he were obliged, under the impact of an unequivocal observation, to believe in something the reality of which had hitherto seemed doubtful. If I may make a slight exaggeration, it was as if someone, walking beside Loch Ness, suddenly caught sight of the form of the famous Monster stranded upon the shore and found himself driven to the admission: "So it really does exist—the sea-serpent we've never believed in!" The second person, on the other hand, was justifiably astonished, because he had been unaware that the real existence of Athens, the Acropolis, and the landscape around it had ever been objects of doubt. What he had been expecting was rather some expression of delight or admiration.[20]

Like Renan before him, the experience of standing on the Acropolis returns Freud to the scene of his own childhood. Renan's description of the windswept Breton coast, for sure, has a more pastoral quality than Freud's recollection of his schoolroom. In Renan's confession, the experience of being in Athens draws him back to his own autobiographical beginnings. His childhood seems to stand in metonymically for the childhood of humanity. In Freud's less lyrical account, the analogy is not so direct. Freud's identification with Athens is mediated through the classroom. Despite its saturation in a much broader philhellenic discourse, Renan's is an immediate and sensual Grecomania; Freud's, by contrast, is a learnt one. For Stathis Gourgouris, the experience that Freud calls "derealization," is, in fact, a self-conscious confrontation with the discourse of philhellenism. "Freud's arrival at this site signals the impossible confrontation between the discourse of the Hellenic ideal, internalized as part of the very process of *Bildung*, and its visual presentation as (the) real."[21] For Freud the encounter with the "real" Acropolis calls into crisis the philhellenic underpinnings of his own education. Freud at one point does seem to be suggesting that the education he received only provided him with a veneer of Hellenism that did not manage to penetrate into his unconscious:

> It would be possible to maintain that it was true that when I was a schoolboy I had thought I was convinced of the historical reality of the city of Athens and its history, but that the occurrence of this idea on the Acropolis had precisely shown that in my unconscious I had not believed in it, and that I was only now acquiring a conviction that "reached down to the unconscious."[22]

20. Freud, *SE* 22:240–41.
21. Gourgouris 1996, 125.
22. Freud, *SE* 22:241

Freud's Bildung, it would seem, was only skin deep. Athens's "fresh and bracing breeze" was able to conjure up repressed memories from the depth of
Renan's subconscious. The effect of Athens on Freud's unconscious serves
merely to call its very existence into doubt. But despite the initial pull of this
explanation, Freud will ultimately reject it:

> It is not true that in my schooldays I ever doubted the real existence of Athens.
> I only doubted whether I should ever see Athens. It seemed to me beyond the
> realms of possibility that I should travel so far—that I should "go such a long
> way." This was linked up with the limitations and poverty of our conditions
> of life in my youth. My longing to travel was no doubt also the expression of a
> wish to escape from that pressure, like the force which drives so many adoles-
> cent children to run away from home. I had long seen clearly that a great part
> of the pleasure of travel lies in the fulfilment of these early wishes—that it is
> rooted, that is, in dissatisfaction with home and family.[23]

It is not so much his Bildung, on Freud's own account, that was called into
question by his experiences on the Acropolis as his "home and family." It
is hardly surprising to find Freud return to the scene of the family. Where
Renan grounds his autobiographical ambivalence in the grand narratives of
historical civilizations, Freud anchors his ambivalent encounter with culture
in an analysis of the family. For Renan his childhood is a metonym for the
childhood of humanity; for Freud, by contrast, the childhood of humanity is
a metonym of his own childhood:

> But here we come upon the solution of the little problem of why it was that
> already at Trieste we interfered with our enjoyment of the voyage to Athens.
> It must be that a sense of guilt was attached to the satisfaction in having gone
> such a long way: there was something about it that was wrong, that from earli-
> est times had been forbidden. It was something to do with a child's criticism
> of his father, with the undervaluation which took the place of the overvalu-
> ation of earlier childhood. It seems as though the essence of success was to
> have got further than one's father, and as though to excel one's father was still
> something forbidden.[24]

"Filial piety, aroused by the sense of oedipal triumph," writes Armstrong of
this passage. But just at the moment that Freud seems to turn what Armstrong
calls the "primal scene of European identity" into an Oedipal encounter at
the Freud family's own crossroads, he decides to place the familial drama

23. Ibid., 246–47.
24. Ibid., 247.

back into a decidedly cultural context.[25] Self-analysis has "by a bold extension" again become the analysis of "the human race as a whole":

> As an addition to this generally valid motive there was a special factor present
> in our particular case. The very theme of Athens and the Acropolis in itself
> contained evidence of the son's superiority. Our father had been in business,
> he had had no secondary education, and Athens could not have meant much
> to him. Thus what interfered with our enjoyment of the journey to Athens was
> a feeling of filial piety.[26]

Gourgouris writes that "the national-cultural underpinnings of this statement, although unacknowledged by Freud, are striking." He suggests that
Freud's guilt in relation to his father stems not from his social ascension but
from a cultural betrayal. Given the association of Greece in Germany with
a certain construction of Wissenschaft, Freud's scientific success is a symptom of his Hellenization and his consequent abandonment of his Judaism.
"Consequently," writes Gourgouris, "this 'feeling of piety' engenders actually
a disturbance of pleasure, which is indeed the source of 'derealization,' as the
(Hebraic) Father returns to punish the Hellenized son."[27]

But Freud does not seem to disguise the "national-cultural" underpinnings of his statement. In the first instance, Freud calls attention to the specificity of his relationship to his father not, as one might imagine, in terms of
their internal psychological dispositions, but rather in terms of their external
social standing. Moreover, Freud gives a particularity to this question of social position by drawing attention to the importance of "the very theme of
Athens and the Acropolis" in terms that can only be understood as cultural.
Freud is precisely calling attention to the pivotal role that Hellenism will play
in establishing the "cultural capital" of his fellow *Gymnasiasts*.[28] He may not
explicitly spell out that it was the Judaism of his father that was the bar to
his cultural assimilation; nevertheless, the focus on the "the very theme of
Athens" as the source of Freud's guilt defines his relationship to his father in
unambiguously cultural terms.

But perhaps one of the most striking elements of Freud's analysis is that
the letter ends not with a sense of alienation from his father but with a profound identification. Judaic filial piety ultimately wins out over Hellenic
Oedipal rivalry: "And now you will no longer wonder that the recollection

25. Armstrong 2005a, 1, 2.
26. Freud, *SE* 22:247–48.
27. Gourgouris 1996, 126.
28. On which see Armstrong 2010.

of this incident on the Acropolis should have troubled me so often since I myself have grown old and stand in need of forbearance and can travel no more."[29] Freud's inability to travel places him in the same position as his father. Where his father could not travel because of his social status—or to follow Gourgouris—his social *and* cultural status, Freud's ability to travel has been curtailed by the more universal fate of growing old. And yet, there seems to be another unacknowledged "national-cultural" underpinning to this statement. Freud, it is true, was by 1936 almost eighty and suffering from throat cancer. Two years later Freud would nonetheless travel again: from Vienna via Paris to London. But Freud's journey to London was far from the fanciful "fulfillment of a childhood wish" nor indeed did it represent the apotheosis of cultural assimilation. Quite the contrary. Freud's exile from Nazi-occupied Vienna is the exact reversal of the Oedipal triumph of Mediterranean travel that he experienced in his successful middle age. Exile is for persecuted Jews, travel is for carefree Greeks. Freud's inability to travel in 1936 may well have had a great deal to do with his old age and ill health, but there was undoubtedly also a "national-cultural" dimension to the restriction on his movements. Freud's final identification with his father was as much enforced as chosen. Moreover, it seems likely that it was this political context that in fact acted as the trigger of Freud's memory. It is far from a coincidence from a "national-cultural" perspective that this memory reoccurred to Freud in 1936.[30]

Renan's and Freud's texts on the Acropolis stand at the book ends of the philological project. They represent respectively the beginning and the end of philology. Renan, as we saw in chapter 3, was one of the most prominent figures in the development of comparative philology. He followed in the tradition of Herder by linking the analysis of linguistics to the study of the historical development of individual cultures and peoples. Through his analyses of the profound connections between language and culture, Renan became one of the most influential figures of historical thought in the nineteenth century. Renan's particular radicalism manifested itself in his application of a rationalist historical scholarship to the Bible. His notorious *Life of Jesus* had heralded a new scientific age. But Renan's philological project was riven by a sense of the bifurcation of European culture. As a Semitic scholar, Renan was preoccupied by the difficulty of applying the insights of the philological method to the Semitic languages. As we have seen, Renan ascribes the extraordinary strides in the "méthode" of philology and comparative linguistics

29. Freud, *SE* 22:248.
30. See Gourgouris 1996, 12.

to the "matière" of its analysis. For Renan a philology of Semitic languages could at best be a poor relation to Indo-European linguistics.

But alongside Renan's worries about the incongruity of his scholarly methodology and the object of his analysis, the "Prayer on the Acropolis" is testimony to a different formulation of this preoccupation. Renan's text voices a strong desire for a sense of unmediated identification, an identification that he feels for the Greeks. Gourgouris writes:

> Approximately a half-century before Freud, Renan would face the ruins of the Acropolis and, similarly awed and disorientated, would exclaim: "It was at Athens, in 1865, that I first felt a strong backward impulse, the effect being that of a fresh and bracing breeze coming from afar." This is no doubt the exuberant confession of a philological psyche yearning for the concreteness of the past.[31]

Gourgouris suggests that for Renan (just as for Freud) the edifice of philology stands in the way of the "yearning for the concreteness of the past." But what Gourgouris refers to as Renan's "philological psyche" is already a psyche, and indeed, a philology in turmoil. For Renan it is not simply a question of a scientific alienation standing in the way of an immediate appreciation of the past. Renan's science, Renan's philology is already internally conflicted. As a scholar of Hebrew, Renan longs for both the easy relationship between science and its object that he associates with the study of the Indo-European languages, and the sense of unambiguous affinity which he feels for the Greeks. In a passing reference to Renan's text, Richard Armstrong has spoken of the "peculiar masochism" of his "Prayer on the Acropolis."[32] Renan's masochism manifests itself at both a scholarly and biographical level and, what is more, these two "masochisms" are profoundly interlinked. Renan's unfulfilled desire for Greece is both a manifestation of a philological career diverted from its true object of philological analysis and of a biography frustrated by an accident of scientific specialism. But for all his self-flagellation, something stands in the way of both his intellectual and spiritual conversion. "Becoming classical," for Renan, for philology, for Europe, is never the easy choice it appears to be. Overcoming Hebraism remains an arduous task even for the man described by his contemporaries as a disaffected cathedral.

Freud's so-called compulsion for antiquity has also recently been firmly linked to the development of the philological method. Jacques Le Rider, for one, has written that "Sigmund Freud was so profoundly steeped in an-

31. Ibid., 132.
32. Armstrong 2001, 107.

cient history and Greek literature that one could define psychoanalysis as an archaeology of the unconscious whose methodology was modeled on philology."[33] Armstrong's masterful analysis of Freud's antiquity traces in detail his relationship to the developments of Altertumswissenschaft. In one particularly compelling chapter in the book, Armstrong uncovers the direct link that Freud establishes between his own methodology and the precepts of "critical history" developed by Niebuhr in his great history of Rome. It has become something of a cliché to argue that Freud turned to the established science of antiquity to lend legitimacy to his anything-but-established science of psychoanalysis. From the Oedipus complex, to the archaeological metaphor to the "cathartic method," the story goes, Freud cloaked the wolf of psychoanalysis in the sheep's clothing of classical learning. And yet, as Le Rider, Armstrong, and others have shown, the engagement with the classical past played a much more integral role in the development of Freud's thought than such a narrative would suggest. "Classical learning" was no mere window dressing for the psychoanalytic project. Freudian psychoanalysis and classical scholarship were grounded in a much wider interrogation of history and historical method that developed throughout the nineteenth century. For Richard Terdiman, Freud's appropriation of antiquity has less to do with the specific needs of the burgeoning science of psychoanalysis and much more to do with the generalized historical malaise of his age. Terdiman universalizes Freud's own experience of a "disturbance of memory" on the Acropolis by postulating that the "long nineteenth century" as was beset with a collective crisis of memory.[34] For a critic like Richard Terdiman, both Freud's psychoanalysis and the triumph of classical philology would just be two symptoms of a wider sense of the uneasy presence of the past in the self-conscious age of modernity.

Both Freud's and Renan's writings on the Acropolis are profound meditations on the intersection between recollection and philology cut across by the opposition between Hellenism and Hebraism. Nevertheless, on the surface of things, they represent diametrically opposed reactions. Where Renan repents his Hebraism, Freud seems, in the final analysis, to renounce his Hellenism. In Renan it is only when he begins to remember in a nonscholarly context that he understands that he is truly a Greek. Philhellenism is, for Renan, a childhood memory—a childhood memory that stands in opposition to his scientific interest in Hebraism. Philhellenism is also a childhood memory for Freud but it is a disturbed childhood memory. Freud will remain alienated

33. Le Rider 2002, back cover.
34. See Terdiman 1993.

from his own memory, it is unable to attain the status of the "real" for him. He appears to feel nostalgia for a philology that is not his own. His reactions on the Acropolis expose philology as a nostalgia in which he cannot participate. Freud's disturbance of memory not only shows a profound disjunction between his own personal memory and the collective memory of philhellenism, but it also seems to go to the heart of the positivistic methodology that underpins the philological project. Freud's disturbance of memory, his inability to believe in the "real" rather than a "constructed" version of Athens, stands in opposition to the desire to experience antiquity *wie es eigentlich gewesen ist.*

The Life of Moses

At the same time that he was drafting his letter to Rolland about his visit to Acropolis, Freud was in the middle of writing his last and in many senses most enigmatic book—a book Freud described to his son as his "first appearance as a historian." Published from his exile in London, *Moses and Monotheism* was to be Freud's last major work. It is here that he develops the now notorious theory that Moses was not a Hebrew but an Egyptian priest who, far from being chosen by the Jewish people as their leader, himself chose the Jewish people to be his followers. The origins of monotheism are then to be discovered in the transposition of the Egyptian religion of Aten via Moses to the Jews. In addition to the suggestion of the Egyptian origin of monotheism, at the center of Freud's provocative rewriting is the claim that the Jews, in their impatience with the harsh strictures of his monotheistic religion, murdered Moses. The history of ancient Judaism is the site of an oedipal murder whose consequences for the Jewish people continued to be felt well into Freud's lifetime. Written on the eve of World War II and only published after Freud had fled Vienna in the aftermath of the Anschluss, the contemporary political implications of this text were not lost on either Freud or the text's many subsequent readers. This work functions as both an investigation of the origins of monotheism and as an exploration of the pathology of anti-Semitism. Freud's characteristically slippery opening has found itself at the center of an impassioned debate about his Jewish identity: "To deprive a people of the man whom they take pride in as the greatest of their sons is not a thing to be gladly or carelessly undertaken, least of all by someone who is himself one of them."[35] Is *Moses and Monotheism* a brave return to his paternal religion at a time of extreme persecution or is it, in one critic's words, "an excavation into

35. Freud, *SE* 23:7.

the Jewish past," which, in the name of a "selfish desire to display the impersonal vigour and superiority of *Wissenschaft*" is "quite to the detriment of his own people on the eve of their greatest catastrophe"?[36]

The debate about Freud's Jewish identity and its relationship to his commitment to Wissenschaft takes on a different resonance if we consider it in conjunction with Freud's and Renan's experiences on the Acropolis. Where Freud's moment of derealization follows forty years after Renan's own troubled visit to Athens, his revisionist account of the life of Moses follows some seventy-five years after Renan's revolutionary *Life of Jesus*. As Yerushalmi writes: "the nineteenth and early twentieth century had left a turbulent legacy of conflicting interpretations [of the bible] at least as radical as Freud's, and sometimes more so."[37] Yerushalmi has in mind the tradition of rationalizing readings of the Bible that have their conventional origins in David Strauss and reach their culmination in Renan. Freud, like Nietzsche, had read David Strauss's *Life of Jesus* in his youth and at that time had become a devoted follower of Strauss's associate Ludwig Feuerbach. Indeed, Freud was so influenced by Feuerbach that he went so far as to proclaim him as "the man whom I revere and admire most among all philosophers." As Armstrong writes, commenting on "the fervor of Freud's adolescence" "one can see why an assimilating Jew would feel an affinity with emergent secular culture's historicizing and materialist apparatus."[38] It is possible to hear the resonance of such a stance of Jewish assimilation in Freud's assurance at the start of *Moses and Monotheism*: "We cannot allow any such reflection to induce us to put the truth aside in favour of what are supposed to be national interests."[39] When Freud decides to "deprive a people of the man whom they take pride in as the greatest of their sons" in the name of *Wissenschaft*, then, he places himself in a line of rationalist historicism reaching back past Renan to the early heroes of his youth.

In his *Life of Jesus*, Renan had marked his historical credentials by differentiating himself from Strauss. Strauss's earlier work of the same name, he claims, "has the fault of taking up the theological ground too much, and the historical ground too little."[40] Indeed, given Strauss's theological interests, Renan cannot understand how his book could have caused the sensation that it did:

36. Armstrong 2005b, 253.
37. Yerushalmi 1991, 23.
38. Armstrong 2005a, 220.
39. Freud, *SE* 23:7.
40. Renan 1904, 10.

It hardly needs repeating that not one word in Mr Strauss' book justifies the strange and absurd calumny by which one has tried to discredit a useful, precise, spiritual and conscientious book to an uninformed readership. It is a book, however, which is somewhat marred in its more general passages by a certain inaccessibility. Not only did Mr Strauss never deny the existence of Jesus, in fact, every single page of this book implies his existence.[41]

But where for Renan and Strauss the historical existence of Jesus was a question of faith, in Freud's writing the problem of Moses' historical existence has a different dimension. "Throughout the nineteenth century the dominant trend in German biblical scholarship had been to deny that Moses was a historical person or, at best, to grant him a grudging and minimal historicity."[42] It is against this background that we should read Freud's assertion at the start of *Moses and Monotheism*:

> The man Moses, who set the Jewish people free, who gave them their laws and founded their religion, dates from such remote times that we cannot evade a preliminary enquiry as to whether he was a historical personage or a creature of legend. If he lived, it was in the thirteenth, though it may have been the fourteenth, century before Christ. We have no information about him except for the sacred books and their traditions as recorded in writing. Although a decision on the question thus lacks certainty, an overwhelming majority of historians have nevertheless pronounced in favour of the view that Moses was a real person and that the Exodus from Egypt associated with him did in fact take place.[43]

In fact, as Yerushalmi argues and is clear from Freud's footnotes, he would have to rely not "on the overwhelming majority of historians" but on the work of Eduard Meyer and particularly the biblical scholar Ernst Sellin, whose *Mose und seine Bedeutung für die israelitisch-jüdische Religionsgeschichte* provided much of the basis for Freud's own narrative. The overtly historical character of the first two essays of *Moses and Monotheism* parade their affiliation to historical writing and historically inspired biblical scholarship. Freud not only draws on historical sources, but he also repeatedly anticipates the objections to his historical method in a manner that recalls the precepts of "critical history" explored by Armstrong. Indeed, Freud's statement that "science today has become altogether more circumspect and handles traditions far more indulgently than in the early days of historical criticism"[44] brings to mind

41. Renan 1965, 39n4.
42. Yerushalmi 1991, 23
43. Freud, *SE* 23:7.
44. Ibid.

the relationship between Freud's analytic model and Barthold Niebuhr's investigation of Livy's early history of Rome which Armstrong has ingeniously teased out:

> A great hallmark of nineteenth-century German historiography was the critical analysis of the Livian narratives of early Rome by Barthold Georg Niebuhr (1776–1831) in his *Römische Geschicte* (1811–32), in which he proclaimed these hallowed accounts to be poetical fictions responding to national *psychological* needs, not historical truth. This type of source criticism became the model for critical history that was to dominate German thought well into the twentieth century. So it is not surprising that *both* the spell of the Livian narrative, and its dispelling could stand behind an account of childhood memory in Freud.[45]

Armstrong is able to track down a direct reference to Niebuhr's methodology in Freud's own *Autobiographical Study*:

> It will be seen, then, that my mistake was of the same kind as would be made by someone who believed that the legendary story of the early kings of Rome (as told by Livy) was historical truth instead of what in fact it is—a reaction against the memory of times and circumstances that were insignificant and occasionally, perhaps, inglorious.[46]

Freud's comments on the historicity of Moses bring to mind not only Niebuhr and his critical investigations of Roman legends but also David Strauss and his historical uncovering of the mythological structure of the Gospels.

Despite its manifest interest in the historical method, the generic complexity of *Moses and Monotheism* can be uncovered in an excavation of its proposed titles. Freud had originally intended to publish the work under the title *The Man Moses and Monotheistic Religion: A Historical Novel*. Yosef Yerushalmi has written extensively about the implications of Freud's generic qualification in this repressed subtitle.[47] The story of the hesitation over the work's title is only one dimension of the difficulty of categorizing *Moses*, a difficulty only compounded by the notoriously complex structure of Freud's last work, which self-consciously displays the difficult circumstances of its own composition. As Samuel Weber argues: "It is as if the nonlinear, discontinuous, repetitive temporality that marks the historical process as Freud construes it had contaminated the structure of the text."[48]

Freud's desire to recount what he will call in one of the last sections of the

45. Armstrong 2005a, 162.

46. Freud, *SE* 20: 35.

47. See Yerushalmi 1989, 1991.

48. Weber 2006, 65.

book the "historical truth" of the life of Moses may place him in a direct line of descent with the rationalizing biblical narratives of David Strauss and Ernest Renan, but Freud's own idiosyncratic understanding of "historical truth" is at odds with the positivistic premises of his nineteenth-century predecessors. What is perhaps more interesting than Freud's always contentious and now largely discredited historical narrative is what this remarkable text has to say about the transmission of the historical record. Freud signals the departure from the historical material of the first two essays toward the analytic focus of the third: "All this, however, is still history, an attempt to fill up the gaps in historical knowledge. . . . Our interest follows the fortunes of Moses and his doctrines, to which the rising of the Jews had only apparently put an end." In other words, the murder of Moses—rather than being the conclusion of his historical story—is only its beginning. Far from being the *telos* of the Freudian analysis, Oedipus is only its starting point. "It might very well have signified the final end of the Moses episode in the history of the Jewish people. The remarkable thing, however, is that that was not the case—that the most powerful effects of the people's experience were to come to light only later and were to force their way into reality in the course of many centuries."[49] Freud's interest in historical reconstruction here departs from the positivist premise of the previous chapters. He has no desire to return to the originary moment of monotheism's conception; nor, unlike in his previous work *Totem and Taboo*, does he want to prove the historicity of the Oedipal complex by designating the murder of the father as a concrete and specific moment in the history of humanity. Freud's primary interest in *Moses and Monotheism* is rather with the complex reception of this event in the long history of the West from antiquity to the present.

"How," Freud asks, "are we to explain a delayed effect of this kind and where do we meet with a similar phenomenon?" It is at this moment that Freud's much-anticipated analogy makes its appearance: "There is no difficulty in finding an analogy in the mental life of an individual corresponding to this process."[50] Moses' stubborn persistence in the historical consciousness of the Jewish people resembles the mind in which nothing "ever passes away" that Freud describes in *Civilization and its Discontents*. The death of one's father, even and especially when he has been murdered, can never be erased from the memory of the son. And yet, despite their seeming similarity, this analogy functions quite differently from the analogy with Rome constructed

49. Freud, *SE* 23:62.
50. Ibid., 66, 67.

in *Civilization and Its Discontents*. In his famous description of Rome as a "psychical entity' it is the recoverability of the past that is foregrounded:

> Now, let us make the fantastic assumption that Rome is not a place where people live, but a psychical entity with a similarly long, rich past, in which nothing that ever took shape has passed away, and in which all previous phases of development exist beside the most recent. For Rome this would mean that on the Palatine hill the imperial palaces and the Septizonium of Septimus Severus still rose to their original height.[51]

There is no doubt that Freud's reconstruction of the past here exists in a chaotic and destabilizing juxtaposition. History becomes a synchrony of discordant historical moments. But what the Freudian account loses in terms of diachrony, what it lacks in reliable historical narrative, it gains in the assumption that nothing that happens in the past is ever truly lost to the historical record. If the tools of the historian or the analyst are sufficiently finely tuned they will be able to recover the concrete historical moments that have left material remains on the physical landscape. Nothing, in this account, "passes away"; there is, therefore, no bar to the onward march of science.

The story of Moses has more in common with the account of repression that Freud develops in *Gradiva*. In Freud's comparison between Pompeii and the human mind, it is not so much what can be recovered as what has been "repressed" that is at the forefront of the analogy:

> There is, in fact, no better analogy for repression, by which something in the mind is at once made inaccessible and preserved, than burial of the sort to which Pompeii fell victim and from which it could emerge once more through the work of spades. Thus it was that the young archaeologist was obliged in his phantasy to transport to Pompeii the original of the relief which reminded him of the object of his youthful love. The author was well justified, indeed, in lingering over the valuable similarity which his delicate sense had perceived between a particular mental process in the individual and an isolated historical event in the history of mankind.[52]

In *Moses and Monotheism*, Freud draws a comparison between delayed recollection and the phenomenon of repressed memories: "On reflection, it must strike us that, in spite of the fundamental difference between the two cases—the problem of traumatic neurosis and that of Jewish monotheism— there is nevertheless one point of agreement: namely, in the characteristic

51. Ibid., 21:70.
52. Ibid., 9:40.

that might be described as latency." What is more, Freud sees this period of "latency" as crucial to the very development of history as such. For history, the process of recording the past is, Freud suggests, the necessary byproduct of the latency period. History is, as it were, the symptom of "latency." But Freud again challenges the positivist notion of history that he seemingly embraced in the earlier sections of his work. Here the phenomenon of repression is absolutely crucial to the emergence of the historical record. As he writes, "the people who had come from Egypt brought writing and the desire to write history along with them; but it was to be a long time before historical writing realized that it was pledged to unswerving truthfulness."[53] Distortion, fantasy, and repression are all integral to the "desire to write history." Freud's distrust of the official historical record seems fully in tune with his hermeneutics of suspicion:

> All the tremendous efforts of later times failed to disguise this shameful fact. But the Mosaic religion had not vanished without leaving a trace; some sort of memory of it had kept it alive—a possibly obscured or distorted tradition. And it was this tradition of a great past which continued to operate (from the background, as it were), which gradually acquired more and more power over people's minds.[54]

It is significant that Freud turns to the history of Greece to explain this "unfamiliar idea":

> With our present psychological insight we could, long before Schliemann and Evans, have raised the question of where it was that the Greeks obtained all the legendary material which was worked over by Homer and the great Attic dramatists in their master-pieces. The answer would have had to be that this people had probably experienced in their prehistory a period of external brilliance and cultural efflorescence which had perished in a historical catastrophe and of which an obscure tradition survived in these legends.[55]

Archaeology, here, is for Freud, no longer functioning as an analogy for psychoanalysis. Freud and Schliemann are rather in competition and in Freud's fantasy chronology the spades of psychoanalysis discovered the remains of Troy long before Schliemann set sail. Homer's *Iliad* is, for Freud, the neurotic symptom of a repressed trauma.

> Early trauma—defence—latency—outbreak of neurotic illness—partial return of the repressed. Such is the formula which we have laid down for

53. Ibid., 23:68.
54. Ibid., 70.
55. Ibid.

the development of a neurosis. The reader is now invited to take the step of supposing that something occurred in the life of the human species similar to what occurs in the life of individuals.[56]

Freud's theory of the return of the repressed functions as a compelling model of historiography. It is as if Freud's so-called Jewish science is providing an alternative account of historical method that challenges the Wissenschaft of a Strauss or a Renan. A complex dynamic between memory and forgetting, revelation and distortion, at the heart of Freud's new account of the encounter with the past is perhaps most interestingly illustrated in his famous comparison of the act of textual distortion to a murder:

> The text, however, as we possess it to-day, will tell us enough about its own vicissitudes. Two mutually opposed treatments have left their traces on it. On the one hand it has been subjected to revisions which have falsified it in the sense of their secret aims, have mutilated and amplified it and have even changed it to its reverse; on the other hand a solicitous piety has presided over it and has sought to preserve everything as it was, no matter whether it was consistent or contradicted itself.[57]

In his description of the biblical text, Freud seems to be creating perfect character sketches of the revisionist and the positivist historian. The revisionist "mutilates" the text with her or his "own secret aims," while the positivist in his or her "solicitous piety" attempts to preserve "everything as it was." However, despite the conscientious historian's desire to "let the text speak for itself" the past cannot help but implicate its receiver in its reception: "Thus almost everywhere noticeable gaps, disturbing repetitions and obvious contradictions have come about—indications which reveal things to us which it is not intended to communicate." In Freud's version it is the positivist who ends up having to confront disturbing contradictions and it is for her or him that authorial intention and original meaning become most difficult to control. When one tries to "preserve things as they are" in Freud's account, the text appears to have an even more transformative power on its reader than when one actively tries to appropriate it. The most transformative readings in Freud's version are the ones that seek to stay closest to the original.

> In its implications the distortion of a text resembles a murder: the difficulty is not in perpetrating the deed, but in getting rid of the traces. We might well lend the word "*Entstellung* [distortion]" the double meaning to which it has a claim but of which to-day it makes no use. It should mean not only "to change

56. Ibid., 80.
57. Ibid., 43.

the appearance of something" but also "to put something in another place, to displace." Accordingly, in many instances of textual distortion, we may nevertheless count upon finding what has been suppressed and disavowed hidden away somewhere else, though changed and torn from its context. Only it will not always be easy to recognize it.[58]

The scholar of the ancient world must always work with texts that are torn from their context, displaced and in disguise. But the ineradicable traces of history always return to haunt the receiver. What is more, the past has a transformative effect on the present no historian can hope to control. Just as the positivist historian can never hope to stand outside her/his object of study, the revisionist can never fully appropriate the text s/he receives. Cathy Caruth has argued:

> For many readers, the significance of Freud's questioning of history has been a tacit denial of history. By replacing factual history with the curious dynamics of trauma, Freud would seem to have doubly denied the possibility of historical reference: first, by himself actually replacing historical fact with his own speculations; and secondly, by suggesting that historical memory, or Jewish historical memory at least, is always a matter of distortion, a filtering of the original event through the fictions of traumatic repression, which makes the event available at best indirectly.[59]

But by reconfiguring history as traumatic history, Caruth suggests, Freud has a more interesting point to make about the relationship between the original historical moment and its reception: "the experience of trauma, the fact of latency, would . . . seem to consist, not in the forgetting of a reality that can never hence be fully known; but in an inherent latency within the experience itself." "For history to be a history of trauma," Caruth concludes, "means that it is referential precisely to the extent that it is not fully perceived as it occurs; or to put somewhat differently, that a history can be grasped only in the very inaccessibility of its occurrence."[60] Freud's understanding of history as history of trauma undermines the opposition between a positivist and more constructivist view of history. In Freud's version the process of reception is fully constitutive of the "original meaning" of an event. This does not mean the denial of history but rather, as Caruth puts it, the recognition of the "inherent latency" within history itself.

In comparing the task of the biblical historian in his attempts to interpret

---

58. Ibid.
59. Caruth 1991, 185.
60. Ibid., 187.

the text to the perpetration of a murder, moreover, Freud cannot have been blind to the Oedipal overtones of this analysis nor indeed could he have failed to recognize that his own text had been launched with the confession of a parricide: "To deprive a people of the man whom they take pride in as the greatest of their sons is not a thing to be gladly or carelessly undertaken, least of all by someone who is himself one of them"—a confession immediately followed by the self-assertion of Wissenschaft: "We cannot allow any such reflection to induce us to put the truth aside in favour of what are supposed to be national interests."[61] In other words, to follow Gourgouris again, Freud cannot have been unaware of the "national-cultural" underpinnings to his statements about historiography. Just as Freud's Judaism stands in the way of his easy assimilation to German philhellenism in the Acropolis text, so Freud's identity as a "one of the people" makes the task of historical Wissenschaft he embarks upon in *Moses and Monotheism* something that is neither "carelessly" or "gladly" undertaken. The tortuous nature of historical record that he uncovers in the work calls into question the possibility of any easy assimilation to the positivist Wissenschaft he inherits from his scholarly contemporaries.

Richard Armstrong launches his analysis of Freud's "compulsion for antiquity" with an exploration of the Acropolis essay but this prelude soon gives way to a more familiar archetype of Freud's engagement with the classical past:

> I will now take as my model . . . someone with a compulsion for antiquity whom Freud himself came to analyse. In his 1907 analysis of the archaeologist Norbert Hanold from Wilhelm Jensen's novella *Gradiva*, Freud was able to sleuth the ruses of repressed desire in Hanold's fascination with a figure of antiquity, the gracefully stepping girl in a bas-relief he names "Gradiva."[62]

Freud's exploration of the novella *Gradiva* is significant because it was his first published work that conducted an extensive analysis of a fictional character rather than one of his patients. It also has an important bearing on the wider relationship to antiquity he develops in his writing. As Armstrong notes: "part of the psychological preparation is to develop the awareness that in the archive of antiquity one confronts the very sexuality that the sublimating drive for professional advancement and "objective knowledge" seeks to repress or co-opt, which is itself a return to the sexual interest that activates the will to know in childhood." Hanold's encounter with the archive of antiq-

61. Freud, *SE* 23:7
62. Armstrong 2005a, 12.

uity, like Renan's, leads him back to the scene of his childhood. As Armstrong observes: "this is made poignantly clear in the very first paragraph of Jensen's story by the intense aesthetic pleasure his protagonist derives from a sculpted female figure that he 'possesses' in a plaster copy in his study (like the one Jensen owned and Freud later acquired), and that unconsciously returns him to his childhood sexual object."[63]

For Hanold, the classical past recalls him to a repressed memory of his childhood; the material remains of antiquity, as it were, function as conduit to lead him back to his true (historical) object of affection. Just as in the wider concept of the "archaeological metaphor," in this version classical antiquity provides a convenient medium for reaccessing a childhood memory that is hidden beneath the layers of adult repression. Despite the distorting effect of the intervening strata, the careful psychoanalyst, like the professional archaeologist, is able to uncover a childhood and a memory intact. Armstrong brilliantly shows how this narrative of personal self-recognition is mapped onto a cultural history of the aesthetics of German philhellenism. And yet, as we have seen, where the metonymy between classical antiquity and childhood memory seems to work in an uncomplicated way for a Renan, a Hanold, or a Jensen, the process is rather more tortured for Freud. Freud may have had a copy of Hanold's bas-relief of Gradiva hanging on his consulting room wall, but just outside his study hangs a different picture: an engraving based on Rembrandt's *Moses Throwing the Tablets of the Law to the Ground*. The relationship to a more traumatic conception of Jewish history fundamentally changes our conception of the role of the ancient archive in Freud's work. Freud's history, Freud's historiography, then, is deeply implicated in a conflict between Athens and Jerusalem, a contest between Gradiva and Moses.

Indeed, the "national-cultural" underpinnings of Freud's historiography come into even greater perspective when one considers that the very content of *Moses and Monotheism* could be seen as the delayed manifestation of an obscured historiographic tradition. Freud's theory of the Egyptian origins of Moses places him at the heart of the debate about the primacy of different ancient cultures (Greek, Roman, Egyptian, Phoenician, and others) that dominated the intellectual landscape of the nineteenth century. For Martin Bernal, Egypt plays the role of the faultline in this competition of ancient cultures. It was this position vis-à-vis Egypt that would define the racial politics of nineteenth-century historiography on the ancient world. What is more, as Jan Assmann has shown, in his privileging of Egyptian culture Freud comes at the end of a long line of Enlightenment thinkers who had invested in Egypt

63. Ibid., 13.

as a "counter-religion" to the dual forces of Christian monotheism and secular European philhellenism.[64]

As Moses comes to occupy the role of Oedipus in Freud's account of the collective psyche, Freud's historical narrative shifts its focus from Hellenism to Hebraism. Freud's investment in the biblical Moses as he approached his death has been interpreted by Yerushalmi, among others, as a return of the Hellenized Freud to the repressed Hebraic religion of his father.[65] But as we have seen, far from a resurrection of the father, *Moses and Monotheism* is launched by a parricide. By making Moses an Egyptian, Freud affirms the Semitic character of the European monotheistic tradition while seemingly denying its specifically Jewish origin. On the one hand, Freud's Moses stands in continuity with a long line of Jews who finally find their acceptance by not being Jews at all. One recalls Lessing: "There must be Jews who are not really Jews." Like his earlier and well-documented identification with the Carthaginian general Hannibal ("To my youthful mind Hannibal and Rome symbolized the conflict between the tenacity of Jewry and the organization of the Catholic church"),[66] in his identification with Moses, Freud's Jewish identity is transposed onto a Semitic tradition that, while existing in opposition to the Greco-Roman civilization, cannot be easily assimilated into the religion of his father. On the other hand, Freud seems to be rejecting the exclusionary rhetorics of the Eurocentric and Judaic accounts alike. In opposition to a long history of thought that had insisted on the purity of *both* the Greek *and* the Jew, Freud creates in the Egyptian Moses a hybrid figure who is certainly not Hellenic but nonetheless confuses the anti-Semitic stereotype of Jew.[67] Written at time when the polemics of the Aryan/Semite debate had reached its most frenzied literalization in the politics of Nazism, *Moses and Monotheism* stands as a provocative example of a universal history—a history, that is, that covered the development of humanity in general without distinctions of race or culture. Freud thus champions a model of historiography that for both scholarly and ideological reasons had been exiled from the academy.

It is notable from this perspective that the ancient historian that Freud cites most extensively in this work is Eduard Meyer (1855–1930), whose own brand of universal history Arnaldo Momigliano identified as an anachronism even though Meyer was writing more than half a century before the publication of Freud's *Moses*:

---

64. See Assmann 1997.
65. See also Robert 1977; Rice 1990
66. Freud, *SE* 4:196; see also Armstrong 2005a, 222–24.
67. This is the basis of the reading which is elaborated by Said 2003.

In the situation that existed around 1880 Meyer's notion of the history of antiquity was therefore in one respect the continuation of an old idea of universal history now in decline, but was in another respect an affirmation of concrete political and cultural relations extending from Mesopotamia to the Iberian peninsula, which were not generally recognised by contemporaries.[68]

Meyer was an increasingly rare late nineteenth-century phenomenon, a scholar who was as familiar with the Semitic cultures of the Near East as he was with Greece and Rome. Meyer thus positioned himself both against the increasing specialization of the academy and the climate of racial intolerance that made the juxtaposition of Semitic and European cultures so distasteful to his contemporaries. But Eduard Meyer's untimely scholarly radicalism went hand in hand with his fierce political conservatism and personal anti-Semitism.[69] Freud, in other words, chose to base his historical account of Moses' Egyptian origins on the writings of an anti-Semite who held on to the belief in the possibility of a universal history long after the political circumstances made this impossible.

The Triumph of Geistigkeit

Both the form and content of Freud's historiography, then, posed a challenge to the precepts of late nineteenth-century Wissenschaft. Freud's philology stands in opposition to the positivistic underpinnings of historicism just as it calls into question the racial exclusionism of its historical narratives. Freud's life of Moses in its pursuit of "historical truth" may at first sight appear to mirror the project of Renan's *Life of Jesus*, but in its idiosyncratic redefinition of the very concept of the "historical" it marks out its distance from its mid-nineteenth-century predecessor. Moreover, in making the origins of monotheism the central question of his work, Freud seems to be offering an even more direct challenge to Renan. Renan had famously made the argument that the Semites had a "monotheistic instinct": "The Semitic conscious is clear but somewhat closed in on itself; it understands unity to perfection but multiplicity is beyond its grasp. Monotheism both sums up and explains all its characteristics."[70] Renan saw Jewish monotheism as demonstrating the same qualities of inflexibility that characterized Semitic languages. As Olender phrases it:

68. Momigliano 1994a, 213. See also Marchand 2009, 206–11.
69. See Calder and Demandt 1990, 446–504, and Momigliano 1994a, 207–22.
70. Renan 1855, 5.

Since the spirit of a people is inextricably intertwined with its linguistic system, "their very thought is monotheistic." More precisely, since language for Renan was first of all a question of race, a "mold" as decisive in its influence as was the shape of the cranium for adepts of physical anthropology, the Semitic languages became "the organs of a monotheistic race."[71]

So for Renan, the Jews were racially predisposed to adopt a monotheistic attitude, a religious attitude that was at the source of their "absence of philosophical and scientific culture":[72]

One doesn't invent monotheism: India, which has thought such profound and original thoughts, has still not reached this stage today. The whole impetus of the Greek spirit did not suffice to bring humanity back to monotheism without the cooperation of the Semites. At the same time, one has to say that the Semites would have never conquered the dogma of divine unity had they not encountered it in their very instincts and in their spirit and in their hearts.[73]

For Renan, monotheism could never be an invention, for an invention would require the exercise of reason and creativity, two features that he emphatically denied to the Semitic peoples: "The critical, independent, rigorous, brave and philosophical search for truth seems to have been attributed to this Indo-European race which from the depth of India to the extreme ends of the Occident and in the North, from oldest antiquity until our current days, have sought to explain God, man and the world through a rational system."[74] In the distribution of attributes the Semites may be credited with "monotheism" but it is not an attribute in which they can take any pride. Unlike the Indians and the Greeks, who can congratulate themselves for their "depth" and their "originality," the Jews have no agency and therefore can take no responsibility for their "monotheistic instinct." What is more, it is precisely their "monotheism" that is a symptom of their more generalized intellectual stagnation.

Freud, on the other hand, will view precisely the "invention of monotheism" as a symptom of the "advance in intellectuality" that he attributes specifically to the Jews. For crucial to the Mosaic conception of monotheism was one prohibition in particular:

71. Olender 1992, 57.
72. Renan 1855, 8.
73. Ibid., 5.
74. Ibid., 3.

Among the precepts of the Moses religion there is one that is of greater importance than appears to begin with. This is the prohibition against making an image of God—the compulsion to worship a God whom one cannot see. In this, I suspect, Moses was outdoing the strictness of the Aten religion. Perhaps he merely wanted to be consistent: his God would in that case have neither a name or a countenance. Perhaps it was a fresh measure against magical abuses. But if this prohibition were accepted, it must have had a profound effect. For it meant that a sensory perception was given second place to what may be called an abstract idea—a triumph of intellectuality [*Geistigkeit*] over sensuality [*Sinnlichkeit*] or, strictly speaking, an instinctual renunciation, with all its necessary psychological consequences.[75]

The Mosaic invention of the ban on graven images is for Freud at the center of the intellectual and spiritual advancement of the Jews. Freud's use of the term *Geistigkeit* consciously mimics the language of Hegel and German Idealism, the same language that had declared a triumph of "*Geistigkeit*" an impossibility for Judaism.[76] And yet, despite the irony of Freud's use of the Hegelian vocabulary of Geistigkeit, in his characterization of the Jews' elevation of an "abstract idea" we hear the echoes of Hegel's Noah and the "thought product" with which he attempted to heal the world. Freud, moreover, makes the very "strictness" of Mosaic monotheism, which had been its most backward dimension in Renan's analysis, the source of its greatest advance. In highlighting the active agency of Moses in his development of a particularly strict conception of monotheism, Freud explicitly counters the Renanian assertion about the instinctual nature of Semitic monotheism. Far from being an instinct, monotheism was, for the Jews, the ultimate renunciation of the instincts. The echo of Nietzsche here could not be more striking. Readers of Freud's *Civilization and Its Discontents* would be all too aware that the renunciation of instincts is, for Freud, the necessary precondition for the establishment of civilization. But where the earlier work shares Nietzsche's ambivalence toward this renunciation, Freud seems to represent it in purely positive terms in *Moses and Monotheism*. As Jan Assmann puts it "Freud was trying . . . to present the Mosaic distinction (in the form of the ban on graven images) as a seminal, immensely valuable, and profoundly Jewish achievement, which ought on no account be relinquished, and that his own psychoanalysis could credit itself precisely with taking this specifically Jewish type of progress a step further."[77]

75. Freud, *SE* 23:112–13.
76. Bernstein 1998, 33.
77. Assmann 2010, 87.

While Renan aims to highlight the irreconcilability of Indo-European and Semitic conceptions, Freud, by contrast, uses an analogy from Greek culture to explain this intellectual triumph:

> We can far more easily grasp another process of later date. Under the influence of external factors into which we need not enter here and which are also insufficiently known, it came about that the matriarchal social order was succeeded by the patriarchal one—which, of course, involved a revolution in the juridical conditions that had so far prevailed. An echo of this revolution seems still to be audible in the *Oresteia* of Aeschylus. But this turning point from mother to father points in addition to a victory of intellectuality over sensuality—that is, an advance in civilization, since maternity is proved by the evidence of the senses while paternity is a hypothesis, based on an inference and a premises. Taking sides in this way with a thought-process in preference to a sense perception has proved a momentous step.[78]

It is to the *Oresteia* and its decisive redistribution of gender roles that Freud turns to ground his account of the intellectual advance of the Jewish people.[79] The triumph of "intellectuality" over "sensuality," which Freud saw as key to the advance in civilization represented by the Greeks, has the same relationship to the development of abstract thought that Freud sees as Moses' gift to the Jews. Abstract thought, what Renan will call science and philosophy, is not an exclusive attribute of the Indo-European peoples; it is a phenomenon shared by all civilizations worthy of that name (just as the triumph of patriarchy over matriarchy is). And yet, despite this shared inheritance, in the logic of Freud's argument it is the Jewish tradition that explains the *Oresteia*. Jewish monotheism is the prototype that gives meaning to the Greeks' own advance in intellectuality. In Freud's provocative assertion, it is the Jews who provide the clue to the Greeks' "*Triumph der Geistigkeit.*" Or as Assmann phrases it: "One would not, therefore, be mistaken in summing up Freud's understanding of Judaism and the Jewish contribution to human history in the following statement: If it is the destiny of humankind to advance intellectuality, then the Jews are the ones who lead the way."[80]

That Freud had the Greek/Jew dichotomy in mind when he made this argument seems clear from the closing remarks of this section of *Moses and Monotheism*:

78. Freud, *SE* 23:113–14

79. For an analysis of this passage in terms of Freud's "matriarchy manqué" see Armstrong 2005a, 244–49.

80. Assmann 2010, 89.

> The pre-eminence given to intellectual labours throughout some two thou-
> sand years in the life of the Jewish people has, of course, had its effect. It has
> helped to check brutality and the tendency to violence which are apt to appear
> where the development of muscular strength is the popular ideal. Harmony in
> the cultivation of intellectual and physical activity, such as was achieved by the
> Greek people, was denied to the Jews. In this dichotomy their decision was at
> least in favour of the worthier alternative.[81]

In assigning a "pre-eminence" in "intellectual labours" to the Jews, Freud's
analysis could not stand in starker contrast to Renan's account of the Indo-
European and Semitic races. And yet, a different Greek/Jew antithesis seems
to be operating behind Freud's distribution of labors here. Where the Jews, in
Freud's account, are all spirit, the Greeks in this version have bodies, too: they
combine "cultivation of intellectual and physical activity." They are, in other
words, paradigms of Winckelmannian harmony.

Freud has more in common here with Nietzsche, Heine, and Arnold than
he does with Renan. "All people are either Jews or Hellenes," Heine wrote,
"peoples with ascetic and iconoclastic instincts who are addicted to intellec-
tualizing, or people of a sunny and realistic temperament who take pride in
their own organic growth."[82] Harmony may not have been a luxury that the
Jews can afford, but Freud is clear that they nonetheless chose the "worthier
alternative." It is noteworthy that in a prior version of this section that Freud
published separately as an article his last sentence reads slightly differently:
"In this dichotomy their decision was at least in favour of the alternative that
was more significant culturally."[83] From more "culturally significant alternative" to "worthier alternative," what, one might ask, led Freud to move
from the objective stance of the cultural historian to the partisan defender of
Jewish culture? Perhaps Freud knew, especially at that moment, that when it
came to the Greek/Jew antithesis he would have to take sides.

It is difficult not see Freud's investment in the intellectual labor of the Jews
as a contribution to the wider philosophical debate about Judaism that we
have been tracing in this book. Indeed, as his use of the term *Gesitigkeit* makes
clear, Freud's polemic seems to be addressing itself as much to philosophical
debates about the origins of monotheism as it is to the historical writings of
a figure like Renan. As we have seen, the relationship between monotheism
and the development of rationality had been a concern of philosophers since
the Enlightenment. It is interesting that Freud's position about monotheism,

81. Freud, *SE* 23:115.
82. Heine 1994, 350.
83. See Freud, *SE* 23:115n2.

for instance, contrasts so markedly with that of Feuerbach's, "the man," after all, whom Freud "revered" and "admired" "most among all philosophers." Feuerbach, one recalls, had argued that "science, like art, arises only out of polytheism, for polytheism is the frank, open, unenvying sense of all that is good and beautiful without distinction, the sense of the world, of the universe. The Greeks looked abroad into the wide world that they might extend their vision; the Jews to this day pray with their faces turned towards Jerusalem."[84] Despite the many idiosyncrasies of his characterization of Judaism that we analyzed in the previous chapter, Feuerbach's comments on monotheism and polytheism uncannily anticipate Renan's later writings about Semites and Indo-Europeans. To the fixed inward-looking monotheists, Feuerbach contrasts the dynamic expansive polytheists. Where Renan would later claim that "le désert est monothéiste," Feuerbach had already uncovered the desert of monotheism's intellectual aspirations.

While there are strong parallels, as we have seen, between Feuerbach's and Hegel's depictions of the Jews in their hostility to nature, their respective accounts give a very different weight to the question of the Jews' propensity to abstract thought. Where "theoretical" thought is precisely what Feuerbach's Jews lack, it is Noah's overdependence on abstract thought that forms the basis of Hegel's critique. When Hegel opposes Noah to the "more beautiful pair Deucalion and Pyrrha" it is monotheism's tyranny of "the idea" that comes into conflict with the life-affirming beauty of polytheism. For Feuerbach "science, like art, arises only out of polytheism," Hegel, on the other hand, seems to want to prise these two fields apart, attributing theoretical thought to the Jews and aesthetics to the Greeks. In the context of Hegel's argument in "The Spirit of Christianity" it is Judaism's association with the intellectual tyranny of the Enlightenment that makes Noah's "thought product" so suspect. Judaism was associated by Hegel both with instrumental reason and a Kantian notion of ethics that subjected the individual to an external regime of law and abstract command. Freud's assertion of the intellectual mastery of the Jews, an intellectual mastery that was achieved through the renunciation of instincts, not only looks back to Hegel and Feuerbach but also seems to speak directly to Nietzsche who attributed responsibility for the development of "slave morality" to Judaism. Freud's very different evaluation of this overcoming of the instincts is a pointed reversal of Nietzsche's claims about the "poisonous" Judification of European morality. Nietzsche's poisoned chalice is the antithesis of "the secret treasure" that Freud sees the Jews offering to humanity.

84. Feuerbach 2008, 95–96.

But despite the more obvious echoes of Nietzsche, Freud's preoccupations bring him into dialogue with an older debate about the relationship between Judaism and the Enlightenment. By highlighting how it is to Jewish mono- theism rather than to Greek polytheism that we owe the invention of abstract thought Freud makes a very provocative claim about intellectual history. Freud's Moses can lead us back to another Moses who would make the claim that it was Judaism that offered the world the gift of reason. Like Moses Men- delssohn before him, Freud seems to be reclaiming Judaism as *the* religion of reason. Like Mendelssohn, moreover, Freud makes this argument in the context of a wider discourse of Christian hostility to Judaism. Mendelssohn's conscious fusion of Judaic and Greek reason had led his contemporaries to call for his conversion to Christianity. Freud, for his part, sees the Jews' intel- lectual self-confidence, their superior rationality, as the source of Christian anti-Semitism. Freud one could argue, not only reveals how Jewish reason precedes Greek reason, but he also shows how the exclusive attribution of reason to the Greeks is the product of Christian anti-Semitism. In his relent- less pursuit of the Delphic injunction "know thyself," Freud has often been identified as the Socrates of the twentieth century. Freud's *Moses*, however, reveals his powerful relationship to the Socrates of the eighteenth century.

Between Hannibal and Winckelmann

From his visit to the Acropolis to his encounter with the Egyptian Moses, Freud's relationship to antiquity seems to have been implicated in the wider debates about the opposition between Hellenism and Hebraism, Aryan and Semite, which dominated the intellectual landscape of the nineteenth century. Scholars have frequently noted how as Europe entered its darkest moment Freud would embark on a journey that would lead him away from Oedipus toward Moses. Jacques Le Rider, for instance, traces just such a trajectory:

> The references to ancient Greece gave Freud an opportunity to differentiate himself from the Viennese *genius loci*, which drew on the Baroque and the Roman. But the ultimate voyage takes him away from the Acropolis and leads him back to the Sinaitic covenant. It is not a return to religion, but a search for the new foundations of an ethics and a scientific rationality at a time when European civilization is falling apart.[85]

But as Le Rider's comments make clear, the Greek/Jew opposition in Freud is crucially mediated through Freud's relationship to Christian Rome. Carl

---

85. Le Rider 2002, back cover.

Schorske demonstrates that the trajectory that Le Rider maps out for Freud had already been anticipated long before the official rise of Nazism. "*Moses and Monotheism*, written in the 1930s, explores as history the problem Freud had explored in his own psyche in analyzing his Roman neurosis: the relation between the Jew and the gentile."[86] Freud's preoccupation with Greco-Roman antiquity as the site of the encounter "between the Jew and gentile" precedes both his reflections on his visit to the Acropolis and his account of Moses by some thirty years. In *The Interpretation of Dreams*, Freud reflects upon a series of dreams that were associated with what he saw as his pathological inability to fulfill his desire to visit Rome:

> What I have in mind is a series of dreams which are based upon a longing to visit Rome. For a long time to come, no doubt, I will have to continue to satisfy that longing in my dreams: for residence in Rome must be avoided for reasons of health. For instance, I dreamt once that I was looking out of a railway carriage window at the Tiber and the Ponte Sant' Angelo. The train began to move off, and it occurred to me that I had not so much set foot in the city. The view that I had seen in the dream was taken from a well-known engraving which I had caught sight of for a moment the day before in the sitting-room of one of my patients.[87]

Freud's account of his failure to "set foot in the city" strongly anticipates his brooding doubts about his ability to reach Athens which he articulated some thirty-six years later in his letter to Rolland. Freud's "Athens neurosis," then, has a precursor in the "Rome-neurosis" he had already detailed at length in his first great work of psychoanalysis.[88] Moreover, the realization that the Rome he thought he had experienced in his dreams was in fact merely "a well-known engraving" he had witnessed without ever having to leave Vienna foreshadows the sense of "derealization" that Freud experiences on the Acropolis.

If Freud falls short of being able to experience Athens "*wie es eigentlich gewesen ist*," his access to Rome is even less direct, mediated, as it is, through a popular reproduction of an engraving. But as his account makes clear, Freud's sense of alienation described in this dream was not an isolated occurrence:

> Another time someone led me to the top of the hill and showed me Rome half-shrouded in mist; it was far away and I was surprised at my view of it being so clear. There was more in the content of this dream than I feel prepared

86. Schorske 1998, 207.

87. Freud, *SE* 4:194.

88. For a more psychoanalytic reading of Freud's "Rome-neurosis" see also Robert 1977 and Goldstein 1992.

to detail; but the theme of "the promised land seen from afar" was obvious in it.[89]

As Freud again attempts to experience Rome, its outlines are shrouded in mist. Far away on the horizon it is far and yet uncannily near. Perhaps its unexpected proximity was the result of the familiarity of the "theme" that seemed to give meaning to Freud's nocturnal vision. Freud's Rome is substituted by the more-powerful cliché of "the promised land." Where Freud thinks he is seeing Rome he is actually seeing Jerusalem. The new and longed-for classical city is overlaid by the familiar and "disappointing" biblical "theme." Perhaps for Freud, like Renan before him, his "resolve to become classical eventually drove [him] in the opposite direction." Bluma Goldstein, however, comments: "There is . . . a dream which is especially important . . . because of the dreamer's identification with Moses: but this identification is problematic because in choosing Rome over Jerusalem, Freud carves out a history for himself in Rome amidst classical culture and Christianity, not in Canaan among the Jews."[90] Where Goldstein expects the Jewish Freud to identify with Moses, she finds him instead longing for an assimilation to classical and Christian culture. And yet, it seems to be Freud's inability to assume this subject position that his so-called Rome phobia exemplifies. Indeed in a later passage he makes clear the complexity of his relationship to the "eternal city":

> It was on my last journey to Italy . . . that finally . . . I discovered the way in which my longing for the eternal city had been reinforced by my impressions from my youth. I was in the act of making a plan to by-pass Rome next year and travel to Naples, when a sentence occurred to me which I must have read in one of our classical authors: 'Which of the two, it may be debated, walked up and down his study with the greater impatience after he had formed his plan of going to Rome—Winckelmann, the Vice-Principal, or Hannibal, the Commander-in-Chief?' I had actually been following in Hannibal's footsteps. Like him, I had been fated not to see Rome.[91]

In his desire to conquer Rome, Freud suggests, he could either be replaying the wish-fulfillment fantasies of a Winckelmann or a Hannibal. But when Freud is offered the opportunity to "carve out a history for himself in Rome amidst classical culture" he chooses to identify with Hannibal over the "Vice-Principal." It is not *qua* devotee of classical culture that he wishes to experi-

89. Freud. *SE* 4:194.
90. Goldstein 1992, 70.
91. Freud, *SE* 4:196.

ence Rome. Rather, his passion for Rome has its source in the longings of his youth:

> Hannibal . . . had been the favorite hero of my later school days. Like so many boys at that age, I had sympathized in the Punic Wars not with the Romans but with the Carthaginians. And when in my higher classes I began to understand for the first time what it meant to belong to an alien race, and anti-Semitic feelings amongst the other boys warned me that I must take a definite position, the figure of the Semitic general rose still higher in my esteem. To my youthful mind Hannibal had symbolized the conflict between the tenacity of Jewry and the organization of the Catholic church.[92]

Far from a desire for assimilation with classical and Christian culture, Freud presents his thwarted ambitions to reach Rome as failure to conquer a hostile land. It is as a self-confessed "alien" that Freud experiences his dreams of the eternal city. Like his later analyses in *Moses and Monotheism*, Freud's sense of the conflict between Rome and its Semitic other brings together questions of both race and religion. In his identification with Hannibal, Freud imagines the encounter between pagan Rome and Hannibal as a conflict of race. It is *qua* Hannibal that Freud first understands that he belongs to an "alien race." And yet, he later shifts from this racial typology when he argues that Hannibal and Rome symbolized the conflict between Judaism and the Catholic Church. In *Moses and Monotheism* Freud denies Moses his Jewish origin but recasts him as a Semite, in the *Interpretation of Dreams*, Freud turns the Semitic Hannibal into a Jew.

But despite the reversals of these religious and racial identifications, Freud's analysis seems to self-consciously draw together the two dominant strands we have been analyzing in this book. Throughout the previous chapters we have been attempting to trace how the Greek/Jew opposition has been implicated in the shift from Christian anti-Judaism to secular anti-Semitism. Freud's analyses, however, reveal how both discourses remain deeply implicated in one another. Thus instead of finding a contrast between the preoccupations of his early and late work we find a profound continuity. One might expect that the concern with anti-Semitism would be quite differently expressed by Freud in the *Interpretations of Dreams* and in *Moses and Monotheism* written, as it was, under the shadow of Freud's own personal threat from Nazism. But Freud does not contrast a predominantly Christian attack on Judaism in the late nineteenth century to a secular racial one in the 1930s. Christian anti-

92. Ibid.

Judaism remains a persistent preoccupation of *Moses and Monotheism* just as Freud already represents his relationship to Christian Rome in racial terms in the *Interpretation of Dreams*. Christian anti-Judaism, then, is not superseded by the racial theories of the second half of the nineteenth century; rather, one discourse is grafted on to the other.

But what role does an identification with classical culture play in the developing movements of secularism and anti-Semitism? In the figure of Sigmund Freud we can recognize a "godless Jew" who invests in Greco-Roman antiquity as an alternative to both the dominant Christian society of Vienna and the religion of his father. But in his attempts to conquer Rome or savor the Acropolis, Freud becomes aware that he belongs to an "alien race." Freud's realization of his "alien race," however, continues to be understood in terms of an antagonistic relationship to Christianity. Unlike Marx and Nietzsche, whose "godless" identities lead them to embrace a Hellenism that opposes both Judaism and Christianity on secular grounds, Freud reveals that Hellenism can never be fully secular; it has yet to emancipate itself from its Christian cooption.

When Freud overcame his "Rome-phobia" and did finally travel to the eternal city it was not to the *ersatz* Jew, Hannibal, but to Moses himself that his thoughts would turn. "A few years later, returning to Rome," Carl Schorske writes, "Freud felt again a flash of the apostate's guilt. This time it was confronting Michelangelo's statue of 'Moses.'"[93] Like Freud's later encounter with Moses, his 1914 essay on the statue of Michelangelo announces his long hesitations about publishing the work that was eventually printed anonymously. Freud's earlier Moses, however, shares more than a troubled publication history with his later incarnation. For the same preoccupation with the question of Jewish Geistigkeit seems to lie at the heart of Freud's early Moses analysis:

> The Moses of legend and tradition has a hasty temper and was subject to fits of passion. . . . But Michelangelo has placed a different Moses on the tomb of the Pope, one superior to the historical or traditional Moses. He has modified the theme of the broken Tables; he does not let Moses break them in his wrath, but makes him be influenced by the danger that they will be broken and makes him calm that wrath, or at any rate prevent it from becoming an act. In this way he adds something new and more than human to the figure of Moses; so that the giant frame with its tremendous physical power becomes only a concrete expression of the highest mental achievement that is possible to man, that of struggling successfully against an inward passion for the sake of a cause to which he had devoted himself.[94]

93. Schorske 1998, 203.
94. Freud, *SE* 13:233.

FIGURE 6. Michelangelo, *Moses*, 1513–15, San Pietro in Vincoli

Like in *Moses and Monotheism*, Freud finds his interpretation of Moses to be at odds with the orthodox interpretation of the Bible. Freud rescues from the tradition a Moses capable of extreme instinctual renunciation in the service of the "highest mental achievement." Freud's early Moses thus anticipates the "triumph of intellectuality" he celebrates in his final work. But in Michelangelo's rendition, Moses achieves a "tremendous physical power" that Freud had reserved for the Greeks in *Moses and Monotheism*. Where Freud will later exclude the Jews from the possibility of a (Greek) harmony of physical and intellectual power, it is this harmony that is writ large in Michelangelo's Moses. Moreover, Freud's description of the struggle between inner turmoil and outer calm depicted in Michelangelo's statue could not be more resonant of Winckelmann's supremely famous motto of Greek art: *"edle Einfalt und stille Größe,"* "noble simplicity and sedate grandeur." Freud's description of Michelangelo's Moses resembles nothing so much as Winckelmann's paean to the *Laocoon*:

> The last and most eminent characteristic of Greek works is a noble simplicity and sedate grandeur in gesture and expression. As the bottom of the sea lies peaceful beneath a foaming surface, a great soul lies sedate beneath the strife of passions in Greek figures. 'Tis in the face of Laocoon this soul shines with full lustre, not confined however to the face, amidst the most violent sufferings. Pangs piercing every muscle, every labouring nerve; pangs which we almost feel ourselves, while we consider—not the face, not the most expressive parts—only the belly contracted by excruciating pains: these however, I say, exert not themselves with violence, either in the face or gesture. He pierces not heaven, like the Laocoon of Virgil; his mouth is rather opened to discharge an anxious overloaded groan . . . ; the struggling body and the supporting mind exert themselves with equal strength, nay balance all the frame. Laocoon suffers, but suffers like the Philoctetes of Sophocles: we weeping feel his pains, but wish for the hero's strength to support his misery.[95]

In Freud's Moses we hear the echo of Laocoon's "overloaded groan" his "stifled sigh." At the height of his "Rome-neurosis," Freud had denied the possibility that it was as a new Winckelmann that he longed to conquer Rome. Freud had directly opposed Winckelmann's Roman campaign to that of the Semitic warrior Hannibal. In choosing to associate himself with Hannibal,

95. Winckelmann 1999, 30–31. Winckelmann himself makes the connection between the Laocoon and Michelangelo's Moses elsewhere in the *Reflections* when he writes: "The beard of Laocoon [is] as worthy of your attention as his contracted belly: for every admirer of Greek works, says he, must pay the same respect to the beard of Laocoon, which father Labat paid to that of the Moses of Michelangelo" (1999, 70).

Freud had forgone the possibility of experiencing the classical tradition as an heir to Winckelmann. And yet, when he later assumes a Winckelmannian position, it is not in the service of "becoming classical." Freud appropriates Winckelmann's insights in order to understand a hero not from classical but from biblical culture. Where Winckelmann had considered the Jews' contributions to sculpture minimal and had moreover insisted that the ancient Jews regarded the arts as "superfluous in human life," Freud sees Moses emanating an "*edle Einfalt und stille Größe*" worthy of Laocoon.[96] But perhaps the greatest irony is that if Freud sees Jewish culture reaching the heights of Winckelmannian perfection reserved exclusively for the Greeks, it is only in its representation by a Christian sculptor. Freud's frequent visits to Michelangelo's Moses took him to the heart of a Rome steeped in Christian tradition and history. For as Freud never seeks to hide from us, Michelangelo's Moses is not only placed in the Church of S. Pietro in Vincoli, it is the "fragment of a gigantic tomb which the artist was to have erected for the powerful Pope Julius II."[97] It is only as a Christian that the Semitic Moses could ever hope to achieve the perfection of the classical ideal.

Goldstein finds parallels between Freud's troubled encounter with Moses and the difficulties experienced by another Hellenized Jew.

> Like Heinrich Heine, who stood in Paris before a representation of Hellenic culture, a statue of a pagan goddess, and pondered the importance of that culture for his life, Sigmund Freud spent hours, so he tells us, each day of a three-week visit to Rome, looking at a representation of the most significant biblical figure of Jewish history, . . . and sought an explanation for its powerful intimidating effect on him.[98]

In the aftermath of the failed revolutions of 1848, Heinrich Heine would make a final disheartening pilgrimage to his "old pagan gods" housed in the monument to classical culture of the Louvre:

> It was in May 1848, on the day I went out for the last time, that I said goodbye to the idols I worshiped in more fortunate times. I dragged myself to the Louvre only with great effort, and I almost broke down altogether when I entered the lofty hall where the blessèd goddess of beauty, Our Lady of Milo, stands on her pedestal. I lay at her feet for a long time, and I wept so hard that I must have moved a stone to pity. The goddess also gazed down on me with

96. For Winckelmann's comparatively nuanced pronouncements on the Jews and art see Bland 2000, 69. For a different analysis of the Hellenism of Freud's Roman Moses see Armstrong 2005a, 229–30.

97. Freud, *SE* 13:213.

98. Goldstein 1992, 77.

compassion, but at the same time so disconsolately as if to say: Don't you see that I have no arms and so cannot help?[99]

Robert Holub, among others, has interpreted Heine's renunciation of "his blessèd goddess of beauty" in the "Postscript" to his final book of poetry *Romanzero* as the culmination of Heine's spiritual and political disenchantment with the culture of German philhellenism. His realization that his mutilated idol could hardly offer a hand in the cultural and political rehabilitation of postrevolutionary Europe was allied to Heine's growing ambivalence toward secularism and his abandonment of his own Jewish identity. Where Renan kneels before the blue-eyed goddess Athena and renounces his Hebraism, Heine prostrates himself before his goddess of beauty and finally comes to terms with his abandonment of Hellenism. Heine, like Freud, is another failed Winckelmann. He comes to worship at the altar of beauty only to find his inner Semite reassert itself. Godless Jews both, Freud and Heine had turned in hope to Hellenic culture only to ultimately find it impotent in fending off the violence of cultural and political forces of European history. And like Freud, the baptized Heine also finds Christianity standing in the way of his Hellenic communion. It is no surprise that when Heine kneels before "Our Lady of Milo," she replies, "don't you see that . . . I cannot help?"[100]

---

99. Heine 1982a, 696. For detailed discussion of this passage see Holub 1981, 174ff.; Schneider 1980; and Goldstein 1992, 27–28, 77–78.

100. Heine 1982, 696.

"Metaphors we live by . . ."

"Are we Jews? Are we Greeks?" asks Jacques Derrida. "We live," he writes, "in the difference between the Greek and the Jew, which is perhaps the unity of what we call history."[1] Even in the age of postmodernity, it would seem, the opposition between Athens and Jerusalem remains inescapable. How else can one make sense of Derrida's decision to launch his 1967 essay "Violence and Metaphysics," written almost exactly a century after *Culture and Anarchy*, with a quotation from Matthew Arnold? "Hellenism and Hebraism, —between these points of influence moves the world. At one time it feels more powerfully the attraction of one of them, at another time of the other; it ought to be, though it never is, evenly and happily balanced between them."[2] In "Violence and Metaphysics," Derrida uses a contrast between Emmanuel Lévinas's ethics of Judaism and Martin Heidegger's Hellenic metaphysics to reveals how an antithesis between Greeks and Jews had been central to the very definition of philosophy. Derrida's essay starts with a famous interrogation of the limits of philosophy: "That philosophy died yesterday, since Hegel or Marx, Nietzsche, or Heidegger . . . or that it has always lived knowing itself to be dying." Derrida's questioning of philosophical discourse per se, however, is soon troped as an exploration of the *Greek* limits of philosophy. For, as he quotes Heidegger:

> The word *philosophia* tells us that philosophy is something which, first of all, determines the existence of the Greek world. Not only that—*philosophia* also determines the innermost feature of our Western-European history, the often heard expression 'Western-European philosophy' is, in truth, a tautology.

1. Derrida 2001, 191.
2. Arnold 1993, 126; cited in Derrida 2001, 97.

Why? Because philosophy is Greek in its nature; Greek in this instance, means that in origin the nature of philosophy is of such a kind that it first appropriated the Greek world, and only it, in order to unfold.[3]

For Heidegger, "the entirety of philosophy is conceived on the basis of its Greek source." But, Derrida contends "this amounts neither to an occidentalism, nor to a historicism. It is simply that the founding concepts of philosophy are primarily Greek, and it would not be possible to philosophize or to speak philosophically outside this medium." To speak philosophically is to be confronted with the inevitability of a Greek lexicon. For reasons, suggests Derrida, which are neither ideologically motivated nor strictly historically contingent, Heidegger affirms the impossibility of an exit from the Greek premise of philosophy. "It is at this level," writes Derrida, "that the thought of Emmanuel Lévinas can make us tremble. . . . In Greek, in our language, in a language rich with the alluvia of its history . . . in a language that admits to its power of seduction while playing on them unceasingly, this thought summons us to a dislocation of the Greek logos, to a dislocation of our identity, and perhaps of identity in general."[4] Lévinas speaks "our" language—that is to say, Greek—but it is in this very language that he calls into question the inevitability of the association of thought with its Greek legacy. Indeed, Derrida characterizes Lévinas's thought as:

> A thought which . . . seeks to liberate itself from the Greek domination of the Same and the One (other names for the light of Being and phenomenon) as if from oppression itself—an oppression certainly comparable to none other in the world, an ontological and transcendental oppression, but also the origin and alibi of all oppression in the world.[5]

In Lévinas, Derrida identifies a figure who confronts philosophical thought with its other, an other who is other by virtue of not being Greek. Lévinas's thought makes us tremble because this questioning of the Greekness of philosophy has implications well beyond the realm of philosophy *stricto sensu*. Lévinas's thought, by virtue, in part, of its foregrounding of ethical concerns, has something to say about "oppression itself." But can a concept as abstract and abstruse as the "Greek domination of the Same and the One" really be said to be responsible for oppression "in the world"? The Greekness of philosophy itself is held to account for a regime of worldly oppression. Derrida's retreat into metaphor is every bit as conscious as Matthew Arnold's had been,

---

3. Heidegger 1958, 29–31; cited in Derrida 2001, 397n4.
4. Derrida 2001, 100, 101–2.
5. Ibid., 102.

and yet, with his desire to expose the complicity of abstract thought with the practice and experience of domination, Derrida puts the question of the lived reality of exclusion and persecution back on the agenda. In Derrida's hands, the complex interplay between allegorization and political immediacy that had marked the eighteenth- and nineteenth-century discussion of the Greek/Jew antithesis reaches a new level. There could be no starker formulation of the political consequences of the conceptualization of the Athens/Jerusalem polarity than Derrida's provocative remark. And yet, to speak about Jewish suffering in the aftermath of the Shoah as a consequence of the "Greek domination of the Same and the One" and, moreover, to do so in a genealogy which leads Derrida back to Arnold, runs a strong risk of trivialization.[6]

I have written elsewhere about Derrida's use of the Athens/Jerusalem polarity in this essay;[7] what interests me here, however, is Derrida's gesture toward the intellectual genealogy I have been tracing in this book. Can one really place the conflict between Lévinas and Heidegger in the aftermath of the Holocaust under the sign of Arnold's plea for a "balance" between Hellenism and Hebraism in nineteenth-century England? Is Derrida's own willful metaphorization of the Greek/Jew antithesis finding an alibi in Arnold's earlier abstraction? When Derrida writes in his essay that he is concerned with the "historical *coupling* of Judaism and Hellenism" what work of dehistoricization does he need to perform in order to place his debate about postwar philosophy in continuity with Arnold's prescriptions for English culture?[8] It is the same ahistoricism, this same refuge in abstraction, which allows him to exonerate Heidegger from the charge of "occidentalism." As we have seen in relation to Kant and Hegel in particular, Derrida's own work has repeatedly centered on exposing the Hellenism of philosophy as a covert Christianity. It is the complex interplay between philosophical abstraction and worldly reality, the shifting relationship between "transcendental oppression" and "oppression in the world" that Derrida obscures when he removes the historical perspective from his analysis. In concealing this genealogy Derrida's essay becomes all metaphysics and no violence.

What difference would it have made if Derrida had started his 1967 essay with a quotation from Moses Mendelssohn rather than Matthew Arnold? This is, at one level, the question raised by *Socrates and the Jews*. Does Mendelssohn's challenge to philosophy, his questioning of a philosophy as steeped

6. See Lambropoulos (1993, 224–34), who responds to this provocation. On Lambropoulos see also Boyarin 1996, 131–39.

7. See Leonard 2006 and 2010.

8. Derrida 2001, 192.

in the precepts of Protestantism as it was in the lexicon of Hellenism, have the potential like Lévinas's "to make us tremble"? Mendelssohn's identification as the "German Socrates" had unexpected consequences. The assimilation of this practicing Jew to the hero of the fifth-century Athenian Enlightenment had implications both for Mendelssohn's contribution to philosophy and for his engagement with the political sphere. In his rewriting of Plato's dialogue on the immortality of the soul, Mendelssohn simultaneously reinvested Judaism with spiritualism and attempted to move away from religious particularism toward a universal rational religion. Mendelssohn's Christian readers, however, interpreted his work as a prelude to his conversion to Christianity. In approaching the (non-Judaic) question of immortality, Mendelssohn was seen to acquiesce in the superiority of Christianity, while at the same time his depiction of a highly spiritual Socrates recalled the traditional identification of the Athenian sage as a precursor to Christ. Lavater's challenge to Mendelssohn encapsulates the desire of Protestant theology to appropriate Hellenism—an appropriation that would lead to a further marginalization of Judaism. The legacy of Lavater's proto-Christian Socrates is felt not just in Nietzsche's later depiction of the philosopher but also in Hegel's wider philosophy of history where Christianity is seen as the spiritual heir to Greece and in Renan's project of rescuing Christianity from its Semitic ancestry.

The consequences of Mendelssohn's participation in political debates were no less ambivalent. There is no doubt that Mendelssohn was a transformative figure for the Jews both in his own city of Berlin and perhaps even more concretely through his later reception in the French Revolution. But his most sustained contribution to Jewish political philosophy, *Jerusalem*, had a complex legacy. In presenting Jerusalem as a paradigm for the modern secular city, Mendelssohn offered an alternative to the model polities of Athens and Rome. And yet, in advocating a highly politicized interpretation of Judaism, Mendelssohn would unwittingly also provide the basis for its later critique. Kant's claim that Judaism was not, in fact, a religion but rather a political organization is only the first in a series of philosophical treatments of Judaism that would emphasize its inability to move beyond worldly aspirations. Hegel's suggestion in his early theological writings that the Jews are incapable of citizenship may at first sight appear to be the exact inversion of Kant's assertion but it is in fact predicated on the same denial of a moral basis to Judaism and the same reduction of Judaism to a regime of worldly tyranny. When Feuerbach and Marx speak of Judaism as synonymous with egoistical materialism, they too, ironically, show themselves to be the heirs to Mendelssohn's *Jerusalem*.

The cultural conflict between Athens and Jerusalem also had a crucial role to play in the critique of the Enlightenment. For those who rebelled against the universalism of Enlightenment philosophies, the opposition between Greek and Jew would help to define the project of isolating cultural and historical particularism. The development, for instance, of romantic nationalism in Herder's writings would have a decisive influence on Renan who, through the introduction of the categories of Indo-European and Semitic, would make the question of racial difference central to nineteenth-century discussions of historical progress. While Matthew Arnold's much more abstract conceptualizations of "Hellenism" and "Hebraism" are notoriously difficult to pin down, it is clear that they are every bit as deeply implicated in a discourse of nationalism. On the eve of World War II, Freud's *Moses and Monotheism* would cast a critical gaze back on these nineteenth-century preoccupations: "To deprive a people [*Volkstum*] of the man whom they take pride in as the greatest of their sons is not a thing to be gladly or carelessly undertaken, least of all by someone who is himself one of them. But we cannot allow any such reflection to induce us to put the truth aside in favour of what are supposed to be national interests."[9] It is difficult not to see Freud's opening statement as a direct rebuttal of the kind of nationalist fervor that had reached its apotheosis in Nazi Germany. By making Moses into an Egyptian, Freud calls into question the very ideology of the "Volk," which was at the center of the National Socialist assault on his people. But the identity of Moses was not just a question of nation, it was also crucially one of race. Freud's Egyptian Moses also acts as an affront to the racial typologies that had marked the study of the Old Testament since Renan.

While the Greek/Jew antithesis helped Hegel, Marx, Nietzsche, and Freud to articulate a rupture with the Enlightenment philosophies of reason and universalism, certain important continuities persist across this divide. The ambivalent role of Protestantism in defining the contours of German philhellenism remains a constant in their works. Thus it becomes apparent that Lavater's response to Mendelssohn, which saw the Greek transposed into a new vision of Christianity, will remain important not just for Arnold but also, surprisingly, for Nietzsche, too. Nietzsche reveals how it is Christianity's stubborn tenacity, its ability to subsume even Dionysus under the sign of the Crucified, which has made it so pernicious. It is precisely because German reason, that is to say, German Hellenism, had not been able to liberate itself from Protestantism that the return to Greco-Roman paganism is so urgent for Nietzsche. But in Nietzsche's own writings the origins of Christianity become an obsession while the Greek world remains, he concedes, ultimately

9. Freud, *SE* 23:7.

"foreign." Despite the Aufklärung, despite the age of reason, the promise of a genuine secularism rooted in the rediscovery of classical antiquity is beyond the grasp of even a Nietzsche, a Feuerbach, or a Marx. Moreover, while I have been arguing that Hellenism played a significant role in the progression from anti-Judaism to anti-Semitism, the examples of Nietzsche and Freud show how the reference to Christianity continues to be the focus of even these most atheistic of philosophies. Just as Nietzsche chose to write a genealogy of Christianity, Freud decided to write a life of Moses that strongly recalled the historical studies of Jesus in the nineteenth century. Both Freud's and Nietzsche's accounts are marked to the core by the new racial vocabulary of anti-Semitism but both, nevertheless, remain in dialogue with a philosophical critique of Judaism which has its roots in the Protestant Aufklärung.

The dogged hold of Christianity on European intellectuals may be one reason why the Enlightenment formulation of the Greek/Jew opposition remained a central preoccupation of post-Enlightenment philosophy. I argue that the ongoing debates surrounding the "Jewish question" are the other factor that explains its continued relevance. I have been concerned not only to trace the relationship between specific philosophical debates and their political manifestations, but also to show how the act of allegorization itself has had important political implications. The metaphorization of Jewish experience had an effect on political and cultural questions of assimilation. The abstraction of Arnold's terms "Hellenism" and "Hebraism," for instance, is essentially the symptom of the "culturalization" of a formerly political debate. Arnold's idiosyncratic formulation expresses the still-unresolved question of cultural difference that persisted after the political emancipation of Jews in British society. Similarly, while Marx appears to support the granting of civil rights to the Jews, by making them a metaphor for capitalism he places Judaism at the center of the more important and still-unresolved problem of economic emancipation.

The reappearance of the opposition in postwar twentieth-century philosophy is a marker of its tenacity. As we have seen, for all-too-understandable reasons, the opposition of Athens and Jerusalem reaches a new height of abstraction in the wake of the Shoah. But while Derrida gives a wholly figurative characterization of Greek thought, Jean-Francois Lyotard reserves his most metaphorical prose for the "Jews": "'The 'jews' are within the 'spirit' of the Occident . . . (they) are what resists this spirit . . . its accomplishments, projects and progress. . . . They are what cannot be domesticated in the obsession to dominate . . . in the passion for empire, recurrent since Hellenistic Greece and Christian Rome." As Max Silverman writes, "There are a number of problems that arise from this allegorical use of the 'Jew'" or as Geoffrey

Bennington puts its more wryly: "I would have liked to talk about quotation marks."[10] But the continuity between the nineteenth- and twentieth-century desire to allegorize perhaps masks an even more problematic tendency. As Silverman argues: "the judaizing of alterity in postmodern theory frequently relies on the same metaphors as those employed in modernity, and re-enacts the very binary terms it critiques."[11] If Greeks and Jews have become metaphors we live by, it is in part because we have accepted and naturalized the legacy of a nineteenth-century racialization of cultural discourse. By making these terms even more disembodied, these same postmodern writers seem intent on disavowing this history. Turning Athens and Jerusalem into ever more abstract ideas, they simultaneously rescue the antithesis and detoxify it by reversing the binary.

But what could and should the Greek and the Jew signify today? If we have truly entered a secular age, if we have really escaped from the shadow of the Aryan and Semite, if we live, moreover, in a globalized world with an infinite number of possible identifications, how are we to understand the compulsive recurrence of the polarity? As Jonathan Boyarin puts it, "The fact that the place of the Jews in Europe can still be a current question (as it evidently is) suggests that, for reasons that are contingent but remarkably durable, debate over the place of the Jews indicates not an immaturity in the liberal conception of the state, but part of its constitutive discourse."[12] The "remarkable durability" of this debate should not in the end surprise us: for the Carthaginian Tertullian, the contrast between Athens and Jerusalem was already a powerful and inevitable cliché. Perhaps we can take some heart from the fact that the "constitutive discourse" of European identity was first formulated in Africa.

10. Lyotard 1990, 22; Silverman 1998, 198; Bennington 1998, 188. For a challenging exploration of the relationship between Jews, alterity, and abstraction see Benjamin 2010.

11. Silverman 1998, 198–99.

12. Boyarin 1996, 138.

Works Cited

Aarsleff, Hans. 1982. *From Locke to Saussure: Essays on the Study of Language and Intellectual History*. Minneapolis: University of Minnesota Press.

Adams, Robert Merrihew. 1998. "Introduction." In Kant 1998, vii–xxxiii.

Adler, Hans, and Wulf Koepke, eds. 2009. *A Companion to the Works of Johann Gottfried Herder*. Columbia, SC: Camden House.

Altmann, Alexander. 1973. *Moses Mendelssohn: A Biographical Study*. London:Routledge.

———. 1983. "Introduction." In Mendelssohn 1983, 3–29.

Anderson, Amanda. 2001. *The Powers of Distance: Cosmopolitanism and the Cultivation of Detachment*. Princeton: Princeton University Press.

Arendt, Hannah. 2007. *The Jewish Writings*. Edited by Jerome Kohn and Ron H. Feldman. New York: Schocken Books.

Armstrong, Richard. 2001. "Review Essay." *Psychoanalysis and History* 3:93–108.

———. 2005a. *A Compulsion for Antiquity: Freud and the Ancient World*. Ithaca, NY: Cornell University Press.

———. 2005b. "Contrapuntal Affiliations: Edward Said and Freud's *Moses*." *American Imago* 62 (2): 235–57.

———. 2010. "Marooned Mandarins: Freud, Classical Education and the Jews of Vienna." In Stephens and Vasunia 2010, 34–58.

Arnold, Matthew. 1960–1977. *The Complete Prose Works of Matthew Arnold*. Edited by R. H. Super. 11 vols. Ann Arbor: University of Michigan Press.

———. 1962. *Lectures and Essays in Criticism*. Vol. 3 of *The Complete Prose Works of Matthew Arnold*, ed. R. H. Super. Ann Arbor: University of Michigan Press.

———. 1993. *"Culture and Anarchy" and Other Writings*. Edited by Stefan Collini. Cambridge: Cambridge University Press.

Arnold, Thomas. 1842. *Introductory Lectures on Modern History*. Oxford: J. H. Parker.

Assmann, Jan. 1997. *Moses the Egyptian: The Memory of Egypt in Western Monotheism*. Cambridge: Harvard University Press.

———. 2010. *The Price of Monotheism*. Stanford: Stanford University Press.

Avineri, Shlomo. 1963. "A Note on Hegel's Views on Jewish Emancipation." *Jewish Social Studies* 25 (2): 145–51.

Bar-Yosef, Eitan and Nadia Valman. 2009. *"The Jew" in Late Victorian and Edwardian Culture: Between the East End and East Africa.* Chippenham: Palgrave Macmillan.

Barner, Wilfied and König, Christoph. 2001 *Jüdische Intellektuelle und die Philologien in Deutschland 1871–1933.* Göttingen: Wallstein.

Barnett, Stuart. 1998. *Hegel after Derrida.* London: Routledge.

Bauman, Zygmunt. 1998. "Allosemitism: Premodern, Modern, Postmodern." In Cheyette and Marcus 1998, 143–56.

Behm, Britta. 2002. *Moses Mendelssohn und die Transformation der jüdischen Erziehung in Berlin.* Münster: Waxmann.

Beiber, Hugo. 1956. *Heinrich Heine: A Biographical Anthology.* Translated by Moses Hadad. Philadelphia: Jewish Publication Society of America.

Beiser, Frederick C. 1987. *The Fate of Reason: German Philosophy from Kant to Fichte.* Cambridge MA: Harvard University Press.

Benjamin, Andrew. 2010. *Of Jews and Animals.* Edinburgh: Edinburgh University Press.

Benjamin, Walter. 1973. "Theses on the Philosophy of History." In *Illuminations,* trans. Harry Zohn, 253–64. London: Fontana.

Bennington, Geoffrey. 1998. "Lyotard and 'the Jews.'" In Cheyette and Marcus 1998, 188–97.

Bernal, Martin. 1987. *Black Athena: The Afro-Asiatic Roots of Classical Civilisation,* vol. 1. *The Fabrication of Ancient Greece 1785–1985.* London: Free Association Books.

Bernstein, J. M. 2003. "Love and Law: Hegel's Critique of Morality." *Social Research* (Summer): 1–19.

Bernstein, Richard. 1998. *Freud and the Legacy of Moses.* Cambridge: Cambridge University Press.

Bland, Kalman P. 2000. *The Artless Jew: Medieval and Modern Affirmations and Denials of the Visual.* Princeton: Princeton University Press.

Blumenkranz, Bernhard, and Albert Soboul, eds. 1976. *Les Juifs et la Révolution Française: Problèmes et aspirations.* Toulouse: Éduoard Privat.

Böhm, Benno. 1966. *Sokrates im Achtzehnten Jahrhundert: Studien zum Werdegang des modernen Persönlichkeits-Bewusstseins.* Neumünster: Kieler Studien zur deutschen Literaturgeschichte, Bd 4.

Bollack, Jean. 1998. *Jacob Bernays: Un homme entre deux mondes.* Villeneuve d'Ascq: Presses Universitaire du Septentrion.

Bourel, Dominique. 2004. *Moses Mendelssohn et la Naissance du judaïsme moderne.* Paris: Gallimard.

Bourel, Dominque, and Jacques Le Rider, eds. 1991. *De Sils-Maria à Jérusalem: Nietzsche et le judaïsme.* Paris: Le Cerf.

Bourgeois, Bernard. 1970. *Hegel à Francfort—Judaïsme, Christianisme, Hégélianisme.* Paris: J. Vrin.

Bowie, Andrew. 2005. "The Philosophical Significance of Schleiermacher's Hermeneutics." In Marina 2005, 73–90.

Boyarin, Jonathan. 1996. *Thinking in Jewish.* Chicago: University of Chicago Press.

Bradley, A. C. 1962. "Hegel's Theory of Tragedy." In Paolucci and Paolucci 1962, 367–88.

Brumlik, Micha. 2000. *Deutscher Geist und Judenhaß: Das Verhältnis des philosophischen Idealismus zum Judentum.* München: Luchterhand.

Calder, William M., and Alexander Demandt, eds. 1990. *Eduard Meyer: Leben und Leistung eines Universalhistorikers.* Leiden: Mnemosyne Supplements 112.

Cancik, Hubert, and Hildegard Cancik-Lindemaier. 1991. "Philhellénisme et antisémitisme en Allemagne: le cas de Nietzsche." In Bourel and Le Rider 1991, 21–46.

Carlebach, Julius. 1978. *Karl Marx and the Radical Critique of Judaism.* London: Routledge.

Carroll, Joseph. 1982. *The Cultural Theory of Matthew Arnold.* Berkeley: University of California Press.

Caruth, Cathy. 1991. "Unclaimed Experience: Trauma and the Possibility of History." *Yale French Studies* 79:181–92.

Cheyette, Bryan. 1993. *Constructions of "the Jew" in English Literature and Society.* Cambridge: Cambridge University Press.

———. 2004. "On Being a Jewish Critic." *Jewish Social Studies* 11 (1): 32–51.

Cheyette, Bryan, and Laura Marcus. 1998. *Modernity, Culture and "the Jew."* Cambridge: Polity Press.

Cheyette, Bryan, and Nadia Valman, eds. 2004. *The Image of the Jews in European Liberal Culture, 1789–1914.* London: Vallentine Mitchell.

Cohen, Joseph. 2005. *Le Spectre Juif de Hegel.* Paris: Galilée

Cohen, Matin. 1994. "Nietzsche, Hebraism, Hellenism." *International Studies in Philosophy* 26 (3): 45–66.

Collini, Stefan. 1988. *Arnold.* Oxford: Oxford University Press.

Cowling, Mark, and James Martin, eds. 2002. *Marx's "Eighteenth Brumaire": (Post)Modern Interpretations.* London: Pluto.

Critchely, Simon. 1997. "A Commentary upon Derrida's Reading of Hegel in *Glas.*" In Barnett 1998, 197–226.

Curtius, Ludwig. 1954. *Humanistisches und Humanes: Fünf Essays und Vorträge.* Basel: Schwabe.

Davison, Neil R. 1996. *James Joyce, Ulysses, and the Construction of Jewish Identity: Culture, Biography, and "The Jew" in Modernist Europe.* Cambridge: Cambridge University Press.

DeLaura, David J. 1969. *Hebrew and Hellene in Victorian England: Newman, Arnold, and Pater.* Austin: Texas University Press.

Delpech, François. 1976. "Les Juifs en France 1780–1840: État des questions et directions de recherche." In Blumenkranz and Soboul 1976, 3–46.

Derrida, Jacques. 1986. *Glas.* Translated by John P. Leavey Jr. and Richard Rorty. Lincoln, Nebraska: University of Nebraska Press

———. 1991. "Interpretations at War: Kant, the Jew, the German." *New Literary History* 22:39–95.

———. 1994. *Spectres of Marx.* London: Routledge.

———. 1998. "Faith and Knowledge: The Two Sources of 'Religion' at the Limits of Reason Alone." In *Religion*, ed. Derrida and Vattimo, 1–78. Cambridge: Polity Press.

———. 2001. "Violence and Metaphysics: An Essay on the Thought of Emmanuel Lévinas." In Derrida, *Writing and Difference*, trans. Alan Bass, 97–192. London: Routledge.

Doull, James. 1973. "Comment on Fackenheim's 'Hegel on Judaism.'" In O'Malley et al. 1973, 186–95.

Dunn, Geoffrey. 2004. *Tertullian: The Early Church Fathers.* London: Routledge.

Eliot, T. S. 1968. *The Use of Poetry and the Use of Criticism.* London: Faber and Faber.

Erlin, Matt. 2002. "Reluctant Modernism: Moses Mendelssohn's Philosophy of History." *Journal of the History of Ideas* 63 (1): 83–104.

Evangelista, Stefano. 2009. *British Aestheticism and Ancient Greece: Hellenism, Reception, Gods in Exile.* Chippenham: Palgrave Macmillan.

Fackenheim, Emil L. 1973. "Hegel and Judaism: A Flaw in the Hegelian Meditation." In O'Malley et al. 1973, 161–85.

Faverty, Frederic E. 1951. *Matthew Arnold, the Ethnologist.* Evanston: Northwestern University Press.

Feldman, David. 1994. *Englishmen and Jews: Social Relations and Political Culture, 1840–1914.* New Haven: Yale University Press.

Feuchtwanger, Ludwig. 2003. "Das Bild Mendelssohns bei seinen Gegnern bis zum Tode Hegels. Ein Beitrag zum Neuaufbau der geistigen Gestalt Mendelssohn." Reprinted in Ludwig Feuchtwanger, *Gesammelte Aufsätze zur jüdischen Geschichte,* ed. Rolf Rieß, , 17–43. Berlin: Duncker & Humblot.

Feuerbach, Ludwig. 2008. *The Essence of Christianity.* Translated by George Eliot. Mineola, New York: Dover.

Foucault, Michel. 1966. *Les mots et les choses: Une archéologie des sciences humaines.* Paris: Gallimard.

———. 1970. *The Order of Things: An Archaeology of the Human Sciences.* Translated from the French. London: Tavistock Publications.

———. 2003. "What Is Enlightenment?" In *The Essential Foucault: Selections from the Essential Works of Foucault 1954–1984,* ed. Paul Rabinow and Nikolas Rose, 32–50. New York: Penguin.

Fraisse, Simone. 1979. *Renan au pied de l'Acropole: Du nouveau sur la "Prière."* Paris: Editions A.G. Nizet.

Freeman, E. A. 1884. *The Office of the Historical Professor.* London: Macmillan and Co.

Freud, Sigmund. 1953–1974. *The Standard Edition of the Complete Psychological Works of Sigmund Freud.* Edited and translated by James Strachey et al. London: The Hogarth Press.

Funkenstein, Amos. 1993. *Perceptions of Jewish History.* Berkeley: University of California Press.

Galchinsky, Michael. 2004. "Africans, Indians, Arabs, and Scots: Jewish and Other Questions in the Age of Empire." In Cheyette and Valman 2004, 46–60.

Gay, Peter. 1967. *The Enlightenment: An Interpretation; The Rise of Modern Paganism.* London: Weidenfeld and Nicholson.

Gilman, Sander. 1991. *The Jew's Body.* New York: Routledge.

Glucker, John, and André Laks, eds. 1996. *Jacob Bernays: Un philologue juif.* Villeneuve D'Ascq: Presses Universitaire du Septentrion.

Goetschel, Willi. 2004. *Spinoza's Modernity: Mendelssohn, Lessing, and Heine.* Madison: University of Wisconsin Press.

———. 2007. "Mendelssohn and the State." *MLN* 122:472–92.

Goldhill, Simon. 2001. *Victorian Culture and Classical Antiquity: Art, Opera, Fiction, and the Proclamation of Modernity.* Princeton: Princeton University Press.

Goldstein, Bluma. 1992. *Reinscribing Moses: Heine, Kafka, Freud and Schoenberg in the European Wilderness.* Cambridge MA: Harvard University Press.

González, Justo L. 1974. "Athens and Jerusalem Revisited: Reason and Authority in Tertullian." *Church History* 43 (1): 17–25.

Gossman, Lionel. 1994. "Philhellenism and Anti-Semitism: Matthew Arnold and His German Models." *Comparative Literature* 46 (1): 1–39.

Gotzmann, Andreas, and Christian Wiese. 2007. *Modern Judaism and Historical Consciousness: Identities, Encounters, Perspectives.* Boston: Brill.

Gourgouris, Stathis. 1996. *Dream Nation: Enlightenment, Colonization, and the Institution of Modern Greece.* Stanford: Stanford University Press.

Grafton, Anthony. 1981. "Prolegomenon to Friedrich August Wolf." *Journal of the Warburg and Courtauld Institutes* 44:101–29.

———. 1999. "Juden und Griechen bei Friedrich August Wolf." In *Friedrich August Wolf: Studien, Dokumente, Bibliographie*, ed. Reinhard Markner and Giuseppe Veltri, 9–31. Stuttgart: Franz Steiner.

Grafton, Anthony and Weinberg, Joanna. 2011. *"I have always loved the Holy Tongue": Isaac Casaubon, the Jews, and a forgotten chapter in Renaissance Scholarship*. Cambridge, MA: Harvard University Press.

Graham, John. 1979. *Lavater's Essay on Physiognomy: A Study in the History of Ideas*. Bern: Lang.

Gruen, Erich, S. 2009. "Hellenism and Hebraism." In *The Oxford Handbook of Hellenic Studies*, 129–39.

Güthenke, Constanze. 2008. *Placing Modern Greece: The Dynamics of Romantic Hellenism 1770–1840*. Oxford: Oxford University Press.

Hamacher, Werner. 1998. *Pleroma—Reading in Hegel*. Translated by Nicholas Walker and Simon Jarvis. Stanford: Stanford University Press.

Hamann, Johann Georg. 1967. *Socratic Memorabilia*. Translated with a commentary by James C. O'Flaherty. Baltimore: Johns Hopkins University Press.

Hamilton, Paul. 2002. *Historicism: The New Critical Idiom*. London: Routledge

Hanfmann, George M. A. 1951. "Socrates and Christ." *Harvard Studies in Classical Philology* 60: 2057–2233.

Harris, H. S. 1972. *Hegel's Development: Toward the Sun 1770–1801*. Oxford: Clarendon Press.

Harrison, Paul R. 1994. *The Disenchantment of Reason: The Problem of Socrates in Modernity*. Albany, New York: State University of New York Press.

Hartog, François. 2005. *Anciens, Modernes, Sauvages*. Paris: Galaade Éditions.

Harvey, Van A. 1995. *Feuerbach and the Interpretation of Religion*. Cambridge: Cambridge University Press.

Hegel, G.W.F. 1902. *The Philosophy of History*. Translated by J. Sibree. New York: P.F. Collier and Sons.

———. 1907. *Hegels theologische Jugendschriften*. Edited by H. Nohl. Tübingen: JCB Mohr.

———. 1942. *Philosophy of Right*. Translated by T. M. Knox. Oxford: Clarendon Press.

———. 1948. *Early Theological Writings*. Translated by T. M. Knox. Chicago: University of Chicago Press.

———. 1957. *Lectures on the History of Philosophy*. Translated by J. Sibree. New York: Dover.

———. 1974. *Lectures on the History of Philosophy*, vol. 1. Translated by E. S. Haldane and Frances H. Simpson. London: The Humanities Press.

———. 1977. *Phenomenology of Spirit*. Translated by A. V. Miller. Oxford: The Clarendon Press.

———. 1984. *Three Essays: The Tübingen Essay, Berne Fragments, The Life of Jesus*. Edited and translated by Peter Fuss and John Dubbins. Notre Dame, Indiana: University of Notre Dame Press.

———. 1986. *Vorlesungen über die Ästhetik I–III. Werke*, vols. 13–15. Frankfurt: Suhrkamp.

———. 1997. *Premiers Ecrits (Francfort 1797–1800)*. Edited and translated by Olivier Depré. Paris: Vrin.

Heidegger, Martin. 1958. *What Is Philosophy?* Translated by William Kluback and Jean T. Wilde. London: Vision Press.

Heine, Heinrich. 1954. *Heinrich Heines Werke: In Einem Band*. Edited by Hermann R. Leber. Salzburg: Das Bergland Buch.

———. 1968–1976. *Sämtliche Werke*, Edited by K. Briegleb et al. Munich: Hanser Verlag.

———. 1982a. *Poetry and Prose*. Edited by Jost Hermand and Robert C. Holub. London: Continuum.

———. 1982b. *The Complete Poems of Heinrich Heine: A Modern English Version*. Translated by Hal Draper. Oxford: Oxford University Press.

———. 1994. *Werke*, vol. 4. Frankfurt: Suhrkamp.

Helleman, Wendy. 1994. "Tertullian on Athens and Jerusalem." In *Hellenization Revisited: Shaping a Christian Response within the Greco-Roman World*, ed. Helleman. Lanham: University Press of America.

Hengel, M. 1974. *Judaism and Hellenism: Studies in Their Encounter in Palestine during the Early Hellenistic Period*. 2 vols. London: SCM Press.

Herder, Johann Gottfried. 1790. *Briefe das Studium der Theologie betreffend*. Frankfurt und Leipzig.

———. 1877–1913. *Sämtliche Werke*. Edited by B. Suphan. Berlin: Weidmann.

———. 1968. *Reflections on the Philosophy of the History of Mankind*. Edited by F. Manuel and translated by T. O. Churchill. Chicago: University of Chicago Press.

———. 2004. *Another Philosophy of History and Selected Political Writings*, edited and translated by Ioannis D. Evrigenis and Daniel Pellerin. Indianapolis: Hackett Publishing.

Heschel, Susannah. 1998. *Abraham Geiger and the Jewish Jesus*. Chicago: University of Chicago Press.

———. 2008. *The Aryan Jesus: Christian Theologians and the Bible in Nazi Germany*. Princeton: Princeton University Press.

Hess, Jonathan M. 2002. *Germans, Jews and the Claims of Modernity*. New Haven: Yale University Press.

———. 2007. "Moses Mendelssohn and the Polemics of History." In Gotzmann and Wiese 2007, 3–27.

Hilfrich, Carola. 2000. *"Lebendige Schrift." Repräsentation und Idolatrie in Moses Mendelssohns Philosophie und Exegese des Judentums*. München: Fink Wilhelm.

Hodgson, Peter. 2005. *Hegel and Christian Theology*. Oxford: Oxford University Press.

Holub, Robert C. 1981. *Heinrich Heine's Reception of German Grecophilia*. Heidelberg: Winter.

Honig, Bonnie. 2009. *Emergency Politics: Paradox, Law, Democracy*. Princeton: Princeton University Press.

Horkheimer, Max, and Theodor W. Adorno. 2002. *Dialectics of Enlightenment: Philosophical Fragments*. Edited by Gunzelin Schmid Noerr and translated by Edmund Jephcott. Stanford: Stanford University Press.

Jameson, Frederic. 2009. "Filming Capital." *New Left Review* 58 (July/August): 109–17.

Janicaud, Dominique. 1975. *Hegel et le déstin de la Grèce*. Paris: Vrin.

Jenkyns, Richard. 1981. *The Victorians and Ancient Greece*. Oxford: Blackwell.

Jones, William. 1788. "On the Hindus: The Third Anniversary Discourse." *Asiatik Researches* 1:415–31.

Joyce, James. 1990. *Ulysses*. With a foreword by Morris L. Ernst. New York: Random House.

Kain, Philip. 1982. *Schiller, Hegel and Marx: State, Society and the Aesthetic Ideal of Ancient Greece*. Montreal: McGill University Press.

Kant, Immanuel. 1929. *Critique of Pure Reason*. Translated by Norman Kemp Smith. London : Macmillan.

———. 1967. *Philosophical Correspondence 1759–1799*. Edited and translated by Arnulf Zweig. Chicago: University of Chicago Press.

————. 1979. *The Conflict of the Faculties*. Translated by Mary Gregor. New York: Abaris Books.

————. 1998. *Religion within the Boundaries of Mere Reason; and Other Writings*. Edited and translated by Allen Wood and George di Giovanni. Cambridge: Cambridge University Press.

Kearney, R. 1984. *Dialogues with Contemporary Continental Thinkers*. Manchester: Manchester University Press.

Kirchhoff, Markus. 2006. "Erweiterter Orientalismus. Zu euro-christlichen Identifikationen und jüdischer Gegengeschichte im 19. Jahrhundert." In *Jüdische Geschichte als allgemeine Geschichte*, ed. Raphael Gross and Yfaat Weiss, 99–119. Göttingen: Vandenhoeck and Ruprecht.

Kohn, Hans. 1945. *The Idea of Nationalism: A Study in its Origins and Backgrounds*. New York: Macmillan.

Kofman, Sarah. 1994. *Le mépris des Juifs: Nietzsche, les Juifs, l'antisémitisme*. Paris: Galilée.

————. 1998. *Socrates: Fictions of a Philosopher*. Translated by Catherine Porter. London: Athlone.

Lacan, Jacques. 1991. *Le séminaire, VII; Le transfert*. Paris: Seuil.

Lambropoulos, Vassilis. 1993. *The Rise of Eurocentrism: Anatomy of Interpretation*. Princeton: Princeton University Press.

Lamm, Julia A. 2005. "The Art of Interpreting Plato." In Marina 2005, 91–108.

Lavater, Johann Caspar. 1775. *Physiognomische Fragmente*. Leipzig: Ben Weidmanns Erben und Reich, und Heinrich Steiner und Compagnie.

————. 1848. *Essays on Physiognomy: Designed to Promote the Knowledge and the Love of Mankind*. Translated by Thomas Holcroft. London: William Tegg.

Legros, Robert. 1997. "Sur l'antijudaïsme et le paganisme du jeune Hegel." In Hegel 1997, 11–45.

Leonard, Miriam. 2005. *Athens in Paris: Ancient Greece and the Political in Post-War French Thought*. Oxford: Oxford University Press.

————. 2006. "Oedipus in the Accusative: Derrida and Lévinas." *Comparative Literature Studies* 43 (3): 224–51.

————. 2010. "Derrida between 'Greek' and 'Jew.'" In *Derrida and Antiquity*, ed. Leonard, 135–58. Oxford: Oxford University Press.

Le Rider, Jacques. 2002. *Freud, de l'Acropole au Sinaï: Le retour à l'Antique des Modernes viennois*. Paris: Press Universitaires de France.

Lerousseau, Andrée. 2001. *Le judaïsme dans la philosophie allemande*. Paris: Presses Universitaires de France.

Lévinas, Emmanuel. 1963. *Difficile liberté*. Paris: Albin Michel.

————. 1986. "The Trace of the Other." In *Deconstruction in Context*, ed. M. Taylor, 345–59. Chicago: University of Chicago Press.

Librett, Jeffrey S. 2000. *The Rhetoric of Cultural Dialogue: Jews and Germans from Moses Mendelssohn to Richard Wagner and Beyond*. Stanford: Stanford University Press.

Lifshitz, M. 1938. *The Philosophy of Art of Karl Marx*. Translated by R. B. Winn. New York: Pluto Press.

Lincoln, Bruce. 1999. *Theorizing Myth: Narrative, Ideology, and Scholarship*. Chicago: Chicago University Press.

Lukács, Georg. 1975. *The Young Hegel: Studies in the Relations between Dialectics and Economics*. Translated by Rodney Livingstone. London: Merlin Press.

Lyotard, Jean-François. 1990. *Heidegger and the "Jews."* Minneapolis: University Minnesota Press.

Mack, Michael. 2003. *German Idealism and the Jew: The Inner Anti-Semitism of Philosophy and German-Jewish Responses.* Chicago: University of Chicago Press.

Mahoney, Patrick. 1989. *On Defining Freud's Discourse.* New Haven: Yale University Press.

Manuel, Frank. 1992. *The Broken Staff: Judaism through Christian Eyes.* Cambridge MA: Harvard University Press.

Marchand, Suzanne L. 1996. *Down from Olympus: Archaeology and Philhellenism in Germany, 1750–1970.* Princeton: Princeton University Press.

———. 2003. "From Liberalism to Neoromanticism: Albrecht Dieterich, Richard Reitzenstein and the Religious Turn in Fin de Siècle German Classical Studies." In *Out of Arcadia*, ed. Martin Ruehl and Ingo Gildenhard, 129–60. British Institute of Classical Studies Supplement 79.

———. 2009. *German Orientalism and the Age of Empire.* Cambridge: Cambridge University Press.

Marchand, Suzanne, and Anthony Grafton. 1997. "Martin Bernal and His Critics." *Arion* 5 (2): 2–35.

Marina, Jacqueline. 2005. *The Cambridge Companion to Friedrich Schleiermacher.* Cambridge: Cambridge University Press.

Marx, Karl. 1967. *Writings of the Young Marx on Philosophy and Society.* Translated by L. Easton and K. Guddat. Garden City, NY: Doubleday.

———. 1975. "Doctoral Dissertation: Difference between Democritean and Epicurean Philosophy of Nature in General." In Karl Marx and Friedrich Engels, *Collected Works*, 1:25–108. London: Lawrence and Wishart.

———. 1992. *Early Writings.* Translated by Tom Nairn. London: Penguin.

———. 2000. *Selected Writings.* Edited by David McLellan. Oxford: Oxford University Press.

———. 2002. "The Eighteenth Brumaire of Louis Bonaparte." Translated by Terrell Carver. In Cowling and Martin 2002, 19–112.

Marx, Karl, and Friedrich Engels. 2004. *The German Ideology, Part 1.* Edited and translated by C. J. Arthur. London: Lawrence and Wishart.

Massey, Marilyn Chapin. 1983. *Christ Unmasked: The Meaning of the Life of Jesus in German Politics.* Chapel Hill: University of North Carolina Press.

McCarthy, George E. 1990. *Marx and the Ancients.* Savage, Maryland: Rowman and Littlefield.

———. 1992. *Marx and Aristotle: Nineteenth-Century German Social Theory and Classical Antiquity.* Savage, Maryland: Rowman and Littlefield.

———. 1994. *Dialectics and Decadence: Echoes of Antiquity in Marx and Nietzsche.* London: Rowman and Littlefield.

Meinecke, Friedrich. 1972. *Historism: The Rise of a New Historical Outlook.* Translated by J. E. Anderson. London: Routledge and K. Paul.

Mendelssohn, Moses. 1843. *Gesammelte Schriften.* Edited by G. B. Mendelssohn. 7 vols. Leipzig: F. A. Brockhaus.

———. 1929–1938. *Gesammelte Schriften Jubiläumsausgabe.* Edited by I. Elbogen, J. Guttmann, and E. Mittwoch. 7 vols. Berlin: Akademie-Verlag.

———. 1983. *Jerusalem or on Religious Power and Judaism.* Translated by Allan Arkush. Hannover: University of New England Press.

———. 2007. *Phädon, or On the Immortality of the Soul.* Translated by Patricia Noble. New York: Peter Lang.

Mirabeau, Le comte de. 1968. *Sur Moses Mendelssohn sur la réforme politique des Juifs*. Reprinted as *La Révolution Française et l'émancipation des Juifs*, vol. 1. Paris: Editions d'histoire Sociale.

Misrahi, Robert. 1972. *Marx et la question juive*. Paris: Gallimard.

Momigliano, A. D. 1994a. *Studies on Modern Scholarship*. Edited by G. W. Bowersock and T. J. Cornell and translated by T. Cornell. Berkeley: University of California Press.

———, ed. 1994b. *Essays on Ancient and Modern Judaism*. Translated by M. Masella-Gayley with an introduction by S. Berti. Chicago: University of Chicago Press.

Montuori, Mario. 1981. *Socrates: Physiology of a Myth*. Amsterdam: Gieben.

Morley, Neville. 2009. *Antiquity and Modernity*. Oxford: Blackwell.

Mossé, Claude. 1989. *L'antiquité dans la Révolution Française*. Paris: Albin Michel.

Mosse, Werner. 1981. *Revolution and Evolution: 1848 in German-Jewish History*. Tübingen: Mohr.

Müller, Max. 1862. *Lectures on the Science of Language*. London: Longman, Green.

———. 1864. *Lectures on the Science of Language*, vol. 2. London: Longman, Green.

Munk, Reiner. 2006. "Mendelssohn and Kant on Judaism." *Jewish Studies Quarterly* 13:215–22.

Musto, Marcello. 2008. "History, Production and Method in the 1857 'Introduction.'" In *Karl Marx's* Grundrisse: *Foundations of the Critique of Political Economy 150 Years Later*, ed. Musto, 3–32. London: Routeldge.

Myers, David N. 2003. *Resisting History: Historicism and Its Discontents in German-Jewish Thought*. Princeton: Princeton University Press.

Nancy, Jean-Luc. 2005. "Préface." In Cohen 2005, 11–17.

Nehamas, Alexander. 1998. *The Art of Living: Socratic Reflections from Plato to Foucault*. Berkeley: University of California Press.

Nelson, Eric. 2010. *The Hebrew Republic: Jewish Sources and the Transformation of European Political Thought*. Cambridge MA: Harvard University Press.

Newman, Amy. 1993. "The Death of Judaism in German Protestant Thought from Luther to Hegel." *Journal of the American Academy of Religion* 61 (3): 455–84.

Nicholls, Angus. 2006. *Goethe's Concept of the Daimonic: After the Ancients*. Rochester, NY: Camden House.

Nietzsche, Friedrich. 1969. *On the Genealogy of Morals*. Translated by Walter Kaufmann and R. J. Hollingdale. New York: Random House.

———. 1979. "The Struggle between Science and Reason." In *Philosophy and Truth: Selections from Nietzsche's Notebooks of the early 1870s*, trans. Daniel Breazale, 127–48. Atlantic Highlands: Harvester Press.

———. 1993. *Beyond Good and Evil*. Translated by R. J. Hollingdale. New York: Dover.

———. 1997. *Untimely Meditations*. Edited by Daniel Breazeale and translated by R. J. Hollingdale. Cambridge: Cambridge University Press.

———. 1998. *Twilight of the Idols or How to Philosophize with a Hammer*. Translated by Duncan Large. Oxford: Oxford University Press,

———. 1999. *The Birth of Tragedy*. Edited by Raymond Geuss and Ronald Speirs and translated by Ronald Speirs. Cambridge: Cambridge University Press.

———. 2001. *The Gay Science*. Edited by Bernard Williams and translated by Josefine Nauckhoff. Cambridge: Cambridge University Press.

———. 2005. *The Anti-Christ, Ecce Homo, Twilight of the Idols and Other Writings*. Edited by Aaron Ridley and Judith Norman. Translated by Judith Norman. Cambridge: Cambridge University Press.

O'Flaherty, James C. 1967. *Hamann's Socratic Memorabilia: A Translation and Commentary.* Baltimore: Johns Hopkins University Press.

Olender, Maurice. 1992. *The Languages of Paradise: Race, Religion, and Philology in the Nineteenth Century.* Cambridge MA: Havard University Press.

O'Malley, J. J, K. W. Algozin, H. P. Kainz, and L. C. Rice, eds. 1973. *The Legacy of Hegel: Proceedings of the Marquette Hegel Symposium 1970.* The Hague: Nijhoff.

Osborn, Eric. 1997. *Tertullian, First Theologian of the West.* Cambridge: Cambridge University Press.

Paolucci, Anne, and Henry Paolucci, eds. 1962. *Hegel on Tragedy.* New York: Harper and Row.

Peyre, Henri. 1973. *Renan et la Grèce.* Paris: A.G. Nizet.

Psichari, Henriette. 1956. *La Prière sur l'Acropole et ses Mystères.* Paris: Éditions du Centre Nationale de la Recherche Scientifique.

Pöggeler, Otto. 1974. "Hegel's Interpretation of Judaism." *Human Context* 6:523–60.

Poliakov, Leon. 1974. *The Aryan Myth: A History of Racist and Nationalist Ideas in Europe.* Translated by E. Howard. London: Chatto and Windus.

Porter, James I. 2000. *Nietzsche and the Philology of the Future.* Stanford: Stanford University Press.

———. 2008. "Erich Auerbach and the Judaizing of Philology." *Critical Inquiry* 35 (1): 115–47.

———. 2010. "Odysseus and the Wandering Jew: The Dialectic of Jewish Enlightenment in Adorno and Horkheimer." *Cultural Critique* 74 (Winter): 200–213.

Potts, Alex. 1994. *Flesh and the Ideal: Winckelmann and the Origins of Art History.* New Haven: Yale University Press.

Pulzer, Peter. 1988. *The Rise of Political Anti-Semitism in Germany and Austria.* Cambridge MA: Harvard University Press.

Rajak, Tessa. 2001a. "Jews and Greeks: The Invention and Exploitation of Polarities in the Nineteenth Century." In Tessa Rajak, *The Jewish Dialogue with Greece and Rome.* Leiden: Brill.

Reill, Peter Hans. 1975. *The German Enlightenment and the Rise of Historicism.* Berkeley: University of California Press.

Renan, Ernest. 1855. *Histoire générale et système comparé des langues sémitiques.* Paris: Chez Benjamin Dupra.

———. 1904. *The Life of Jesus.* Complete edition with a preface by Charles T. Gorham. London: Watts and Co.

———. 1929. "Prayer on the Acropolis." In *Ernest Renan: Recollections of My Youth,* trans. C. B. Pittman, 49–64. London: Routledge.

———. 1947. *Oeuvres Complètes.* Edited by Henriette Psichari. Paris: Éditions Louis Conard.

———. 1965. *Vie de Jésus.* Paris: Calmann-Lévy.

Rice, Emanuel. 1990. *Freud and Moses: The Long Journey Home.* Albany: State University of New York Press.

Ritter, Joachim. 1982. *Hegel and the French Revolution: Essays on the* Philosophy of Right. Translated by Richard Winfield. Cambridge MA: Harvard University Press.

Robert, Marthe. 1977. *From Oedipus to Moses: Freud's Jewish Identity.* London: Routledge and Kegan Paul.

Rose, Gillian. 1993. *Judaism and Modernity: Philosophical Essays.* Oxford: Blackwell.

Rose, Paul Lawrence. 1990. *Revolutionary Antisemitism in Germany from Kant to Wagner.* Princeton: Princeton University Press.

Rosenstock, Bruce. 2010. *Philosophy and the Jewish Question: Mendelssohn, Rosenzweig, and Beyond.* New York: Fordham University Press.

Rotenstreich, Nathan. 1964. *The Recurring Pattern: Studies in Anti-Judaism in Modern Thought*. New York: Wiedenfeld & Nicolson.

———. 1984. *Jews and German Philosophy: The Polemics of Emancipation*. New York: Schocken Books.

Russell, George W. E. 1895. *The Letters of Matthew Arnold 1848–1888*. 2 vols. London: Macmillan.

Said, Edward. 1978. *Orientalism*. London: Routledge and Kegan Paul.

———. 2003. *Freud and the Non-European*. London: Verso.

Salbstein, M.C.N. 1982. *The Emancipation of the Jews in Britain: The Question of the Admission of Jews to Parliament, 1828–1860*. Rutherford: Fairleigh Dickinson University Press.

Sannwald, Rolf. 1957. *Marx und die Antike*. Zurich: Einsiedeln.

Santaniello, Weaver. 1994. *Nietzsche, God and the Jews: His Critique of Judeo-Christianity in Relation to the Nazi Myth*. Albany: State University of New York Press.

Schechter, Ronald. 2003. *Obstinate Hebrews: Representations of the Jews in France, 1715–1815*. Berkeley: University of California Press.

Schlegel, Friedrich. 1991. *Philosophical Fragments*. Translated by Peter Firchow. Minneapolis: University of Minnesota Press.

Schleiermacher, Friedrich. 1836. *Schleiermacher's Introductions to the Dialogues of Plato*. Translated by W. Dobson. Cambridge: Cambridge University Press.

Schmidt, James. 1989. "The Question of Enlightenment: Kant, Mendelssohn and the Mittwochsgesellschaft." *Journal of the History of Ideas* 50 (2): 269–91.

Schneider, Manfred. 1980. "Die Angst des Revolutionärs vor der Revolution: Zur Genese und Struktur des politischen Diskurses bei Heine." *Heine Jahrbuch* 19: 9–48.

Schorske, Carl. 1998. *Thinking with History: Explorations in the Passage to Modernism*. Princeton: Princeton University Press.

Sedgwick, Sally. 2011. "Hegel on the Empty Formalism of Kant's Categorical Imperative." In *A Companion to Hegel*, ed. Stephen Houlgate and Michael Baur, 265–80. Oxford: Wiley-Blackwell.

Shapiro, Gary. 1982. "Nietzsche Contra Renan." *History and Theory* 21 (2): 193–222.

Shavit, Yaacov. 1997. *Athens in Jerusalem: Classical Antiquity and Hellenism in the Making of the Modern Secular Jew*. London: Littman Library of Jewish Civilization.

Sheehan, Jonathan. 2005. *The Enlightenment Bible*. Princeton: Princeton University Press.

Shookman, Ellis, ed. 1993. *The Faces of Physiognomy: Interdisciplinary Approaches of Johann Caspar Lavater*. Columbia SC: Camden House.

Silverman, Max. 1998. "Re-Figuring 'the Jew' in France." In Cheyette and Marcus 1998, 197–207.

Stegmaier, Werner and Daniel Krochmalnik, eds. 1997. *Jüdischer Nietzscheanismus*. Berlin: W. de Gruyter.

Steiner, George. 1961. *The Death of Tragedy*. London: Faber and Faber.

———. 1984. *Antigones*. Oxford: Oxford University Press.

Stephens, Susan, and Phiroze Vasunia, eds. 2010. *Classics and National Cultures*. Oxford: Oxford University Press.

Stray, Christopher. 1998. *Classics Transformed: Schools, Universities and Society 1830–1960*. Oxford: Clarendon Press

Terdiman, Richard. 1993. *Present Past: Modernity and the Memory Crisis*. Ithaca: Cornell University Press.

Tesdorpf, Ilse-Maria. 1971. *Die Auseinandersetzung Matthew Arnolds mit Heinrich Heine, des Kritikers mit dem Kritiker*. Frankfurt am Main: Athenäum Verlag.

Theoharis, Constantine Theoharis. 1988. *Joyce's "Ulysses": An Anatomy of the Soul*. Chapel Hill, NC: University of North Carolina Press.

Tibebu, Teshale. 2008. *Hegel and Anti-Semitism.* Pretoria: University of South Africa Press.

Tomasoni, Francesco. 2003. *Modernity and the Final Aim of History: The Debate over Judaism from Kant to the Young Hegelians.* Dordrecht: Kluwer Academic.

———. 2004. "Mendelssohn and Kant: A Singular Alliance in the Name of Reason." *History of European Ideas* 30 (3): 267–94.

Trabant, Jürgen. 2009. "Herder and Language." In Adler and Koepke 2009, 117–39.

Trapp, Michael, ed. 2007a. *Socrates from Antiquity to the Enlightenment.* Aldershot: Ashgate.

———. 2007b. *Socrates in the Nineteenth and Twentieth Centuries.* Aldershot: Ashgate.

Tree, Stephen. 2007. *Moses Mendelssohn.* Reinbek: Rowohlt Taschenbuch Verlag.

Trousson, Raymond. 1967. *Socrate devant Voltaire, Diderot et Rousseau. La conscience en face du mythe.* Paris: Minard.

Turner, Frank. 1984. *The Greek Heritage in Victorian England.* New Haven: Yale University Press.

Vidal-Naquet, Pierre. 1990. *La démocratie grecque vue d'ailleurs: essais d'historiographie ancienne et moderne.* Paris: Flammarion.

———. 1995. "Renan and the Greek Miracle." In *Politics Ancient and Modern*, trans. Janet Lloyd, 177–99. Cambridge: Polity.

Vieillard-Baron, Jean-Louis. 1974. "Le Phédon de Moses Mendelssohn." *Revue de Métaphysique et de Morale* 79 (1): 99–107.

———. 1979a. *Platon et l'Idéalisme Allemand 1770–1830.* Paris: Beauchesne.

———. 1979b. "Platonisme et paganisme au XVIIIe sciècle." *Archives de Philosophie* 42:439–56.

Voltaire. 1994. *Dictionnaire de la pensée de Voltaire par lui-même.* Edited by André Versaille. Paris: Complexe.

Weber, Samuel. 2005. *Targets of Opportunity: On the Militarization of Thinking.* Ashland, Ohio: Fordham University Press.

Wechsler, Judith. 1993. "Lavater, Stereotype, and Prejudice." In Shookman 1993, 104–25.

Williamson, George. 2004. *The Language of Myth in Germany: Religion and Aesthetic Culture from Romanticism to Nietzsche.* Chicago: University of Chicago Press.

Wilson, Emily. 2007. *The Death of Socrates.* Cambridge, MA: Harvard University Press.

Winckelmann, Johann J. 1999. *Reflections on the Painting and Sculpture of the Greeks.* Translated by Henry Fusseli. London: Routledge/Thoemmes Press.

Witte, Bernd. 2007. *Jüdische Tradition und literarische Moderne.* München: Carl Hanser.

Wood, Allen W. 1992. "Rational Theology, Moral Faith and Religion." In *Cambridge Companion to Kant*, ed. Paul Guyer, 394–416. Cambridge: Cambridge University Press.

Yack, Bernard. 1986. *The Longing for Total Revolution: Philosophical Sources of Social Discontent from Rousseau to Marx and Nietzsche.* Princeton: Princeton University Press.

Yerushalmi, Yosef Hayim. 1989. "Freud on the 'Historical Novel': From the Manuscript Draft (1934) of *Moses and Monotheism.*" *International Journal of Psycho-analysis* 70:375–95.

———. 1991. *Freud's Moses: Judaism Terminable and Interminable.* New Haven: Yale University Press.

Young, Robert. 1995. *Colonial Desire: Hybridity in Theory, Culture and Race.* London: Routledge.

Yovel, Yirmiyahu. 1998. *Dark Riddle: Hegel, Nietzsche and the Jews.* Oxford: Polity.

Zac, Sylvain. 1989. *Spinoza en Allemagne: Mendelssohn, Lessing et Jacobi.* Paris: Méridiens Klincksieck.

Zammito, John. 2009. "Herder and Historical Metanarrative: What's Philosophical about History." In Adler and Koepke 2009, 65–92.

Index

Ingram Content Group UK Ltd.
Milton Keynes UK
UKHW012011130323
418508UK00005B/453